# By Way of Canarsie

## A Memoir

Rob Cuccurullo

ISBN: 978-0-578-52712-3

Cover Design:
JT Lindroos
www.oivas.com
juha@oivas.com

Content Editing:
Marisol Gonzalez
gonzam4@nv.ccsd.net

Final Editing:
Karen LeBlanc
mskmlb57@outlook.com

Photographs:
Yong Dawson Photography
www.yongdawson.com

Interior and Ebook Design:
Steven W. Booth
GeniusBookServices.com
steven@geniusbookservices.com

# Table of Contents

# Acknowledgments

I want to thank the most special person in my life, my mother Ellen Pavlatos-Cuccurullo. Even during my darkest days she never lost faith in me, and without her love and support I could have never gotten to where I am today.

I want to thank my father Gennaro Cuccurullo, who did the very best he could to raise us and always made sure we had everything we needed, and then some. It wasn't until I was an adult that I realized what my father had to go through as a young child and how it affected him. He was the glue that kept our family together and he is sorely missed.

I want to also thank my siblings Warren, Stephanie, and Jerry. I love you guys and I'm hoping that this book helps bring us back together.

I want to acknowledge all of you who appear in my story. Thank you for being a part of my life for better or worse.

Most of all I need to thank the two people who saved my life, my daughter Ava and my son Robert. It was fatherhood that changed me, and from the moment they were born all I wanted to do was give them everything I could. As a part-time father, I still made many mistakes but when I was given custody of my son I became obsessed with being a great parent. It forced me to reevaluate my life, which in turn motivated me to pursue my dreams.

For Bob… my best friend<br>
For all my students past, present & future… learn from my story<br>
In memory of<br>
Police Officer Cecil Frank Sledge NYPD<br>
1944-1980

# By Way of Canarsie

# Chapter 1
# Sons of Italy

The police car pulled up in front of our house on East 94th Street. As I looked out the living room window I saw my brother Warren in the backseat. He'd been falsely accused of vandalizing the synagogue near our house and two policemen were escorting him to our front door. They told my father their version of events as I watched Warren fume with anger. Fourteen at the time, he was the oldest of my three siblings. When the cops drove off, dad went ballistic and screamed, "You fuckin' punk!" while grabbing Warren by the shirt collar and yanking him through the house and down the stairs. Warren struggled to pull himself away as my father forced him into the garage yelling, "I'll fuckin' kill you, you punk!" As my siblings and I cried hysterically, my sister Stephanie screamed out, "Daddy, please stop. Don't hit him!" Dreading the inevitable, I ran outside to escape my brother's screams.

Friends were now gathering on the street near our house, and as I tried to divert them away, the sound of the garage door being violently yanked opened and my father screaming at the top of his lungs immediately made them turn back to watch the drama unfold. My father launched a full-scale assault on Warren as my mother screamed for him to stop. By this time, half of our block was witnessing this while I cried uncontrollably and screamed at my father, "Leave him alone! Please Dad! Please stop!" I even made a feeble attempt to physically intervene, but my father easily pushed me aside. My dad continued to pummel Warren with closed fists as my repeated pleas to stop went ignored. Warren kept yelling, "I didn't do anything!" but his protests fell on deaf ears. Finally, our next door neighbor pulled dad off my brother who was now sporting a ripped shirt, black eye, and bloody lip.

Born in 1933, my Italian father was the product of an extramarital affair and had been abandoned by his father. Raised by his promiscuous mother, he was eight years old when his father had a change of heart and took custody of him. His father already had a daughter with his wife in America, but she was unable to bear any more children, and he always wanted a son to pass on the family name. My father's mother was hesitant to give up custody at first, but my grandfather offered to pay for her divorce from another man she had married, and she eventually agreed. He placed my father in a private Catholic school in his hometown of Nocera Inferiore while he built his produce business in America. For nine years my father was raised by the nuns, getting a visit from his father only in the winter. He would tell me many years later that he was regularly beaten during his years at the school and even showed me a huge scar on his backside that he claimed was caused by a priest's belt buckle. Dominus Vobiscum.

In 1950, at 17 years of age, my father Gennaro Michael Cuccurullo arrived in America. Months after his high school graduation and after spending time with his mother, my father came to New York City to work with the father he barely knew. At first, he moved in with his father and his father's wife, but she wanted nothing to do with the product of her husband's affair, so he shared a room with a few guys he had come to America with. My grandfather had intended to divorce that woman two years earlier but after accidentally killing a young boy who ran out in front of his truck, he had feared a lawsuit and put all his assets in his wife's name.

Within two years, my father would meet my mother, Ellen Pavlatos, and after dating for six months they married in August 1952. After living in Germany during my dad's two-year stint with the U.S. Army, my parents would settle in the Canarsie section of Brooklyn, New York where my mother had lived most of her life.

In the days following my brother's beating, my mother threatened to divorce my father if he ever hit one of us like that again. My father never hit Warren after that "incident," but he continued to beat my brother Jerry and me with his belt. It seemed he was mad all the time and the slightest thing would set him off. Every day I would pray to God that he wouldn't lose his temper because I'd cringe in fear if he started yelling. Whenever he went into one of his rages, he'd turn beet red and slam his fist down or throw something. One day he didn't like how my mother made dinner, so he called her a fucking whore then flung his entire dinner plate across the room and against the wall. She didn't say a word. As violently tempered as he was, he never laid a finger on my mother or my sister.

Not all my childhood memories of my father were unpleasant. By the time I was nine years old I had become a big New York Mets fan, mainly because my father and brothers rooted for them. During September of the 1973 season, the Mets went on a winning streak and made it to the last day of the season needing a win to clinch the National League Eastern Division title. The 2 pm start time on a school day meant I would miss most of the game since I didn't get home from school until after three. I was devastated that I couldn't watch the game and was depressed the entire day. As I was sitting in gym class at around 1 pm I saw my father walk into the gym. Before I could even react, my gym teacher came over to me and said, "Robert, grab your things…you're going home."

At first, I thought something bad had happened, but when I saw my father grinning from ear to ear I was confused, mainly because I rarely saw my father smile. "Are you ready to watch the game?" he asked as we walked to the car. "Is your boss going to be mad at you for leaving work early?" I asked my father. "I don't care if he is," my dad replied. The man who I was deathly afraid of was now making me the happiest kid on the planet. The Mets won that day and would eventually make it to the World Series. My father got tickets through his job and took me to Game 4 of the 1973 World Series at Shea Stadium. After that magical season, I was hooked on baseball and everything New York Mets and dreamt of one day playing centerfield at their hallowed venue.

During the spring and summer, my friends and I played baseball all day every day on the street directly in front of my house. We all had matching authentic Mets uniforms with the number of our favorite player. I wore #41 for Tom Seaver, their best pitcher. We made bases with chalk and had to adjust our field depending on where the cars were parked. When a car was approaching, someone would yell "Heads up!" meaning get out of the way or get run over. We used a rubber-coated baseball to eliminate car window damage and would pitch the ball underhand on a bounce to the batter. If you hit the ball over the second sewer it was a home run. Occasionally, the ball would go down the sewer. We'd use an open wire hanger and stick our hand through the grate to retrieve it but sometimes the smell was so bad we'd just end the game and buy another ball.

We were huge New York Ranger fans so when the fall and winter months arrived we played roller hockey. We wore Chicago-style skates with the metal wheels along with some other equipment the pros used, costing our parents a small fortune. Just like our baseball games, we had to adjust to the street. But in hockey we'd use the parked cars as sideboards, trying to check our opponent into them with full force. And, just like in real hockey, this would cause fights between us and we'd punch it out like the pros. But they were just "hockey fights" and after the game we'd all be friends as if nothing had ever happened. When I was ten I got hit in the face with a puck. I broke my nose, had two black eyes, seven stitches, and had to wear a huge bandage on my face. It happened two days before the start of the fourth grade.

We'd play sports all day and cause mischief at night. One of our favorite things to do was make "thread traps." We'd steal dark colored thread from our mothers' sewing kits and wrap them around two opposing signposts, making an invisible barrier. We'd watch from behind the bushes and laugh uncontrollably as unsuspecting people walked through the trap, struggling to free themselves. Some of the people caught on and began using the other side of the street, or went around the poles, so we'd set traps on multiple corners. One time a guy, thinking he'd outsmarted us, turned around and yelled, "Not this time," only to get caught in a trap we'd set on the next block.

Whenever it snowed, we loved to stand on the corner and throw snowballs at the cars passing on Glenwood Road. We'd make dozens of snowballs and hide behind the same bushes, and when someone would yell "car" we would all stand up and throw the snowballs in rapid-fire motion. Our main goal was to get someone to stop and chase us because we usually got away. Occasionally, some young guy would catch us, but since we were kids he'd just threaten us. Once a year on Halloween we would throw eggs instead of snowballs which caused lots of folks to get out of their cars and chase us. During the Christmas holidays, we would wear dark clothes and go around the neighborhood unscrewing and stealing the colored light bulbs from people's houses so we could throw them against the wall and listen for the popping sound.

We could also be cruel as we used to make fun of some old guy who lived down the block. He walked like an ape and had bushy white hair and a scruffy beard. Whenever we saw him walking home we would scream out "Monkey Man" and run away. We did this for months until one day he snapped and chased us. He cornered me and my friend, and the "Monkey Man," with rage in his eyes, just said, "Why do you kids hate me? I never did anything to you." I immediately felt bad and apologized to him. It turns out that his real name was Frank and that he was a retired police officer who had been injured on the job, which was the reason he walked funny. After that, he would occasionally stop and talk to us on his way home. We never called him the "Monkey Man" again.

I was also quite the entrepreneur as a preteen. Whenever it snowed, my friends and I would make money by shoveling the neighbors' sidewalks and driveways. If it snowed on a Saturday, we would wake up early and hit the local businesses as they opened and shoveled their sidewalks. I also made money every week selling the local paper, the Canarsie Courier. Each copy cost ten cents and you could sell them for a quarter or more. During the summer, I'd sell lemonade in front of my house. When our dad wasn't home, Warren's band would rehearse in our garage and the driveway would fill up with neighborhood kids wanting to watch. Even at ten years old I saw the financial possibilities and immediately raised the price from ten cents a cup to a quarter. I would sometimes make up to twenty dollars a day which was a king's ransom for a kid in 1974.

Like many kids coming of age in the sixties, Warren got caught up in Beatlemania and wanted to play the guitar just like John Lennon. He begged my mother to buy him one and finally got his first guitar as a Confirmation present when he was ten years old. From that moment on he became obsessed with learning how to play it. Within no time at all, and without any formal training, Warren could imitate any pop song he heard on the radio. Realizing he was quite talented, my mother sent him for lessons at a local guitar school where the teacher determined that he was a prodigy with an exceptional musical ear. As the '60s ended, Warren shied away from the pop songs they were playing on WABC radio and began listening to rock bands like Blue Oyster Cult, The J. Geils Band, and The Doors. At the age of fourteen, Warren started his own band.

My brother Jerry, three years older than me and four years younger than Warren, would watch every day as the guys rehearsed in our garage. Since the band's drummer would leave his kit set up, Jerry would practice every day…or whenever my Dad wasn't home. One day when they took a break, he got behind the drums and started playing. He looked up to Warren and wanted nothing more than to play in the band with him. His persistence paid off. By the time Jerry was a teenager, he was one of the best drummers in his school.

By this time, everyone in my family expected me to learn an instrument and play alongside my brothers. In the early '70s, family bands were popping up everywhere. There were the Osmond Brothers, Sonny and Cher, the Jackson 5, and the made-for-television band the Partridge Family. My brothers wanted me to learn how to play bass guitar and even convinced my mother to buy me one for my birthday. I had no desire to play an instrument, although I liked to sing. I used to watch the Jackson 5 cartoons every Saturday morning and sing along with them. I would fantasize about singing with my brothers just like Michael Jackson, but I was much more interested in playing sports. A week after I got the guitar, I broke it trying to hit my sister who had been teasing me incessantly. That would be the end of my musical career.

During his high school years, Warren blossomed as a guitar player. He was now able to read music and write his own songs. He attended Canarsie High School during the 1970s, and the school would hold a "Battle of the Bands" competition each year with Warren's band winning three years in a row. My father still wasn't crazy about his musical aspirations, but my mother softened him a bit. Dad started letting my brother's band practice in the garage even when he was home.

When my father found out that some of the neighbors were complaining to the police about crowds on the sidewalk, he moved the band to our modest-sized backyard. Without the garage walls to muffle the sound, you could hear them from blocks away. It started to piss off even more of the neighbors. One in particular, a religious nut who my dad called a "Holy Roller," came to our door and threatened to call the police if the band didn't stop. I got scared watching my father's face tighten and turn flush with anger. He looked at her and said, "Call 'em," then slammed the door in her face as he stormed into the backyard. My father started screaming at the top of his lungs, "Keep playing! Louder! Louder!" The kids in the backyard cheered my father on while my brothers and I were sporting ear-to-ear grins because for once his rage was not directed at us. For Warren, it was the first time my father ever showed any support for his music. When the police did finally arrive, one cop told my father, "These guys are too good to stop," and proceeded to watch the band play.

All through high school Warren kept my father happy by working summers with him at his printing job. My brother absolutely hated it, but he knew that it kept my father relatively sane. A few years earlier, Warren had transformed our basement into a 1960s psychedelic music room complete with strobe lights, black light posters, and a fake spiderweb spray painted on the ceiling. He even let his friend draw pictures and write graffiti on the walls of the bathroom. One quote read, "My aim is to clean this bathroom…your aim will help." Not surprisingly, when my father ventured into the basement one day he flipped out. "You let someone draw on my fucking walls? Who the fuck did this? I want to know who the fuck did this!" he screamed. The room went silent. I thought for sure he was going to hit Warren, but he just kept screaming, and eventually my mother got him to go upstairs. Strangely he never made my brother paint the bathroom and never brought it up again.

# Chapter 2
# Up in Smoke

It was during high school that Warren began smoking marijuana. Soon after he brazenly began dealing it from our house. What started out as just selling a little weed to his friends began to get out of control. Within a few months, there were thirty to forty people a day showing up to buy pot. My father would watch through the window as people paraded in and out of the door to the basement. I'm sure my mother knew something was going on, but ever since the incident when my father beat Warren up, she went out of her way to protect him. When my father questioned the traffic going into our backyard she told him they came to see the band, but left when there was no room. But she could only run cover for Warren for so long. When strangers began knocking on my brother's door at all hours of the night, he knew he had to stop dealing.

Warren had many musical influences during his high school years, but it was during his sophomore year that he discovered a musician who would most profoundly influence him. Not only would this man change how my brother played the guitar, he would change his entire life. His name was Frank Zappa.

Warren became obsessed with the musician and the man. The basement room was transformed into a shrine to his guitar god with the walls painted jet black to enhance the strobe lights that illuminated all of Zappa's album covers. Titles such as "Weasels Ripped My Flesh," "Don't Eat the Yellow Snow," and "Lumpy Gravy" greeted Warren's visitors. On another wall, there was a huge poster for the movie "200 Motels," Zappa's first attempt at filmmaking and the title of one of his albums. Surrounding the movie poster and pasted to the wall were more pictures of Zappa from various music publications. Zappa's song lyrics, often quite humorous, criticized the hypocrisy and conformity of American society. This sentiment held great appeal for Warren.

He repeatedly played Zappa's albums in an effort to master the songs. Jerry was now the drummer in Warren's band and they'd spend hours in the basement rehearsing, usually ending up with Warren screaming at Jerry for not playing the way he wanted. Occasionally, they'd let me hang out in the basement and listen to the band. I always felt special hanging out with Warren. Every time I watched my brothers play together I still dreamt of playing alongside them. When they'd come up for dinner all they talked about was Frank Zappa. One day my father lost it and screamed, "Zappa, Zappa, Zappa! That's all I fucking hear in this house!" Complete silence followed.

After Warren graduated from high school in 1974, my father got him a job as a driver's assistant for the printing company where he was now shop supervisor. He told him that if he went to work every day he'd leave him alone about his music. Warren didn't mind as the job was relatively easy, and he was able to play his guitar and practice his music during work. He'd spend most of his print job money traveling to any Zappa concert within five hundred miles of Canarsie and had been to hundreds of his concerts in dozens of U.S. cities. Warren always hoped that one day he'd get to meet his idol.

During Thanksgiving dinner in 1976, my brothers were again talking about Frank Zappa when suddenly my grandmother Antonia blurted out, "I used to know a Zappa family when we lived in Baltimore. Ellen do you remember her?" she asked my mother. "Yeah I do," Mom replied. "She was the old lady who used to hang out in our apartment. I remember playing with the little baby boy who lived with them," she recalled further. "I believe that was her grandson," my grandmother stated. Now visibly excited Warren asked when our family left Baltimore. "On the same day Pearl Harbor was bombed in 1941," my mother answered. Knowing that Zappa was born in Baltimore in 1940, Warren went wild! He ran into the basement and returned with a book on Zappa's life that had photos of his family. He showed it to my grandmother who immediately recognized them. My mother then recalled that the day they left Baltimore the Zappa family bid them farewell. This was unbelievable! Upon hearing this revelation, I remember immediately thinking that fate was involved. Warren was beside himself as was the entire family. He couldn't wait to meet Frank Zappa and tell him that our mother used to play with him when he was a baby.

As 1976 came to a close, life in the Cuccurullo household had sunk to a new low. A few months earlier my father had decided to quit his four hundred dollar a week job as a printing supervisor and borrow six thousand dollars from my maternal grandmother to start his own swatch card business with two other partners. Over the next year or so we were practically broke which, if it was possible, made my father more miserable and unbearable. I remember eating spaghetti and chop meat for dinner almost every night. I was twelve years old and in the sixth grade getting ready to enter my first year of junior high school. That same year turned out to be my last year of childhood innocence.

I was in the sixth grade when I realized that my brothers were getting high in the basement. They still wouldn't let me in, but I could smell it through the door no matter how many towels they stuffed under it to mask the smell. Soon my sister and her friends would come over and smoke pot while my parents were at work. I was living in a pot den and finally smoked it for the first time at age 13. My childhood best friend, Robert Johnson, bought a joint for a dollar from an older kid who would, ironically, become one of my close friends years later. We snuck into the bushes at Canarsie High School and smoked it. I don't remember getting high but I do remember being nervous about getting caught by the cops, recalling how my father had beaten Warren when the police brought him home accused of theft. I didn't take to pot right away, but that all changed when I got to the seventh grade.

I entered Bildersee Junior High School 68 in the fall of 1976. Most of the kids I went to P.S. 242 with now went to a different school, but I still had my best friend Robert who was assigned to the same class. All through grade school, I was an honor student, and they assigned me to the SP or Special Progress class, meaning that I would skip the eighth grade. I remember that I couldn't wait to get to junior high because I'd be able to play school sports. Although I was small in stature I was a very good athlete and extremely fast for my age. Both Robert and I were devastated when we found out that the New York City Board of Education had cut all junior high school sports and there would be no teams for us to join. Robert and I began making new friends and soon realized that many of the kids in school were smoking pot.

Marijuana was everywhere and easy to score. I also knew my siblings were smoking it so I didn't consider it to be a bad thing. Back then, every schoolyard hangout had a pot dealer and you could cop a nickel bag for five dollars, or sometimes buy pre-rolled or "loose" joints for a buck apiece. Canarsie even had a record store on Flatlands Ave and East 105th Street that sold bags of weed right over the counter. To make a purchase you had to buy a record. Nobody seemed to mind because you could buy a 45 single back then for a dollar. On Friday nights there were lines out the door and up the block. I finally I got the nerve to go in and buy a bag of weed and asked for the 45 single called "Boogie Nights," then said in a real low and nervous voice, "I'll take a nickel bag, too." The black guy behind the counter looked down at me and started laughing hysterically. "Get the hell out of here!" he yelled in a Jamaican accent. I dropped the record on the counter and started to walk out. "Hey, man, you can still buy the record," he offered. Surprisingly, they stayed open for about a year before the police raided and shut the place down.

By the end of the seventh grade, I was smoking pot every day. I was still able to pass all my classes, but the school kicked me out of the Special Progress program and put me in a regular class. My mother was devastated because she called me her "Golden Boy" and expected great things from me academically. She'd been an excellent student herself and always regretted not going to college. She would later tell me that of all the siblings she felt I had the best chance academically but during the eighth grade my pot smoking got out of control. I was now smoking it on the way to school every morning. Robert and I would cut class just to get high and, for the first time in my life, I began failing in school. When I didn't have money to buy pot, I'd break into Warren's room looking for money or weed or I'd steal spare change from the shoebox in my father's closet. One day while going through my brother's dresser I hit the jackpot. Sitting in the back of the drawer under a pair of his jeans had to be at least two hundred loose joints stuffed in a plastic baggie.

He was obviously dealing again, and I quickly grabbed about fifteen or twenty joints then put everything back as I'd found it. I brought them to the schoolyard and gave everyone their own joint to light. In a few short months my popularity skyrocketed. Eventually Warren realized something was up and I could no longer find his stash. Ironically, he never confronted me and always blamed my brother Jerry.

Not only did my family's life change during the late 1970s, but so did the neighborhood. Although Canarsie was still a predominantly white middle-class area, the bordering neighborhoods had long been in decline. The Brownsville and East New York sections of Brooklyn which were predominately African-American, bordering Canarsie in the west and north, and were two of the worst crime areas in Brooklyn. Just like many neighborhoods in New York City during the 1960s, "White Flight" had driven residents to other sections of the city or into the suburbs of Long Island. The city's bussing policies of the early 1970s had brought African-American students into Canarsie schools, but the welcome mat was never rolled out for them to live in the neighborhood. While I was growing up there was only one black family in Canarsie, and only because they had been there long before everyone else.

Canarsie was also a hotbed for Organized Crime. Both the Gambino and Lucchese families had crews that operated in and around Canarsie. The Gambino family had a social club on Avenue L that was next to the Canarsie Movie Theater and another crew that hung out at the Gemini Lounge located just outside of Canarsie in the Flatlands section of Brooklyn. The Lucchese family had crews that hung out at two local bars which were a few blocks from each other on Flatlands Ave. They also hung at the Bamboo Lounge on Rockaway Parkway, made famous in the movie "Goodfellas." By then everyone including myself had seen both Godfather movies, so by age 12 I was well aware as to who was connected to the mafia and by way of which "family."

The biggest change that came to my neighborhood, however, was the result of the movie Saturday Night Fever. The movie not only spawned the disco craze of the 1970s, it transformed the entire culture of Canarsie. Although the hard-core rockers like my brothers would never succumb to disco, it seemed that half of the neighborhood made a musical transition, including myself. I cut my shoulder length hair and combed it straight back using a ton of my mother's hairspray to keep every strand in place. I shed my Emerson Lake and Palmer denim jacket for black leather. I ditched my cheap blue jeans and "Fonzie" t-shirt for designer jeans and a collared, terrycloth shirt. I stopped listening to rock music and incessantly played the Saturday Night Fever soundtrack. I wore a gold chain with a crucifix around my neck and started smoking Marlboro Red cigarettes.

By 1978, my father's textile business had begun to flourish and my mother quit her job to help run it. They were now working fourteen hours a day. Since they were never home all of us pretty much did what we wanted. Stephanie was now 19 and a regular in the dance clubs of New York. My brother Jerry was a senior in high school and had become one of the best drummers in Canarsie and continued to play in Warren's band. Warren was still working for my father and planned to follow Frank Zappa who was about to begin his 1978 World Tour. Zappa had scheduled a few New York shows prior to his annual Halloween Concert at Madison Square Garden, and Warren planned to be at all of them. He was still hoping to meet Frank and tell him about the connection between our families. A chance subway encounter on his way to the first show would lead to my brother becoming a "cult hero" among Zappa fans everywhere.

# Chapter 3
# Sofia Warren

I'll never forget the first time Warren told me the "Story of Crisis," as it would soon be known. I remember thinking that if it had happened to me I wouldn't have been able to tell a soul much less fifteen thousand people. She went by her stage name of Crisis, but her real name was Elizabeth Eden. She towered over 5'8" Warren and although she wasn't fat she was a full-set woman with large attributes...particularly her breasts. According to Warren, she was more exotic looking than beautiful, which he found intriguing. As he sat and talked with her on the train heading towards the Garden she told him that she danced at a local club and lived nearby. After flirting for a while she invited him back to her apartment. Since there was plenty of time before the show my brother accepted the offer. He said that within minutes of arriving at her place she was giving him a blowjob. When they finished he noticed that she had newspaper clippings hanging on her wall about a Brooklyn bank robbery that took place several years prior. It turns out that she was the reason for the robbery.

In August of '72, John Wojtowicz and Salvatore Naturale attempted to rob the Chase Manhattan Bank in the Gravesend section of Brooklyn. When they realized the bank had very little money they panicked, and a hostage situation ensued. The whole neighborhood gathered around the bank as television stations arrived and began live coverage. The bumbling bank robbers demanded a ride to the airport and a flight out of the country. Before they got to the plane the police killed Naturale, and Wojtowicz surrendered. In 1975 the movie "Dog Day Afternoon," starring Al Pacino as Wojtowicz, immortalized the attempted robbery. It turns out that Wojtowicz was gay and tried to rob the bank so his boyfriend Ernest Aron could get a sex change operation. Although the robbery was a failure the real-life Wojtowicz was paid $7500 for the rights to his story which he then gave to Aron to have the surgery. Ernest Aron then changed "her" name to Elizabeth Eden.

When Warren arrived at the concert a few hours later he was not sure he wanted to tell anybody what had just happened to him. Although he'd just experienced the strangest event of his life he was more interested in meeting Zappa. After the show, Warren was able to get a backstage pass from one of the crew members who brought him to Frank's dressing room. When Warren recounted our family connections, Frank was mesmerized by the story, and a lasting friendship was forged. Frank gave Warren an All-Access pass for him to use the following night.

Prior to the next evening's show, Warren met with one of the crew members who he had befriended and told him the story of his chance encounter on the subway. Immediately his friend said, "You gotta tell Frank that story, he'll absolutely love it!" After the show, Warren went backstage, and in front of Frank and the rest of the band told them "The Story of Crisis." In detail he told of his chance encounter with the transsexual stripper, who was once the boyfriend of the person who robbed the bank so he could get a sex change operation. As the band roared their approval, Zappa said, "We should put that story to music." A few days later, on Halloween night 1978 at the Felt Forum in Madison Square Garden in New York City, Warren told the "Story of Crisis" dressed in drag in front of 15,000 fans as Zappa and the band played in the background. That night Zappa dubbed my brother "Sofia Warren" and recruited him to tell the story at several more of his concert dates.

While Warren was becoming a folk hero among Zappa fans I continued a downward spiral as my drug use escalated. Not only was I smoking pot every day, but I'd started drinking alcohol. My parents weren't big drinkers but sometimes kept liquor in the house. On a few occasions I'd sneak a sip, but always hated the way it tasted. Marijuana was my choice of high and I only started drinking to look cool and fit in with the crowd. When I started hanging out at the schoolyard near my house there were always local guys hanging around who looked old enough to buy alcohol. There was a mom and pop liquor store on Flatlands Avenue where the old couple sold liquor to just about anybody. Every weekend we'd chip in and buy the cheapest bottles of liquor and find ourselves drinking low-shelf classics like Thunderbird, Wild Irish Rose, Blackberry Brandy, and something we called Tango. It was a mix of Vodka and the powdered, orange-flavor drink called Tang. One night I got so sick from drinking Tango that I couldn't smell, let alone drink orange juice for months.

Around this time I also started to experiment with pills. In the late 1970s, Quaaludes, or "Ludes," had become a popular party drug and were all over Canarsie. They had a similar effect as alcohol, and were very inexpensive on the street, usually selling for three or four dollars apiece. The first time I ever tried Quaaludes, I almost overdosed.

Robert Johnson and I had gone to Bildersee Park looking to buy weed before we went to the new teen disco that had recently opened in Canarsie. Unable to find any pot, we ran into a guy who said he had Quaaludes. Although we had never done them, Robert bought six pills for twenty bucks. On our way to the disco, I popped all three of my Quaaludes having no idea of their potency. We walked into the club still sober, but within twenty minutes things went terribly wrong. As I played a game of pinball while enjoying the song "I Got My Mind Made Up," the room began to spin. I can recall the song slowing down, then seeing dozens of spinning blurred faces staring at me. I suddenly found it impossible to stand and slumped on top of the pinball machine. That was my last memory of the night.

My friends told me later that I could barely walk and my words were incomprehensible. Robert was also high, but he had taken only one pill and could still function. The club owner, Mr. Zorros, was furious. "You guys are bombed!" he screamed at Robert. "Get your buddy out of here now!" Passed out and unresponsive, Robert and another friend carried me to my house instead of an emergency room. Luckily, my parents were away that evening, so they dragged me up to my room and threw me on the bed. I slept for over twelve hours and was still high when I woke up.

You'd think that an experience like that would have scared me to death, but that wasn't the case. I did stay away from Quaaludes for a while, but I continued to get high and skip school. By the time I reached the end of eighth grade my attendance was so bad they had no choice but to hold me back. For someone who was supposed to skip the eighth grade, I was now doing it for the second time. School rules stipulated that anyone left back had to attend a non-language class. It was another name for the dumb class. I was embarrassed and humiliated.

I was so hell-bent on getting back to the ninth grade that I started coming to school on a regular basis and finished the marking period with a 95 average. Everyone, including my parents, thought that I'd made a remarkable turnaround and was ready to change my life. The truth was that the classes were so ridiculously easy I could ace every test without ever picking up a book. The school had no choice but to put me back into the ninth grade where within weeks I was back to my old habits. Not sure what to do with a student with college-level test scores but failing grades, the school allowed me to "graduate." It also helped that my cousin Dorothy was the school's guidance counselor.

By the summer after high school, things had begun to change at home. My father's swatch card business was flourishing, and it seemed to have transformed him. Now that he didn't have to worry about money or bills he wasn't as miserable and angry as he'd been in the past. And he was no longer mocking and ridiculing my mother. She was the one now running the financial end of the operation and he knew that without her there would be no business. It seemed that overnight my father went from a typical blue-collar worker to the president of his own company. Gone were the grimy clothes, dirty fingernails and slicked back hair, replaced by designer suits, manicures, and a fancy new coif. Instead of taking the "Double L" subway line to the city, they now drove to work every morning in a brand new, leased Cadillac Eldorado.

As my father was realizing the American dream his children would begin a quest to achieve their own. Warren continued to follow Zappa, hoping he'd one day play for his band. My brother Jerry, who had just graduated from high school, still played drums in Warren's band with dreams of becoming a professional musician. My sister Stephanie continued her pursuit of performing on Broadway and was now taking expensive professional acting and dancing lessons in the City.

The only dream I had at fifteen was the same one I had when I was eight. I wanted to play centerfield for the New York Mets. Although I was getting high all the time I never lost my love for the game and was still playing in local leagues. Some coaches told me that I was too small to make it, but others said I was already close to major league speed and would naturally get faster as I matured. That always made me believe the dream was attainable. Now that I'd be able to play high school sports I was hoping it would motivate me to change my ways.

# Chapter 4
# Crazy Sal

In July 1979, Warren received a phone call that forever changed his life. He had now known Frank Zappa for close to two years who had in turn heard Warren play guitar numerous times. Zappa himself called, extending an offer for Warren to audition for his band. Zappa told Warren that a flight was reserved for him, and a car would be waiting at the airport to take him to Zappa's home and studio. I was in my bedroom and heard my mother scream. Thinking something bad had happened I rushed downstairs to see my mother hugging Warren and my father grinning from ear to ear. He immediately apologized to my brother for doubting him and gave him his full support. Warren left for his audition three days later, and never looked back.

He was hired to play rhythm guitar and do some backup vocals on Zappa's latest project, "Joe's Garage," scheduled for release in October. When Warren's best friend from Canarsie, Alan Malkin, went out to Los Angeles to visit him during the recording sessions that summer, Zappa took an immediate liking to him and hired Alan to do some speaking roles on the album. In the song "Catholic

Girls," including a Cuccurullo shout-out, Warren made his singing debut using the names of two girls he knew from Canarsie. One of them was our next-door neighbor, Carmenita Scarfone. When Carmenita's mother found out her daughter's name was on the record, she asked my mother to play it for her. The problem was the line following her daughter's name. After Warren sings, *"Carmenita Scarfone,"* Alan Malkin then says, *"Hey, she gave me VD."* My mom played it for her but knew when to cut if off.

Most of my friends had never even heard of Frank Zappa. My brother was playing guitar for a musical genius in a band of top-flight musicians but none of them were even slightly impressed, except for the fact that my last name was in a song. Whenever I tried to play the album for them they'd be disinterested within minutes. The only parts they liked were when Zappa used profanity. To be honest, if my brother wasn't on the album I probably wouldn't have listened, either. While Warren was in Los Angeles recording the album that summer, I had just "graduated" from the ninth grade and was spending most of my time getting high and hanging out at the schoolyard a few blocks from my house.

One-Fourteen Park, as we called it, was located adjacent to Public School 114 on the corner of Remsen Avenue and Glenwood Road. It was a combination of the actual schoolyard used by the school and a public park directly next to it run by New York City. In the middle of the park was a strange looking concrete building with a slanted roof that the city used for storage. Next to that was a long tall concrete wall that was used for playing handball. Behind the wall and out of view from the cops was a sandbox where we'd drink and smoke pot. The far corner of 114 Park was our favorite spot to smoke weed. The rear of the property bordered the backyards of the houses on East 92nd Street, separated by a chain link fence. We'd clipped the bottom in a few discreet spots that allowed us to get away from the police if they came into the park to bust us.

According to the cops at the 69th Precinct in Canarsie, the neighbors referred to our hangout at 114 schoolyard as "Needle Park." It was a wholly inaccurate label. With all the drugs that we *did* do in that park over the years never once did we think of shooting heroin. Occasionally, the police would swing by to check on us. One particular cop in our neighborhood had a reputation for being a hardass who enjoyed breaking up the teenage hangouts. His name was Officer Cecil "Frank" Sledge, but the neighborhood kids knew him as just Sledge. Officer Sledge, who was from Alabama, had a thick southern drawl that made us hate him even more.

114 Park was our domain, our epicenter. There were about 15 to 20 of us, both girls and boys, who hung out there every day. We were all between the ages of fourteen and sixteen with most of us just starting high school. Most of the boys wore their hair in a D.A. ("duck's ass") with every hair combed straight back and in place. The rest of us, including myself, whose hair was too straight to comb back, wore it parted in the middle with "wings." We all dressed alike in designer jeans with names like Jordache and Sergio Valente, white t-shirts, and either blue or white "decks," which were cheap sailor sneakers. In the winter we all wore brown leather bomber jackets, and from a distance, you could barely tell us apart. Then, when we went out to the teen disco, we'd dress like twenty-five-year-olds. We wore polyester slacks, silk shirts with funky designs, complete with black leather jackets and dress shoes with two-inch heels. To stand out from my friends I begged my mother to buy me a fedora hat and a silk scarf that made me look like a baby-faced gangster from the 1940s.

On school days we'd hang out at the park from 3:00 pm until dinner, and then everyone would return around 6:30 and stay out until about eleven. On weekends, we were there all day and night. If it got too cold in the winter, we'd find refuge at Michael's Pizzeria or Al's Candy Store where we played video games like Asteroids and Space Invaders. When we weren't drinking and smoking pot we were playing handball, touch football or a game we called Ring-Alivio, which was a contest where each team would try to hide and avoid capture. We even had our own tackle football team complete with matching uniforms that had the name "114 PARK" printed on the front. We'd play semi-organized games against some of the other hangout groups in Canarsie. In the summer we'd hitchhike on the Belt Parkway to Neponset Beach in Far Rockaway, Queens, where we'd smoke pot, blast our music, and bake our bodies with baby oil and sun reflectors.

After a day at the beach, my friends and I would usually head to the park to hang out. One day we noticed a strange person in his early twenties sitting by himself in the back of the park where we did our pot smoking. Initially, we were going to confront him and ask what he was doing but, as we got closer, we realized that might be a bad idea. Although he wasn't that tall he was extremely muscular with what looked like jailhouse tattoos on both arms. He had a classic Mediterranean look with his thick black curly hair, long dark eyebrows, square jaw and prominent Roman nose. What was most intimidating about him was the look in his eyes. He had that deep blank stare, the kind often used to describe a psychopath. As we moved closer he greeted us in a somewhat friendly manner with his deep, raspy Neanderthal-type voice, "Hey guys, I'm Sal." As soon as he spoke in that distinctive voice something told me that I had met this person before, but I couldn't place him.

His name was Salvatore Desarno or "Crazy Sal" as most people in Canarsie called him. He was twenty-two years old and lived with his mother around the block from 114 Park on Remsen Avenue. A few days earlier he'd left Rikers Island Prison after serving two and a half years for robbing a woman at knifepoint. Prior to his prison stint, Sal had earned his nickname simply because he wasn't afraid to do or try anything. He was constantly in trouble with the police for various offenses, and now that he was on parole they kept a close eye on him, especially Officer Sledge. According to Warren, who was the same age as him, "Crazy Sal" was the only guy who had the nerve to walk alone at night into the dangerous, all-black neighborhood of Brownsville to buy marijuana. When Sal needed money for pot he would rob people at random. After Warren told me that I remembered where I had previously met Sal. A few years earlier he'd robbed my friends and me at the Canarsie Movie Theater when we tried to buy pot from him. After he took our money he said to us in that Crazy Sal voice, "You tell anyone, you get this," making a gun gesture with his hand down by his waist.

Once Sal found out that we smoked pot we couldn't get rid of him. He was at the park all the time and would even follow us into Al's Candy Store when we tried to ditch him. With Sal in the park, Officer Sledge watched us even closer. He even came into the park one night and chastised us for hanging out with Sal. He warned us to stay away from him because eventually, something bad would happen. Although we hated having Sal in the park, what we hated even more was some ball-busting redneck cop telling us what to do. What we didn't realize at the time was that Sledge was trying to protect us from a sociopath. I would soon find out the hard way.

Having Crazy Sal at the park did have some advantages. He was able to buy liquor for us and he'd walk into the black neighborhood by himself to buy us weed, but only if we bought a bag for him. On many occasions, he never returned with the pot or our money. After a few months, we weren't that afraid of him anymore and he somewhat became our "protector." Unfortunately for me, when Sal found out I was Warren's brother I became his new best friend. Sal, who had gone to junior high school with Warren, was a huge Frank Zappa fan and would bug me every day to get him a signed copy of the soon-to-be-released "Joe's Garage" album. He became so obsessed with the fact that my brother was in Zappa's band that he started calling me Warren.

By the end of the summer of '79, Warren had completed the recording of "Joe's Garage Act I" and decided to come home for a few weeks. I hadn't seen my brother in months and was thrilled that he was coming back to visit. While Warren was home I got to hear all about his new life in Los Angeles, including all the girls and all the sex. Warren usually did all the talking, but I didn't mind because I idolized him. I could listen to him all day. When he finally did get around to asking about what I was doing, I told him I was still playing baseball and that I was excited for the high school tryouts that were coming up soon. When I got around to telling him about Crazy Sal, his face turned deathly serious and he said to me in an angry voice, "Stay away from that motherfucker, he's bad news." I never mentioned Sal to him again.

A few days later Frank Zappa called Warren and told him he was flying to New York to promote the album. Zappa was scheduled to land at Kennedy Airport, about twenty minutes from Canarsie, and then he'd take a limo to his Manhattan hotel. When Warren told Frank that our house was close to the airport, Zappa replied, "How about I stop over and meet your family?" When Warren told us at the dinner table that Frank Zappa was coming to our house for Sunday dinner, the family was ecstatic! We were all fighting for the phone wanting to call everyone we knew and tell them who was coming to dinner. My father immediately yelled out to all of us, "Don't tell the whole fuckin' neighborhood, only family and close friends." I couldn't wait to tell everyone at the schoolyard about Zappa coming to my house until I realized that there was one person I didn't want finding out.

Although I did tell my close friends that Frank Zappa was coming, I begged them not to mention anything to Sal. In the days leading up to Zappa's visit, I tried to stay away from the park to avoid seeing Sal. My mother spent the days before "the visit" fixing up and cleaning the house, making sure everything was perfect.

She made the traditional Italian Sunday meal complete with pasta, meatballs, sausage, and veal cutlets. She also bought an espresso maker when she found out that Frank was a big espresso drinker. The black limousine pulled up in front of our house on East 94th Street at about noon. Frank Zappa along with his bodyguard John Smothers, a very large, bald African-American man, exited the car. Zappa had a video camera in hand and began filming his own arrival and continued to do so as we all entered the house.

Throughout the day various people came over to meet Zappa. It was mostly friends of Warren who all listened to Zappa's music. Most of my friends from the schoolyard had no desire to meet Zappa so I didn't bother inviting anyone except my best friend, Robert. After dinner, I got on my moped and drove past the park and saw some of the girls we hung out with. I asked them if they wanted to meet Zappa, but only one showed any interest. I drove her back to our house, and after a short visit drove her back. As I was about to pull away I noticed Crazy Sal coming into the other side of the park. I begged the girls not to say anything as I sped off.

As I pulled up to the house I noticed a crowd starting to gather in front. Word was spreading through the neighborhood, and a stream of people were trying to come in to meet Zappa. My father came outside and apologized to the crowd, explaining that house wasn't big enough for everyone, and returned inside. Frank was engaging our living room guests, drinking espresso and smoking his Winston cigarettes, when the doorbell rang again. As my father went to answer the door, I peeked out the window and saw Crazy Sal! Terrified he'd be livid with me for not telling him, I stayed where he couldn't see me and listened as my father opened the door. "Is Warren here?" Sal asked my dad. "I'm sorry," my father said in a friendly voice, "I don't have enough room for anyone else." As my father was closing the door and Sal stepped off the porch, I heard him ask, "What about little Warren?" He didn't return, but now I was afraid to see him.

I avoided the park for a few days but knew I'd eventually run into Sal. Surprisingly, when I did see him he didn't mention coming to my house but instead kept bugging me to get him an autographed album. Not wanting to piss him off, I promised to arrange it. Sal's behavior began getting stranger by the day. By late October, he'd become extremely paranoid and kept going on about how Officer Sledge was out to get him. He even went so far as to file a formal complaint with the police department claiming harassment by Sledge. Now that Sal had access to his mother's car he was spending less time at the park. It was a huge relief for all of us. He'd still come by occasionally either looking for pot or just someone to smoke it with him. We were Sal's only "friends," but certainly not by choice. One evening as my pal Richie and I were sitting in the park, Sal pulled up in his mother's car and called us over. He asked us if we wanted to smoke. Thinking he meant at the park we said yes. "Get in, take a ride. We gotta go get it." As much as we didn't want to go with him, you didn't say no to Crazy Sal.

Luckily, we were able to buy pot in Canarsie and didn't have to drive to the black neighborhood to get it. Sal may have been fearless, but as an undersized 15-year-old I was deathly afraid to even go near the Canarsie border with Brownville, nevertheless go deep into the heart of the ghetto. Since he was too paranoid to smoke in the park, Sal took Richie and me to his mother's house. We went upstairs to his room and began to smoke. Suddenly out of nowhere Sal took out a .38 caliber handgun, pointed it in my face and calmly told me to look inside the barrel. Although I had no idea if the gun was loaded, I froze in absolute terror. "Isn't that sick?" Sal calmly said with a smile on his face. Realizing he wasn't going to shoot me I nervously replied, "Yeah Sal, that's sick." Then he pointed the gun in Richie's face and asked him the same thing. As Sal was putting his gun away he muttered, "Let him try to get me now." I knew he was referring to Officer Sledge.

Two months after Zappa's visit to Canarsie, my brother called home to tell us that Zappa was again coming to our house, this time for Thanksgiving dinner. After the crowd that had accumulated during the last visit, my father demanded that we only invite immediate family. Deathly afraid that Sal would try to come over again, this time with a gun, I told only a few close friends about Zappa's impending visit. Zappa once again arrived with his bodyguard John Smothers along with a German television crew filming a documentary called what else but "Thanksgiving with Frank Zappa."

From the moment he walked into our house, Zappa began directing us to do and say random things about Warren. He then brought us all in the basement and directed the entire family to talk about Warren as fast as we could and all at the same time. When it was time for dinner, Zappa sat at the head of the table usually reserved for my father, and even helped my mother carve the turkey. It was all so surreal. Only three years earlier we'd realized at Thanksgiving Dinner that there was a connection to Frank Zappa and our families back in Baltimore. Now he was having Thanksgiving dinner in our house in Canarsie while my intoxicated grandmother flirted with big John Smothers. I was convinced that fate had brought Warren and Zappa together.

Even though we tried to keep Zappa's visit quiet, a crowd of about twenty people had begun to gather in front of our house. The entire day I was worried that Sal would find out and try to come over, and I kept peeking out the window looking for him. I did invite a few of my friends from the park, with strict instructions not to tell Sal if they saw him. When Zappa met my friends, he got a huge kick from the fact that we all looked alike. A few weeks earlier a bunch of us from the park had shaved our heads for no apparent reason. Zappa even mentioned us on the radio when he was a guest disc jockey on the rock station WNEW. He called us "the guys from Canarsie with the funny haircuts." Crazy Sal never did come over that day, and I finally stopped imagining him coming to our house with a gun demanding to meet Frank Zappa.

Now that Sal had a gun I knew it was only a matter of time before he used it. With winter approaching, Sal could easily conceal his weapon under his jacket. For a guy who complained that the police were watching him you'd never know it by the way he recklessly waved his gun around. One night while a bunch of us were smoking a joint behind the school, Sal came up and asked for some. My friend Vinny made the mistake of telling Sal there wasn't enough for him to smoke. Sal took his gun out of his jacket and pointed it right at Vinny. "Drop your drawers!" Sal ordered. We all froze. "Drop your drawers!" Sal screamed again. As Vinny tried frantically to talk, Sal interrupted, "If you don't drop your drawers right now and run around the schoolyard, I'm gonna shoot you." Fearing for his life, Vinny complied. Although it was hysterical watching him run around with his pants around his ankles we were all scared to laugh until Sal started laughing hysterically. "I'm just kidding," Sal said. "I wouldn't shoot you." Just as Sal said that he turned toward the school, and for no apparent reason fired three shots into the wall about four feet from where my friends and I were sitting. After freezing for a moment, somebody yelled, "Run!" We all darted from the place like Olympic sprinters. My ears rang for an hour. I guess Sledge wasn't watching that night because Sal got away with it.

A few short weeks later, Sal would fire his weapon again, this time it was out on the street and in broad daylight. My friend Richie and I had walked with Sal to the liquor store on Flatlands Avenue so he could buy us a bottle of Blackberry Brandy. We gave him the money and waited across the street. He came out of the store agitated and with nothing in his hand. As he walked across Flatlands Avenue to where we were standing he stopped in the middle of the street, turned toward the liquor store, pulled out his gun, and fired one shot into the large storefront glass window. Luckily, nobody in the store was hurt. As the glass shattered all over the sidewalk, Richie and I ran as fast as we could and didn't stop for about ten blocks. Sal would later tell us that he was pissed because he was thirty cents short, and the old couple who owned the store wouldn't extend him the paltry credit. I guess they were too afraid to call the cops because the police never questioned Sal.

As winter fell and the new decade approached, Sal was now taking his mother's car every day. As usual, he'd drive by 114 Park looking for someone to hang out with him. We made it a point to stay as far away from the street as possible so we'd have time to get away if Sal pulled up. Unfortunately for me, I was the only one Sal knew by name, even though it was my brother's name. "Warren," he'd yell from his car, "take a ride." I was terrified to go with him knowing he had the gun but I was just as afraid to say no. My biggest fear was that he'd take me into the black neighborhood to buy weed and then leave me in the car by myself. Although he would take me there on a few occasions, he was usually able to buy pot in Canarsie. After he bought his weed he would typically smoke a joint with me and then drop me off at the park. Sal wouldn't say much in the car, but every day he asked me about getting him the signed copy of Zappa's new album. I told Sal that I was going to visit Warren in California in a few weeks and would be able to get him the signed album. I thought he'd be happy, but he didn't react. He just said, "I want you to give Warren a letter."

In the weeks leading up to my trip to Los Angeles I was with Sal almost every day, but not by choice. Even when I tried to hide out at the candy store, he would come in and tell me to take a ride with him. He was constantly worried about Officer Sledge and I think felt safer with somebody in the car with him. On a few occasions Sledge would follow us in his patrol car but for some reason never pulled us over. Perhaps it was the fact that Sledge knew that Sal had a young kid in the car with him and didn't want to confront him while I was there. Whatever the reason, I was always relieved when Sledge would pull away, because not only did we have pot on us but because Sal kept his .38 caliber handgun directly under his seat.

On January 27, 1980, my brother Jerry and I flew out to California to visit Warren for a week. On the day we left, Sal gave me the letter that he had written for Warren. When we arrived in Los Angeles that night I gave Warren the letter from Sal and he read it aloud. Riddled with spelling and grammatical errors you could tell that the letter exposed Sal as the paranoid sociopath we suspected. In the letter, he described how Officer Sledge was harassing him unfairly, and that Sledge wanted him dead. The next day I got a phone call from my mother who told me that Crazy Sal had murdered Officer Sledge.

On the night of January 28, following a routine traffic stop on Flatlands Avenue and East 78th Street in Canarsie, Salvatore Desarno shot Officer Sledge four times. As Sal attempted to flee, Sledge's uniform caught the car's undercarriage, and Sal dragged the wounded police officer over a mile before he crashed into a woman's front yard. After a brief hostage situation where Sal held a gun to the head of the woman who lived in the house, the police talked him out and arrested him. Officer Cecil "Frank" Sledge, a decorated 12-year veteran of the NYPD, died in the line of duty. He was 35 years old. To this day I can't help but think that I could have been with Sal that night had I not gone to California to visit my brother.

My visit to Los Angeles could not have come at a better time. Not only did I distance myself from Crazy Sal on the night he killed Officer Sledge, I avoided the onslaught of the police questioning my friends at 114 Park. Richie told me that following Sledge's murder the cops were at the park every night asking questions about Sal and wanting to know about "Warren." Not surprisingly, my friends didn't tell the detectives anything. When I found out the police may be looking for me I talked my mother into letting me stay in

California for a couple more days. It wasn't that I wanted to protect a cop killer; I just wanted the whole Crazy Sal segment of my life to be over.

# Chapter 5
# Destination Unknown

Jerry and I spent ten days in Los Angeles following the murder of Officer Sledge. During that time, I had a recurring nightmare in which I was with Crazy Sal on the night of the shooting. In the dream, I'm trying to run away after seeing Sledge get shot, but my legs won't move. I feel as if I'm about to get caught from behind, and then I would wake up in a panic. Embarrassed to be associated with a cop killer, I didn't talk to anyone about hanging out with Sal. I did, however, smoke a ton of pot with my brother.

Since Warren was living in a studio apartment on Hollywood Boulevard, he arranged for Jerry and me to stay in a motel. I was disappointed as I had envisioned my brother living like a rock star in a fancy apartment. Zappa paid his musicians a salary of $400 per week, so a $90-a-week dump was all that Warren could afford. His basement apartment came complete with a view of a brick wall behind the curtain and messages on his front door written in pen and marker by some of his friends. Somebody had written in big letters, "This is the home of Warren Cockarullo," a play on our last name and a nod to his generously-sized penis.

During my visit, I met Warren's friend, Dale Bozzio, who worked with him on the Joe's Garage album. Dale was married to Terry Bozzio, Frank Zappa's former drummer. Dale was an absolute knockout. She was 24 years old with natural blonde hair and an adorable Boston accent. I was smitten with her from the moment we met. She had already done some nude modeling, appearing on the cover of Hustler Magazine, and was just finishing her second Hustler shoot. This time she would be the featured centerfold in the upcoming February 1980 issue.

Although I had seen naked pictures of Dale in the previous issue, the triple page pullout centerfold with her legs spread wide open and her hand on her pussy was too much for a horny fifteen-year-old virgin. The most memorable part of my trip was when Dale would smoke pot with me. Knowing I had a mad crush on her, she would purposely tease me by giving me "shotguns," putting her lips on mine and blowing the smoke into my mouth. On one occasion, I was so aroused that I grabbed the copy of Hustler and jerked off in her bathroom.

Dale and Warren began writing songs together. When Terry's group broke up the three of them decided to start their own band. Although Dale had never sung a day in her life she was able to create her own distinct singing style and took full advantage of her killer body and drop dead gorgeous looks. She dyed her hair platinum blonde with blue streaks and created her own skimpy outfits complete with metallic, micro-mini skirts and nothing but clear plastic cones covering her breasts. The original name of the band was U.S. Drag which I absolutely hated but they soon changed it to the much cooler name Missing Persons, as in missing from Frank.

I had promised my mother that when I returned home I'd make up the schoolwork I missed while away. I had started Canarsie High School in September, and with tryouts held in the fall, I'd already made the junior varsity baseball team for the upcoming season. All I had to do was maintain a passing average and go to class. I was fine for the first few months, maintaining a "D" average, but after returning from Los Angeles I wasn't the same. I couldn't shake the Crazy Sal nightmares and found myself constantly drinking and smoking pot. When the baseball coach informed me that I wouldn't be allowed to play because of my attendance, I stopped going to school altogether.

I turned 16 that summer and my pot smoking was now chronic. I'd smoke from the moment I woke up and continue all day and night. When I ran out I would either steal money from my father's change box or steal weed from Jerry. My friends and I continued to drink and pop Quaaludes on the weekends, but that changed when someone introduced us to mescaline which was a hallucinogen like LSD. We loved doing mescaline because it made us laugh hysterically. Sometimes fifteen or twenty of us would all pop a tab of mescaline and walk around Canarsie for hours tripping out of our minds. I also experimented a few times with the drug PCP, known on the street as Angel Dust. The drug, which was a white crystal powder that we mixed with marijuana, caused hallucinations, even in small doses. Following a scary experience where I literally could not remember my name for what seemed like forever, I swore I would never smoke Angel Dust again.

It was also during that summer that I got high by "huffing paint," as it was called. There was a specific brand of spray paint called Red Devil 707 Gold which when sprayed into a paper bag and inhaled caused a dream-like state. If you inhaled too much you would pass out, unable to remember what happened when you came around. It happened to me on a few occasions. Since anyone could buy spray paint regardless of age it became an easy way to get high if we couldn't find pot. Thank god the craze didn't last long as the paint stores in Canarsie realized that teenagers were buying Red Devil 707 Gold spray paint in droves. They soon stopped selling it to minors and the brand was eventually discontinued.

As September rolled around I decided to give school another chance. A friend of mine was trying out for the junior varsity football team and encouraged me to go with him. I had always excelled in our "street" football games so I tried to use my love of sports as a motivation to return to school. Not only did I pass the tryouts, I was the fastest player on the team, and the coach had me starting on both offense and defense. I just had to show up for school and pass my classes. Although my drug use didn't keep me from going to practice, it did keep me from going to class. After my parents would leave for work I'd get stoned, sleep all day, and wake up for practice at 2:30 in the afternoon. Following the second game of the season, the coach found out I had stopped attending class and kicked me off the team. That was the end of my high school career. Somehow, I was able to talk my mother into signing me out of school. I know she was devastated, but the fact that we had a successful family business that I could be a part of probably made it easier for her.

After dropping out of high school my father demanded that I start working for him immediately. The thought of working in a hot, sweaty printing factory performing menial tasks was depressing so I was pleasantly surprised when my father told me I would be the driver's assistant on his delivery truck. The guy who drove the van was Warren's friend Vinny who lived in Canarsie. He'd pick me up every morning at 7 am. Vinny was also a regular pot smoker and from the moment I stepped in the van, he'd have a hit ready for me to smoke from his pipe. After making our morning deliveries, Vinny would drive to the far west side of Manhattan near the water where we'd get high during lunch. On the way home to Canarsie, we'd smoke again before he dropped me off. After dinner, I'd go straight to the park and smoke with my friends. Clearly, there was a pattern emerging. Now that I was working I had my own money to buy pot, but still found myself broke because I was getting everyone else high for free. I decided to do what Warren did and went into business for myself.

On payday, I purchased my first ounce of marijuana for $40 from a friend of my brother Jerry. It was bad commercial pot with a ton of seeds and stems that needed to be cleaned. We used Burger King trays to clean the pot, and a few close friends and I would have joint rolling parties at my house when my parents were out. We'd use double sheets of EZ Wider rolling paper to make the joints look fatter. At first, they looked like pregnant fish, but after rolling hundreds of joints we became quite proficient. I'd sell each joint for a dollar or six for five bucks. The first night I went to the park with twenty joints and sold out in two hours. Within a few weeks, I had several regular customers from outside the park and was selling out within minutes. With all the pot I was smoking, I was just breaking even so I decided to step it up.

I used my paycheck to buy a half pound of weed for $300, and because I had the moped I decided to drive around to the other hangouts and expand my business. My scooter was a Honda 50 motorized bike that my father had bought me after my first moped was stolen. It was bright orange and did about 50 miles an hour at top speed. Mopeds were still kind of new so they weren't required to have license plates, nor did you need to wear a helmet. The seat would lift to reveal a secret compartment where I would stash about 100 joints wrapped in a plastic bag. I would start my night at 114 Park meeting my regular customers. When business died down, I got on my moped and drove to various hangouts in Canarsie to sell the rest of my stash. Within weeks, I began buying a pound at a time. Even with all the pot I was smoking I was making more money dealing pot than I was working for my father. Unfortunately, my booming business would be short-lived.

With mopeds becoming quite popular, New York passed a law that required registration and helmets to be worn. Foolishly ignoring the new law, I went out on my moped with over 100 joints stashed under my seat and started at 114 Park as usual. As I pulled into the park, a police car followed me and pulled me over. The officer gave me a ticket for no registration, no helmet, and driving on the sidewalk. He told me I needed to walk the moped home and if he saw me driving it again unregistered he would confiscate it. I gladly obliged as I had enough pot under my seat to be arrested for the sale and distribution of marijuana, at the time a felony in the state of New York. I would sell the moped a few days later, infuriating my father who claimed I had no right. I used the money towards paying the tickets.

Although my moped marijuana business was over I continued to sell joints at 114 Park. Some of the people who I delivered to now began coming to me. I often had lines of people waiting to buy weed from me in the back of the park. I kept the joints hidden in the bushes in case the police came, and still had my escape routes through the back fence. Even without the moped and smoking a good chunk of my profits, I was still earning over $150 a week. In Canarsie, when word gets out that you're making money illegally, it's not just the police you have to worry about.

As soon as they approached me in the park that night I knew they were connected to the mob. I didn't know them personally but I knew of them. They were in their late teens or early twenties and were part of Little Nicky's Canarsie crew that operated under the umbrella of the Gambino Crime Family. They greeted me in a friendly manner, then one of them said with a smile on his face, "Either you start paying us or you stop dealing." I froze in terror even though they were still smiling at me. Before I could even say a word, one of them said, "We want $50 a week right now and we'll take it from there." He paused and then said, "Or you can deal for us, and we'll protect you." I nervously asked them, "What if I just stop?" "You can do that," one responded, "but we rather you didn't." Still smiling they calmly walked away. The fact they were as polite as they were made the experience that much more terrifying. I felt at any moment they were going to hit me. I immediately stopped dealing and stayed away from the park for a few days. Even though many people in the neighborhood told me that if I stopped dealing I had nothing to worry about, I was still afraid and wanted nothing more than to leave Canarsie for a while. A few weeks later I got my wish.

Unable to land a record deal, Missing Persons decided to produce their own four-song extended play or EP record which would be recorded in Frank Zappa's brand-new studio in Los Angeles. My parents financed the entire recording, and the band self-promoted the EP, eventually selling over seven thousand copies. Missing Persons also appeared in the movie Lunch Wagon and became a must-see band among the Los Angeles live music crowd. After touring mainly in California, the band decided to book shows on the East Coast beginning in January 1981. To help finance the tour, the band started selling merchandise at their concerts. Since it was my father footing the bill, he wanted someone he could trust with the money. I think he sensed something was wrong with me, but he never came out and said it or asked. He just told me one day that I'd be going on tour with Missing Persons for a few weeks to sell t-shirts and albums. I was ecstatic. Not only would I get away from Canarsie but I'd be able to hang out with Warren who I desperately missed. More than anything though, it was my father's trust in me that meant everything. I wasn't going to let him down.

# Chapter 6
# Mr. Canarsie

I spent almost a month on tour with Missing Persons and had the time of my life. I fell in love with their music, although that wasn't always the case with the fans. Without a record contract, they were forced to be an opening act for more popular bands. There were many nights when I heard the crowd boo and scream derogatory things at Dale, calling her a bimbo or slut. Sometimes people would come over to where I was selling the merchandise and tell me how bad the band was and that they wouldn't bother coming back. It gnawed on me at first, and when I told Warren about it, he just laughed and said, "The price of fame."

Knowing I'd be gone for over three weeks I made sure to bring enough pot to last. I still had plenty left over from dealing so I didn't have to buy any. But within a week I had gone through my entire stash playing the "big shot" and smoking with everybody. Since I was away from home I had no idea where to get any and was scared to ask strangers for fear of being arrested. Dale was the only one in the band who smoked pot. She shared with me what little she had, but I smoked that up in two days. With no weed and no prospects, I tried to drink at the venues but that was difficult given the fact that I was sixteen and looked thirteen. Without the pot, I had a hard time falling asleep. While I stared at my motel room ceiling for hours, all I could think about was finding weed. It was during one of those sleepless nights toward the end of the tour that I realized for the first time that I might have a problem.

On the ten-hour bus ride back to New York I had a lot of time to reflect on my life. My time with the band made me yearn for that lifestyle. The very thought of working in my father's business depressed me. I felt I was destined for greater things. Warren was on the verge of a recording contract, my sister Stephanie was performing in a dance company, and Jerry was playing for an up-and-coming band in L.A. that Warren had hooked him up with. I was still young enough and believed that I could achieve my dream of playing professional baseball. I continued to play in local leagues, but without regular practice I noticed my skills diminishing, although I was still considered the fastest guy in the neighborhood. I knew the pot smoking was a problem, but I really didn't know how to stop. I thought about confiding in my parents, but it seemed that they were consumed with their business and trying to help Warren's career. I was also still afraid of my father, even though he hadn't hit me since I was twelve. I felt lost and all alone.

When I returned to Canarsie I was still afraid of returning to the park even though I wasn't dealing anymore. A friend told me that the two guys who came to shake me down had passed by the park a few times, but he hadn't seen them in a while. I also found out that these guys weren't official or "made" members of the Mafia, but up and coming guys we called "wannabes." According to unofficial mob protocol, drug dealing by made members was prohibited by Gambino Crime boss Paul Castellano, punishable by death. To get around this rule, some of the local captains had their "wannabes" shake down local drug dealers. The bottom line was that I wasn't in any danger because nobody would come looking for me if I wasn't dealing.

With few other options, I went back to work with my father and fell right back into my schoolyard routine. Now that I wasn't dealing, every day was a mission to buy weed. With more drug dealers being shaken down by the "wannabes," it was harder to buy pot in Canarsie. We knew of a bodega on Remsen Avenue, a few blocks past the Canarsie border in the black neighborhood, that sold nickel bags over the counter. Since white guys walking in the black area wasn't safe and meant only one thing to the cops, we couldn't walk there. Since all of us were too young to drive we always depended on finding some older guy to shuttle us there. It wasn't an easy task.

In February 1981, a new novelty store opened across the street from the park on Glenwood Road. At first they sold cheap household items and discount clothing to the old neighborhood ladies. The store owner must have noticed all the kids in the park across the street and soon had a sign in the window that read, "We sell candy and soda." Naturally, that gave me and my friends a reason to go in and we soon became friendly with the store owner. His name was Joe Milo. According to my mother, who knew him growing up, he was a lifelong Canarsie resident whose family had money. She told me he was once a popular, handsome young man with a fancy car who the girls in the neighborhood once dubbed "Mr. Canarsie." My mother had no idea how he wound up single, childless, and making pennies selling junk to old ladies.

Joe immediately saw an opportunity and turned his novelty store into a kid-friendly hangout. He cleared out some of the merchandise that had been sitting there unsold for months and added video arcade games. Along with the candy and soda, he began selling other snacks, and even added a microwave and began selling burgers and nachos. He always told us not to mention he was selling food because he didn't have a license. His secret was safe with us. Joe was cool to the kids and let us to hang out in store when it was cold even if we didn't have money. The only thing we didn't like about him was that he was cheap. Although we'd constantly ask, he'd never extend us credit--for any amount. One day I was short a measly nickel for a soda. No sale.

After a few months, we'd gotten so comfortable with him that we got the nerve up and asked him to take us to buy pot in the black neighborhood. He was hesitant at first but when I offered him five dollars for gas he immediately agreed. We packed about six of us in his huge, late-model 1970s Ford, and he drove us the few blocks to the pot-selling bodega on Remsen Avenue and Avenue A. My friends came to the consensus that I should go in make the purchase with the reasoning that I was the fastest and would be able to get away if the cops came. As I walked into the bodega for the first time it reminded me of the day a few years back when I tried to buy pot from the record store in Canarsie and was laughed out of the place. This time the guy didn't hesitate and slid a nickel bag through the bulletproof glass counter after I gave him the five dollars. I was in and out of the bodega and back in Joe's car in less than thirty seconds.

As long has he got his gas money Joe would drive us to the bodega whenever we asked. In what seemed to become a nightly routine, we'd all pool our money and wait for Joe to close his store so he could drive us to buy weed. This went on for a few weeks, and on one of the return trips back from the bodega Joe asked me, "How do dealers make a profit by selling pot?" I explained to him that an ounce of weed cost about thirty-five to forty dollars. The dealers could then make about eight or nine "nickel bags" which sold for five dollars each, earning a ten-dollar profit on every ounce. Or they could sell joints which was even more profitable. At the time I thought he was just curious, but a few days later he shocked me when he pulled me to the side and whispered, "I have nickel bags of pot if you want." He then secretly showed me a small, yellow bag in his hand.

Joe Milo was now our own personal pot dealer selling us nickel bags from behind the counter of his store. At the time it didn't feel wrong because we thought we were adults, but Joe was a grown man selling drugs to underage kids in the middle of a neighborhood run by Organized Crime. We were convinced that Joe had the backing of the mob because nobody could be that stupid and brazenly sell pot from a legitimate business. For the next several weeks Joe sold us pot almost every day. As usual, when we had no money we asked him for credit. As usual, he said "no." On a late Saturday morning, I came to the park hungover and broke, having spent my entire paycheck the night before. Desperate to get high, I waited for Joe to open his store and begged him to "front" me a nickel bag. He wouldn't budge. I left the store determined to find five dollars to buy some weed.

I waited in the park by myself for about an hour but soon the regular crew trickled in. Naturally, I asked all of them if they had money or weed, but they were as broke as me. My good friend Albert also wanted to smoke and had an idea that since it was Saturday we could break into the school and find something of value to sell. As much as I wanted to smoke, I had no intention of embarking on a burglary career and immediately refused. Undeterred, Albert started looking for a way into the school and soon forced open one of the back doors and slid inside. He waved his arm to signal me to follow him, but I was too afraid and stayed behind. About twenty minutes later, Albert came out carrying a few boxes and placed them next to the dumpster behind the school. They were boxes of glass panes. I had no idea what they were used for but decided to see if I could sell them. I went straight to Joe Milo.

Joe told me that he would trade me a nickel bag for one of the boxes of glass panels so I walked back across the street to retrieve one of the parcels by the dumpster. As I was walking back to Joe's store a police car pulled right into the park. I continued to walk as if I'd nothing wrong but the officer got out of his car and asked me what I was carrying. I calmly told him that I'd found it by the dumpster and was going to sell it. I played it cool and offered to show him where I "found" it. The officer was friendly and was calmly eating grapes as he walked around the dumpster then began checking doors. "We had a report that someone broke into the school," he said as he walked up to the door that Albert had pried open. "If I don't see any forced entry, I'll assume it was trash and let you go." As soon as he said that, he opened the door and noticed it had been forced. The officer calmly went back to his squad car, placed his grapes on the front seat and proceeded to put my hands behind my back and handcuff me. "I never went into the school, I swear I found these," I declared in my defense. "Doesn't matter," the officer said. "You're under arrest for possession of stolen property."

As I was riding in the back of the police car to the 69th Precinct, all I could think about was how my father was going to react, recalling the day Warren was brought home by the police. But this was different. I was sixteen years old and would be charged as an adult, meaning that mommy and daddy couldn't pick me up and take me home. They took me into a room and began questioning me about the items. I insisted that I wasn't the one who broke into the school. Looking to cover my ass and get home before my father found out, I said to the officer, "Look I swear I found those by the dumpster. What if I tell you who really broke into the school?" I was so afraid of my father that I was willing to sell out my own friend. "We don't care, now we know the goods were stolen," and he proceeded to read me my Miranda rights. I probably deserved it for what I was about to do.

After being processed at the 69th Precinct, I was placed in the back of a police van along with three other guys and transported to

Central Booking in downtown Brooklyn. After getting fingerprinted they took my mug shot and placed me in a cell with about seven older black guys who were all *much* bigger than me. I was terrified as I walked in but tried to act as cool as possible. I was small but very muscular and had tattoos that I'd gotten over the past year on both my calves and upper arm. I didn't look like a pushover. Surprisingly, they were cool with me and asked why I was there. "Possession of stolen property," I slyly said. "You must be hooked up with the Italians," one of the guys in the cell blurted out. "They're the only white guys you see in here." He couldn't have done me a bigger favor. I wasn't afraid anymore.

After about three hours in the cell, I heard an officer yell out my name, "Cuccurullo!" I immediately jumped up. "You're getting out, someone's here to pick you up," he said. I was thrilled to be getting out but terrified that my father was on the other side of the door. As they walked me out of the cellblock and into the visiting area, I was relieved to see my aunt's boyfriend, Louie, and not my father. Louie had been dating my Aunt Linda for a while and had become friends with my mom and dad. He was also connected to the Lucchese Crime family although I never really knew to what extent. I do know that it was Louie who got me out early. I wasn't supposed to get released until I saw a judge, but it was magically arranged that I only receive a desk appearance ticket. On the way home all I could think about was my father beating me up just as he did to Warren years ago. When I got to the house I was too afraid to go in so I stayed out front, pacing the sidewalk. When my father came out he had rage in his eyes and I immediately bolted from the front steps and hauled ass down the street. Louie tried to run after me but took two steps and realized the futility.

I returned home hours later after I called my mother who promised me that my father wouldn't hit me. The first thing out of his mouth was, "If you needed the fuckin' five dollars that bad, why didn't you fuckin' ask me?" his voice rising on the question. "I give you guys every fuckin' thing you need, and you get arrested for five fuckin' dollars? What the fuck is wrong with you?" I sat there silently. He then surprised me when he screamed, "I know you're smokin' that shit. I knew all you guys did, but after your brother made it I didn't think it was a big deal. I figured you'd all grow out of it." My first response was, "I don't smoke pot." That made my father angrier as his voice raised even higher. "Do I look like a fuckin' moron to you? Do I? If I catch you smoking that shit again, you're out of this fuckin' house!" I knew he'd never kick me out of the house at sixteen, but I got the point. Sort of. I stayed away from the park and didn't smoke for three days, but eventually caved and went back to getting high.

I walked into Milo's store and to my delight he was still selling nickel bags. He asked about my arrest but all he seemed concerned with was whether I mentioned his name to the police. I hadn't. After buying the weed, Albert and I went into the back of the park to smoke. When we were finished we headed back to the store to play video games. As Albert was watching me play, he took a piece of gum out of his pocket and ate it. Suddenly Joe grabbed Albert by the arm and yelled, "You didn't pay for that! Get out of my store!" Joe towered over Albert and easily dragged him towards the door, while Albert screamed, "What the fuck are you doing? It was my gum! Let go of me!" Joe tossed Albert out of the store so hard that he fell to the ground and scraped his knees. As I followed Albert out of the store and helped him up, he said in a low angry voice, "I'm telling my stepfather on this guy."

What I didn't know at the time was that Albert's stepfather was a "made man" in the Gambino Crime family. Albert went home and told his stepfather what had happened. He also told him that Joe was selling pot to the kids in the park. The following Saturday afternoon, I was in Joe's store with two of my friends playing video games. As the front door hit the bells that were placed there to alert

Joe of customers, I turned around and saw a short stocky well-groomed Italian guy in his mid-twenties wearing a designer jogging suit walking into the store. Without saying a word to Joe, he looked at us and calmly said, "You kids go across the street in the park for a while, I gotta talk to Joe." Although none of us knew him we knew he was mob connected by the way he looked and talked. Without any hesitation or thought, we followed his orders and headed to the back of the park.

A few minutes later we watched as a blue Lincoln Continental pulled up in front of the store. The man in the jogging suit calmly walked out of the store and got into the car. As the car drove off my two friends and I began walking back to the store to continue playing our games. I entered the store first and immediately saw Joe Milo lying on the floor face up, gasping for air with blood pouring from his chest. I was in shock and didn't know what to do. As I stood over him, he just looked up at me and said in a garbled voice, "I can't believe I'm going to die." As my friend Charlie followed me into the store and saw Joe lying on the floor he yelled out "Holy fucking shit!" We immediately ran out of the store and up the side street as fast as we could. I remember running for blocks and when I turned around my two friends were nowhere in sight. I went straight home and stayed in my bedroom for about an hour, but my curiosity or my stupidity made me return to the scene of the crime. As I came closer to the store I noticed that the police had already taped off the area and a crowd of about forty or fifty people was outside the barricades trying to get a look. About twenty minutes later they carried out Joe Milo's covered body and placed it in the ambulance. Detectives were now quizzing people in the crowd asking if anyone saw anything. A detective came within two feet of me but didn't talk to me. I was just another curious bystander.

Joe Milo's murder in the spring of 1981 signified an end to my days hanging out at 114 Park. I was about to turn seventeen and was now driving. His murder had a profound effect on me as I couldn't get the image of a dying Joe Milo out of my head. I didn't realize it until days later, but I was the last person Joe saw before he died. I had finally shaken the Crazy Sal nightmares but now had something else haunting my dreams. Although I know now that it was his actions that got him killed, I couldn't help but feel somewhat responsible for his death being the one who told him how to make money selling pot. I also had strong feelings of guilt for running away and not calling for help. For years I thought that I might have saved him if I'd called an ambulance, but as I got older I realized that nobody survives four bullets to the chest at point-blank range. It would be many years before I told a soul that I saw the man who killed him. His murder was never solved, and years later with the advent of the internet I decided to research it. Strangely, I was unable to find anything relating to the murder of Joe Milo.

# Chapter 7
# The Fun House

Now that I was driving, for the first time in my life I was able to go wherever I wanted, whenever I wanted. Jerry and I shared the 1973 Gold Cadillac Coupe Deville that my father had purchased for $800. But he was still living in Los Angeles so basically the car was all mine. I was able to keep my father happy by going to work and not bringing pot in the house. Instead, I stashed my weed in the spare tire in the trunk and kept a good supply of Binaca, cologne, and Visine in the glovebox. With many of my friends from the park going their own ways, my friend Richie and I started hanging out on Avenue L near the Canarsie Movie Theater where I became friendly with a new crew of guys.

Although disco was now dead my friends and I were still into the dance scene and loved going to the clubs in the City. The problem for me and a few of my friends was that at seventeen we were still a year away from the legal drinking age. Most of us had purchased fake IDs in Times Square but they didn't work on Manhattan bouncers. I'd used Jerry's license before because they didn't have pictures at the time, but with him away that was no longer an option. Occasionally, depending on the club, you could slip the bouncer either a ten or twenty dollar bill to let you in but usually I couldn't spare it. I was able to get into the clubs on some occasions but also found myself standing outside nightclubs for hours on end because I couldn't get in and didn't drive yet. A few months before the Milo murder my buddy Robert Johnson took me to a new club that turned out to be one of the greatest experiences of my young life.

The name of the club was the Fun House, and it was located on West 26th Street in Manhattan. I got into the Fun House for the first time at age sixteen by handing a ten-dollar bill to the bouncer working the door. The first person I encountered when I walked up to the cashier to pay the $15 cover charge was a short, flaming gay man with blond hair who would not stop staring at me. While having second thoughts about going inside, Robert whispered to me that his name was Ronnie and he was one of the owners.

As we walked past the cashier and into the club I was mesmerized. The music was louder than anything I had ever heard, and I could feel the bass pulse right through me as I passed one of the huge speakers located throughout the club. The place was exceptionally dark but had spinning and flashing strobe lights that enabled you to see your way through the crowd. Near the entrance, dealers were brazenly selling their drugs. Within a radius of about twenty feet, you were able to purchase everything from pot to pills, Quaaludes, and mescaline. As I walked past one guy, he said, "Yo man, I got blow." I'd never done cocaine before but tried to buy some anyway. When the dealer told me it was fifty dollars a bag I wound up settling for two "Black Beauties" for three dollars each. Black Beauties were amphetamines or "uppers," which I was told had a similar effect as cocaine.

Robert, who had been there before, took me upstairs to the balcony where everyone got high. As soon as you walked up the stairs the smell of marijuana and angel dust hit you in the face. There was a long bar where people were openly snorting cocaine. Robert broke open our Black Beauties and dumped the white powder on the bar and broke it into four lines. He rolled up a bill and snorted two lines then handed the bill to me. When I asked him why we were snorting them, he replied, "It makes us look cool, like we're doing coke." I didn't argue with him and proceeded to snort the two lines. Within a few seconds, I started to feel the effects. Suddenly I couldn't stand still and felt my heart begin to palpitate. I started to get nervous until Robert assured me it was the desired effect. "Go get a drink and walk around the club, you'll be fine," he assured me. "I'll catch up with you later." Wired out of mind and on my own in a strange club, I took a tour of the Fun House.

The back of the balcony was an extremely dark area that had pillowed couches where people were doing drugs and making out. As I looked down on the club, there was a giant dance floor that had a huge twenty-foot clown face covering the DJ booth. People were dancing on a huge stage in the middle of the room which they also used for live performances. They had a large game room in the back that consisted of about forty or fifty of the latest video games and pinball machines. The arcade also featured an area where you could purchase Fun House items with the signature clown logo, and replica bumper cars that you could sit in. It also had a huge punching bag game where for a quarter you could measure how hard you punched. As I walked across the main dance floor I noticed a cute girl who was wearing a shirt that had the name of a song on it. It read "Push, Push, In the Bush."

After talking to her for a few minutes we spent the next hour or so dancing next to the giant clown. When we finished dancing she grabbed my hand and led me upstairs to the balcony where we started making out on one of the fuzzy red couches. Then she asked me if I wanted to do cocaine. "Why? You have some?" I asked. With that, she took out a small glass vile and unscrewed it to reveal a tiny spoon attached to the cap. She scooped out some of the coke and placed it under my nostril so I could snort it. She gave me another one in the other nostril and then took two hits herself. Before she put it away she placed a tiny amount on my tongue, which tasted absolutely disgusting. Within a minute my mouth was numb with an unbelievably euphoric feeling that I had never experienced from any drug.

I was talking a mile a minute until she grabbed my neck and started making out with me again. She put her hand over my crotch and started rubbing me over my pants. I immediately got an erection. She then proceeded to slide her hand under my pants. Before I knew it, she pulled out my dick and started giving me a blowjob. I was worried that someone would see us until I realized that it was so dark it was a moot point. She finished me off within a few minutes and then we casually returned to the dance floor to end the night. Except for a few feeble attempts by past girlfriends, that was my first real sexual experience.

Unfortunately, not long after that night the Fun House was shut down for numerous alcohol infractions, mainly underage drinking. The same owners would reopen the club in the spring of 1981 minus the alcohol and fuzzy red couches. There was really no need for liquor as most of the kids who went to the Fun House were doing drugs and couldn't afford Manhattan drink prices anyway. They also relaxed the dress code to allow people to wear whatever they liked. The best change to the Fun House was the new resident deejay that they hired. His name was John "Jellybean" Benitez. He was a master remixer and created his own unique sound by fusing disco, funk, and R&B with the new electric sound of the '80s. Within months word spread about the amazing new DJ at the Fun House, and they began to draw up to three thousand people every Friday and Saturday night.

Saturday night soon became a weekly ritual for me and my friends as Friday nights were for the girlfriends. All week we would practice new dance moves to show off at the Fun House. Gone were the days of going to clubs dressed in slacks and shoes. We now dressed to dance and wore satin shorts which only came down to the tops of our thighs, and long white striped tube socks that came up to our knees. We cut off the sleeves on our Fun House t-shirts and cut them halfway up to show off our flat stomachs. We wore rolled up bandanas around our heads with a long-feathered roach clip attached to the back. For some odd reason, with all the dancing we did, we still wore those cheap slip-on sailor sneakers we called "Decks."

Before we left for the City we'd usually meet on Avenue L to get high. About eight or nine of us would drink and smoke big fatties of bad commercial pot that we called "mung" weed. Then we'd all pile into my friend Barry's station wagon with a couple of us having to lay down in the back of his car. We would blast our Fun House tapes and whenever a good part of a song came on somebody would scream "Car break!" and we'd all simultaneously bounce up and down. The car would vehemently shake as we drove through the Brooklyn Battery Tunnel at one hundred miles an hour.

After exiting the tunnel, we'd drive down the West Side Highway through the gay neighborhood. Sometimes a few of my friends would scream derogatory obscenities at them. It always seemed so senseless. On one occasion as one of my friends was taunting a couple of gay men standing on the corner of Christopher Street when someone threw a bottle at the car. Barry stopped the car and two of my friends got out to confront them. Instantly, as though they were expecting us, about twenty gay men dressed in leather biker outfits came charging towards the car. I saw the look of terror on my friends' faces as they desperately tried to get back in the car, barely making it to safety. That was the last time any of us got out of the car in that neighborhood.

Now that the Fun House had no liquor license it was easier to get in if you were under eighteen. I still had a hard time getting in because of my youthful appearance, but after pulling up in my father's newly leased Cadillac Eldorado there was never a problem. The bouncers would let me park the car in front of the club for ten bucks. A few weeks later my father surprised me and Jerry when he leased another Cadillac for us to use. When I pulled up to the Fun House in my new car, the head bouncer said to me, "You're pretty young to be driving around in all these fancy cars. Is your father connected or something?" I knew he was insinuating the mob, so I just smiled and said, "Yup." After that, we never had to wait on line which sometimes went halfway up the block.

Kids from all over New York City and New Jersey came to the Fun House to get high and dance to the music of Jellybean. He was becoming very popular with the Puerto Rican and Italian kids who made up a good portion of the crowd. There were also large groups of Italian kids from Ozone Park, Queens, and the Bronx. Each neighborhood had their own section of the Fun House. The Canarsie contingent, which grew to over seventy-five people at its peak, hung out and danced on the main stage. Although I'm sure there were kids from all different backgrounds, there were never any black kids in the club. I was in line once when I heard the bouncer tell a black couple who were obviously of age that the Fun House was a private club that required a membership card to be admitted. It was complete bullshit.

Even with three thousand teenagers all doing various drugs there were rarely any fights at the club. It helped that they had huge bouncers all over the place, but it seemed that all anyone cared about was getting high, hooking up, and dancing. The bouncers were the ones allowing the drug dealing because they were all getting a cut. If they caught you dealing without their permission, you'd find yourself being literally thrown out the door head first. One guy made the mistake of punching one of the bouncers breaking up a fight, and I watched as three huge bouncers pummeled this guy until he was lying on the floor unresponsive. To add insult to injury, they picked him up and threw him on the sidewalk outside the club.

I was always convinced that the reason for the minimal number of fights was that there was no alcohol served. I watched my own friends over the years get extremely rowdy and start many fights whenever they drank, but usually not when they got high on other drugs. I never got violent on any drug including alcohol, and always tried to avoid confrontations. There was a small contingent of guys who smoked Angel Dust in the balcony, and there were always a few guys passed out on Quaaludes scattered around the club, but most people in the Fun House were doing drugs that kept you dancing into the early morning hours. Mainly mescaline and cocaine.

I had done cocaine on a few occasions since my first Fun House adventure about a year prior, but because it was expensive I usually resorted to taking what the dealers called double barrel purple mescaline. The drug we started taking years ago to make us laugh was now the drug that fueled our hours of nonstop dancing. Mescaline was only five dollars a hit and lasted for close to four hours after taking about an hour to take effect. I would usually take a hit on the car ride to the club so it would hit me right when I got there. Mescaline had the speedy effect which kept you dancing, but it was also a hallucinogenic that could play tricks with your mind.

There were nights when I was tripping so hard that I felt everyone around me moving in slow motion amplified by the continuous strobe lights. The drug also took away every ounce of social skills that I possessed. It made me paranoid to talk to anyone, especially girls, because I always assumed they knew I was tripping and were laughing at me. The thing that scared me most about mescaline was that it had a strange effect on my private parts. My penis would shrivel up but only towards the base making it look like an alien, and my testicles looked as if they were fused together as one. There were a few nights where I did the second hit of mescaline somewhere around 4 am and was still high when I got back to Canarsie. Now that I had my own room in the basement I was able to come and go as I pleased and avoid my parents seeing me looking like a zombie.

Going out had always fueled my anticipation that I'd meet some cute girl and hook up with her. Now that I was doing mescaline regularly I found myself avoiding girls and going home with shriveled balls. I always preferred the effects of cocaine but took mescaline for purely economic reasons. I was extremely social on coke when I first started doing it, and it also acted as an aphrodisiac. A fifty-dollar piece was the cheapest you could get, and that was almost one-fourth of my weekly paycheck. To make it more affordable a few of us would chip in and share the bag. With many noses to supply it went fast. Eventually, I began bringing my own piece, sharing with a friend or two or a girl I was trying to pick up. As much as I tried to conserve it, I found myself finishing it all well before closing time. Whenever I ran out of drugs there was always one person I would seek out in the club. He always had coke, no matter the time of night…or morning.

His name was Randy and he was a year older than me. He lived down the block from me in Canarsie and we'd met a few years back. Robert Johnson and I used to hang out in his basement, smoke pot, and repeatedly listen to the Saturday Night Fever soundtrack. Randy worked long hours in his father's popular restaurant so he always had lots of money. He'd bring an eight ball to the club with him every weekend which back then cost about three hundred dollars. He was very generous and would share his coke, not just with me but with many of his friends. It got to a point where almost everyone in the club knew he had coke, and by the early morning hours, almost everyone was begging him for some. It became a major power trip for him but over time he became less generous, selecting only certain people to do it with him. I was among the selected. After Randy was spotted in the deejay booth with Jellybean one night, his friends dubbed him the "Cocaine King of the Fun House."

The party typically rolled on until the early morning. After spending seven or eight hours in a loud, dark club the silence was a welcome reprieve, but the early morning sun always burned my eyes as we walked outside. My car was usually parked directly in front of the club, and sometimes there would be random people from Canarsie waiting nearby looking for a ride home. I always had a full car so on plenty of nights they were stuck taking the subway. If we weren't too exhausted and had money we'd go to the diner. In the summer, we'd occasionally go to the beach and sleep on the sand. But most nights it was me driving with all my friends asleep in the car. By the time the club closed, I wasn't stoned, but I was crashing on cocaine and clearly shouldn't have been driving. On Memorial Day weekend, 1982, while driving home from the Fun House, I experienced something so surreal that I wasn't quite sure it was actually happening.

While heading home that early Sunday morning I turned on the radio and the local station Z100 was doing a Top 100 countdown for the holiday weekend. They were playing the song "Stone Cold." As it faded out the announcer said, "That was number eighty-eight, Stone Cold by Rainbow. Coming up next, Missing Persons have been found." He then broke to a commercial. In my compromised state of mind it took a second to register what I'd just heard. When I realized it was my brother's band I started yelling, "Guys wake up! My brother's song is going to be on the radio!" Complete silence. Again, I yelled, "Yo guys, I'm not kidding, Missing Persons is coming on next!" as I nudged my friend Armando who was passed out in the front seat. All I got from him was a sarcastic and barely audible, "that's great" as my other three friends remained unresponsive in the backseat. When the commercial ended and the announcer came back on I was immediately glued to the radio.

They began talking about the new band from California that was making their top 100-chart debut. My mother had told me a few weeks back that Warren's record would be released soon, but I never imagined they would chart so fast. Thinking they were about to play the song, the announcer instead said, "Here's Missing Persons guitarist Warren Cuccurullo...." I have no idea what they said following my last name, and as Warren started to speak a chill went through my body. I turned the volume up. I felt as if I was all alone in that car and that Warren was sitting behind me talking. It was exciting and scary at the same time as I wasn't sure if what I was hearing was real. After Warren finished speaking of which I remember nothing, the announcer said, "Debuting at number eighty-seven with their new song Words, here's Missing Persons." As the song played and my friends slept I had mixed emotions. I was thrilled for my brother's success, but it made me realize that I was about to turn eighteen and my life was going nowhere.

# Chapter 8
# White Lines

With my father's financial support, two years of hard work, and relentless self-promotion, Missing Persons signed with Capitol Records in March 1982. With label support, they re-released the EP and sold another 250,000 records. In October 1982, they would release the band's first full-length album "Spring Session M," an anagram of their name. They'd already released the single "Words" which spent eleven weeks in the Top 100 charts and peaked at number 42. A month before the release of the album Capitol released the second single, "Destination Unknown," which would spend thirteen weeks in the Top 100, also peaking at 42. They would release two more singles off the album, "Windows" and "Walking in L.A.," and both cracked the top 100. Their popularity grew as their music videos received regular airplay on the new music video channel, MTV. Spring Session M sold over 500,000 records and was certified "Gold" in 1983.

Warren was now officially a rock star and enjoying his new-found fame in Los Angeles while I was on the road to self-destruction. I managed to make my parents happy by getting my high school equivalency diploma and continuing to work for my father. He had taken me off the delivery van and now had me working in the shop, performing menial tasks alongside my father's partner who ran the shop while my dad did outside sales. I was miserable the second I walked into work and stared at the clock all day. I smoked a joint before, during, and immediately after every work day, then got high with my friends at night. Somehow with all the drugs I was using, I continued playing baseball and started playing competitive fastpitch softball. The only thing I enjoyed more than getting high was playing ball. It was the only thing in which I thought I truly exceled.

I continued doing cocaine on the weekends with the same crew of my Fun House friends. One of them was named Mario who I'd known years earlier through playing sports. He was also a good athlete and very smart, having been elected Valedictorian of his graduating class. Although he was only 5'5," he was stocky and had a reputation as one of the toughest guys in Canarsie. Following high school, he enrolled in college and majored in business. I was a little jealous of him because I viewed myself as just as smart and could have accomplished what he did academically. We began playing on the same softball teams together and soon became close friends. He was also a big Missing Persons fan, and I would take him to all the concerts with me. Mario didn't smoke pot, but like the rest of the crew he liked cocaine.

In the beginning, blow was something that added to the fun of whatever we were doing. Usually, we would do it when we went out to the clubs, but sometimes Mario and I would do some lines and cruise around Canarsie in my father's Cadillac. On some nights, my girlfriend Michele and I would snort lines in my car baring our souls to each other for hours. When we were still doing relatively small amounts we would park in semi-deserted areas and do "bumps" in the car. Eventually that became almost impossible as the drug made some of my friends extremely paranoid. I never got paranoid and always thought the safest place to do it was in plain sight. I would pull over on a busy street or sometimes even double park, snort a line or two, and leave before anyone noticed. Ultimately, we realized the repercussions of getting caught and decided to take the party indoors.

Mario and I would hang out with my friend Randy who would throw cocaine parties in his basement every Friday night while his parents were out. There were usually about nine or ten of Randy's friends, both guys and girls, snorting lines as Randy blasted his Fun House music. He'd repeatedly play the new rap song "White Lines" as everyone sang along word for word. Although the song warns against the dangers of cocaine, we didn't care. It became our anthem. Mario and I would usually go there with a fifty-dollar piece that would last us a few hours. Randy always had his eight ball with plenty to spare by the time most of us had blown through our stash. As the weeks progressed Randy started acting more bizarre, constantly stopping the music because he imagined someone was coming into the house. While he did his coke in a small room in the back of his basement, he'd shut off all the lights except for a small purple blackout lamp, making it almost impossible to see. He wouldn't allow anyone to do coke outside that of that room and soon the girls stopped coming over. Eventually, it got so weird that Mario and I stopped going to Randy's house, too.

Over the next few months we hopped around from house to house doing our drugs on weekends, and occasionally during the week. The only thing that kept it under control was that it was expensive and not always easy to get. Sometimes there would be "droughts" in the neighborhood when you couldn't find anything. That all changed for me and my crew when Mario began dealing cocaine. He started out just selling twenty-five and fifty-dollar pieces to his immediate friends but soon expanded his sales to friends of friends. He never sold to anyone he didn't know and carefully operated under the radar to avoid the local mob wannabes. By his sophomore year, he had dropped out of college and taken a job in the city, and continued to deal cocaine. He used his street smarts, self-discipline, and frugalness to build up a very lucrative drug business. Within a year he'd bought himself a brand-new BMW. I used to hang out in his room while he "cut" the cocaine with other substances to increase his profit and would help him package his stash. One day he pulled out a bag from the top of his closet and dumped the contents on his bed. It was just a little over $100,000 in cash.

Mario was all business and would only sell to you if you had the cash. As we became better friends he began extending credit to me and a few of our other close friends. He'd let some of us accrue a couple hundred bucks of debt before he started bugging us for the money. He never threatened any of us, but would cut us off if we couldn't pay. I'd now built up a tolerance to cocaine and needed to do more to get high. I went from spending fifty dollars a week on coke to over two hundred dollars, about half my salary. What made it worse was that Mario began extending me more and more credit, and my "bill" was fast approaching a thousand dollars. We'd become best friends, but Mario would still ask me for money every week. I gave him money when I could, but as much coke as I was doing hardly put a dent in what I owed him.

In the summer of 1983, my parents purchased an oceanfront condominium in Monmouth Beach, New Jersey, about sixty miles from Canarsie. Now that my parents were going to the Jersey Shore every weekend my house became party central on Friday nights. My sister had moved to the City, and with my brother Jerry's L.A. group now disbanded, he was back living in the basement. He was smoking his pot and didn't give two shits about us being there. My friends liked coming to my family's house because we had a big screen television and a videocassette recorder, new technology at the time. Six or seven of them would wait on the corner until they saw my parents pull out of the driveway. The second the car turned the corner they'd come bursting through the door. They brought cheap beer, good vodka, and Valiums to come down from the coke that Mario always brought. The first night we partied at my house on East 94th Street would be the first time that I smoked cocaine.

They called it freebasing, and most of us had never tried it before. Mario had done it a few times and seemed to know everything about it. He knew exactly how much baking soda and water to mix with the cocaine, and how long it needed to cook. Using a straightened-out wire hanger he pulled the entire glob of gooey, freshly cooked freebase out of the test tube and dropped in onto a mirror without leaving a drop behind. He dried it out on the mirror until it got hard and then used a razor blade to break it up into smaller pieces. Mario warned us that since freebase was pure cocaine you had to be very careful with how much you put in the pipe. If you did too much at once it could cause a heart attack.

He took a chunk about the size of a small pebble and placed it into a glass pipe with a long stem layered with metal screens and attached to a round glass bottom with a four-inch mouthpiece. On the side of the pipe it said, "I Love New York," with a heart replacing the word love. Using a miniature blowtorch called a Super Cub, Mario slowly and carefully lit the pipe until the cocaine started to make a crackling sound as the smoke poured into the bottom of the pipe and then into his lungs. After he held it in for a few seconds he then exhaled the smoke. He appeared to "leave us" as he stared straight ahead without saying a word. After a few seconds, he just smiled, shook his head and said, "Wow." Now we all wanted to do a hit.

The immediate high from smoking cocaine was unlike any drug I had ever done, and much more intense than snorting it. The first time I did a hit I couldn't utter a word for half an hour. After another ten or fifteen minutes when the initial effects of the high wore off, I immediately wanted another hit. Since the rest of us were amateurs at smoking it Mario took control of everything. Not only did he cook it, he regulated how much you did, and lit the torch for us. He would instruct you when to inhale, and how long to hold it in. After a few hits we wanted to try it by ourselves, but Mario wouldn't let us. It may have been my house, but it was his pipe, his torch, and his cocaine. When we had finished our last hit we drank beer and vodka and took Valiums to help us come down and sleep.

This immediately became a weekly ritual. Every Friday night it was the same cast of characters and the same routine. Mario would call me up before the night kicked off to ask me how much coke I wanted for the night. I usually asked him to bring me a fifty-dollar piece which was plenty since everyone bought their own. Although all of us owed money to Mario from previous purchases he would still extend us credit. Whenever I told him I was broke he'd say, "Don't worry, I'll put it on your bill." After a while, I didn't even have to ask, and Mario would just bring me the same amount every week. He even stopped asking me for money which reinforced the fact that he was my best friend.

Even though we were only doing it on Friday nights, within months the drug began to get the best of us. After doing your first hit you spent the rest of the night unsuccessfully trying to duplicate it. We began taking bigger and bigger hits that made us run out faster. Since Mario always had double the amount we had, we'd always finish long before him. While we waited for Mario to finish his batch the rest of us would scrape out the brown residue that accumulated on the inside of the glass pipe after each hit. After it dried you could easily get it out in chunks using a wire hanger and re-smoke it. It wasn't as strong as the actual rock, but it not only got us a few extra hits it kept us from begging Mario for more. As soon as we finished I would pack up all the drug paraphernalia and hide it in my sports bag in my bedroom closet. Everyone left before the sun came up after the booze and pills took effect, except my friend Dave who would always sleep over. After everyone left, Dave and I would take out all the pipes and scrape them out again, scavenging enough to last for a couple more hours. When we were done we'd start drinking all over again to come down. There were Friday nights where I got high for fifteen hours straight and then sleep all day Saturday and straight into Sunday. It got to a point that I would blow off hanging out with my girlfriend on Saturdays just so I could recover. She would dump me weeks later.

Things got out of hand as I started freebasing on any given night if I had a place to do it. If we couldn't find somewhere to cook the coke, we'd just hang out and snort it. Whenever I did coke on work nights I'd come home so wired up that I'd stare at the ceiling for hours, unable to sleep. Even smoking pot wouldn't help as sometimes I smoked multiple joints to no avail. Sometimes I'd sneak a drink from my parents' liquor cabinet, but they must have realized what was happening and stopped buying it. Without much TV programming those days, I spent many nights staring at my ceiling, my mind racing a hundred miles an hour, praying that I'd fall asleep and swearing to myself that I'd never do it again. I would look at the clock for what seemed like every minute, dreading the arrival of 6 am when my father came to wake me up for work.

If I hadn't slept there was no way I was going to work. The thought of standing in that noisy, sweaty factory on no sleep having to listen to my father's partner boss me around was unimaginable in my state of mind. I would rather listen to my father scream like a lunatic when I tried to feign illness. I would either force myself to throw up, heat the thermometer up to show a high temperature, or promise my father I would take the subway to work. I did everything in my power just to shut him up and get him to leave so I could go back to bed. On the days when I did promise him I would take the subway I would show up two or three hours late. Eventually, I would just stop showing up altogether. One morning when I refused to get up for work my father snapped.

He grabbed me by the arm and dragged me out of the bed and onto the floor, "Get the fuck up you waste of fuckin' life," my father screamed like a crazy man. "I know you're getting high you fuckin' junkie. Is that what you wanna be? A fucking junkie?" I began crying hysterically as if I was eight and not eighteen. "I'm sorry, I'm sorry dad, I'm so sorry," was all I could say over and over as I laid on the floor. "Is your life so bad that you have to get high?" he asked as his voice got a little lower. "Your brother stopped getting high, why can't you?" he said, referring to Warren's lifestyle change. "Why can't you be more like him?" My father had never compared me to my brother before, and for the first time I was jealous of my brother's success. What hurt the most was that I had let my father down. Maybe I *was* becoming a waste of life.

I did go to work that day and sat in the back of the car with my Walkman on, never say a word on the ride to the City. With no sleep, I struggled to get through the day and immediately crashed on the car ride home. When I got to the house I went straight to bed and woke up refreshed at 5 am the next day. I went upstairs and made breakfast and started the coffee for my parents. When they awoke they were pleasantly surprised to see me up and ready for work. It put my father in a good mood. "The vampire is up early," my father joked as he came in the kitchen. As he began to prepare his coffee he caught me completely off guard when he said, "Maybe you should go stay with your brother for a few weeks." Before I could even react, he said, "Maybe he could help you stop smoking that shit." I was relieved that my father never knew what I was smoking was cocaine and was ecstatic to return to California to see Warren.

My father sent me to Los Angeles in the summer of 1983 to stay with Warren for a few weeks and get my head together. I was happy to get out of Canarsie for a while and knew I needed a break from the cocaine rut I'd fallen into. I was also thrilled to be going back to Los Angeles at a time when Missing Persons was at the height of their popularity. When I landed at the airport I was greeted by my brother's friend, Thomas, since Missing Persons were playing a venue that night in Hollywood. We arrived at Warren's apartment around midnight and I immediately crashed on his couch before he got home. When I woke up hours later there was a cute girl wearing only an oversized t-shirt making coffee in the kitchen.

Already knowing who I was she introduced herself as Jane and asked if I was hungry. I told her I was starving, and she went through all my brother's cabinets looking for something to make. She prepared a huge breakfast and talked with me while Warren soundly slept in the other room. She was the nicest, sweetest girl, and we talked for about a half hour before she gave me a kiss on the cheek and left before Warren woke up. The whole time I was talking to her I couldn't help but think that she looked familiar. When Warren came out of his room he asked me if I had met her. I said, "Yeah, she's a sweetheart, why does she look so familiar?" He calmly replied, "Oh, she's with the 'Go-Go's.'" "We Got the Beat" and "Our Lips Are Sealed" were huge hits at the time and it was at that moment I realized that I recognized Jane from the huge Go-Go's poster that was hanging in my room. Warren would later joke that her lips weren't sealed.

Over the next few weeks, I felt like I was a part of the band and got to experience the life of a rock star. I went to a couple of live concerts and could watch the show from the side of the stage with an "All Access" pass hanging around my neck. I went with Warren when he did radio and television interviews and would join the band when they did promotional appearances at various clubs. At one club I walked into a VIP area with Dale, and within seconds there were over a dozen photographers snapping pictures of us. Whenever we went out to dinner there was always someone asking for an autograph or a picture. When they weren't playing or promoting they were in the studio working on material for their next album. I was having the time of my life, and I didn't want it to end.

As prevalent as it was in Hollywood, during my time in California I was able to stay away from cocaine. Except for Dale who occasionally smoked pot, no one in the band did drugs. I did smoke with Dale the first few days I was there, but when Warren found out he yelled at her for smoking with me. Warren had become a strict vegetarian and was now very anti-drug. And, he was under strict orders from my father to keep me away from pot. Except for a few beers at the concerts, I went the next seventeen days without doing any drugs. On one of the car rides to the studio Warren and I had a long talk for the first time as two adults. "What the fuck are you doing with your life, bro?" he asked. "You're not going to accomplish anything as long as you're smoking that shit." When I confided in him that I was also smoking cocaine, he flipped out on me. "You fuckin' idiot! Do you know you can die from that shit? Are you a fuckin' moron?" I had never seen Warren that mad, and he wouldn't let me get a word in as he continued to chastise me. "I thought you wanted to be a ballplayer. You need to be fuckin' practicing every day and taking care of your body. How the fuck you think I made it? Once I was able to clear my mind I was able to focus on my career. That's what you need to do." I idolized my brother and his words really hit home.

I dreaded returning to Canarsie. I desperately wanted to stay in Los Angeles with Warren knowing he'd keep me away from drugs. I liked being sober and thought that if I stayed in Los Angeles I could get in shape and continue pursuing my dream of playing professional baseball. I begged him to give me a job but he informed me that dad had other plans. On the car ride home from the airport, my father surprised me with some news. While I was away he'd leased a brand new, fully loaded white Cadillac Coupe Deville. Although I did absolutely nothing to earn it, he handed me the keys and told me it was mine. He said, "Just show up for work on time every day, and I'll pay for the car and the insurance." Before I could utter a word, he shocked me when he said, "If you can do that for a year straight, I'll lease you a Porsche." I was blown away by my father's generosity, and repeatedly gushed, "Wow" and "Thank you, dad." I was old enough to know that my father was literally trying to bribe me to stay clean but also realized that it was his way of saying he loved me. Before we arrived at the house my father reminded me of our deal and added, "Your brothers and sister have their careers. Just do the right thing and this business can be yours one day." I was thrilled seeing the Cadillac sitting in front of the house, but the thought of selling swatch cards the rest of my life killed the buzz.

# Chapter 9
# Centerfield

I spent the first few days back in Canarsie driving my new Cadillac around the neighborhood, blasting music and trying to impress the girls. I stayed away from smoking pot. Warren's talk had a huge effect on me, but I also didn't want to give my father an excuse to take back the car. When Friday night rolled around I lied to my friends and told them my parents weren't going to Jersey so they wouldn't bug me to freebase in my house. I was also scared after Warren told me that you could die from smoking cocaine. I had been sober for three weeks now, and for the first time in years, I felt as if I was thinking clearly. The only downside to not smoking pot was that my nightmares about Joe Milo's murder had returned. Other than that, all I could think about was how much I enjoyed my brother's popularity and success and how I wanted the same thing. Since I didn't play an instrument I knew my only shot at stardom was playing baseball. I was nineteen years old and knew that if I was going to make it to the Major Leagues my journey would have to start immediately.

Knowing I would never achieve my dream of playing professional baseball by playing fastpitch softball in Canarsie, I joined a fall baseball team and began practicing with them several times a week. On the days we didn't practice, I went to the batting cages and hit baseballs until my hands were too sore to hold the bat. I noticed that my skills had eroded but I was still very quick. My friends had dubbed me "the fastest guy in Canarsie." I made it from home plate to first base in under four seconds, considered Major League speed. Since I was still able to track down any fly ball hit in my general direction, I concentrated on improving my hitting and throwing. At one of the practices, a guy on the team mentioned that the New York Mets were holding open tryouts in early October, but you needed a recommendation from an established coach to receive an invitation. Knowing it might be my only chance, I decided I *had* to be at that tryout.

As soon as I got home from practice I contacted my former baseball coach who was the one who always told me I had Major League speed. When I asked him for a recommendation he didn't hesitate and assured me he'd take care of it in the morning. I was thrilled and checked the mailbox every day the second I got home from work. Two weeks went by and I hadn't heard anything. I continued to hone my skills and stay sober, no easy feat with my friends bugging me to hang out and smoke every day. With about two weeks until the tryout date, I still hadn't received an invitation and started to get nervous. When I returned home from work one day I noticed that the mailbox was empty. When I came in the house my brother Jerry said, "You got mail from the Mets, I put it on your bed." I ran downstairs so fast I don't think my feet touched the floor. I opened the envelope with the excitement of a little kid on Christmas and proceeded to read it out loud. "Congratulations! You have been invited to take place in the open tryouts at Shea Stadium on Oct. 1, 1983. Please report to the Player's Entrance at 9:45 am sharp." This was it!

My father was excited for me but also kept me grounded. "The odds of making it to the Majors is a million to one...you know that, right?" It's not what I wanted to hear three days before the tryout. I explained to my father that I knew I wasn't ready for the Majors but if they liked me they'd start me out at Class A ball. Then he told me what everyone else was telling me, "You're too small, Rob. The days of guys 5'7 playing in the big leagues are over. The shortstops are now 6'2." I shot back, "There are guys my height playing in the Majors." My father sarcastically responded, "How many? Three?" I knew I was undersized, but I was sure that my speed and base stealing ability would impress the scouts. Base stealing had become a huge part of the game with guys like Rickey Henderson stealing over 100 bases a year. The Oakland A's even put a former sprinter on their roster and called him their "Designated Runner." I was so confident that I began hypothetically tracking how many years of minor league ball I would have to play before I made the Major Leagues.

I could barely sleep the night before the tryout, and even considered smoking pot with Jerry to help me sleep. I was proud of myself for abstaining even as my brother smoked in the next room. I had been sober for six weeks now and I felt better than I had in years. I awoke to a perfect day, with bright sunny skies and the temperature in the 70s. I grabbed my sports bag from the closet and left after eating a bowl of Cocoa Puffs for breakfast. There was little traffic on this early Saturday morning, and I arrived at Shea Stadium in Queens about an hour early. I stretched a little in the parking lot before making my way to the Player's Entrance. I thought there would be a ton of people trying out and was surprised to see only fifty or sixty guys waiting in line. One of my fears was being the smallest guy there, but to my delight, there were more than a few guys around my height, some even shorter. That made me feel more confident as they began to check us in.

As they walked us onto the field I was in my glory. I had been a huge Mets fan since age six, and even at nineteen continued to follow the team. Just being on the field was a thrill, and now I was going to play on it. Since the first time I picked up a baseball all I dreamed about was playing centerfield in this very stadium. Now I was closer than ever to making it a reality. After the coaches explained how the tryout would work they broke us up into three groups and instructed my group to sit in the visiting dugout. I wanted badly to go into the Mets dugout, but it was off limits. My group of about twenty players would field first and was instructed to grab their gloves and warm up. After putting on my cleats I went into my sports bag to grab my glove and was mortified as one of the glass pipes we used to smoke cocaine came flying out of the bag and shattered on the floor. "What was that?" one of the coaches asked. I nervously replied, "It was my juice bottle." "Well clean it up and get your ass on the field," he barked out.

This wasn't happening! How could I have been so careless?! I wanted to cry as I attempted to sweep up the broken glass with my glove. As I went to close my bag I noticed that all the drug paraphernalia was still in it, including the torch, dozens of screens, and the wire hangers we used to scrape out the pipes. The sight of it made me nauseous. I quickly zipped up the bag and ran out to centerfield. Fortunately, nobody saw anything but as I waited my turn to take fly balls, I suddenly felt like an imposter who had no business being there. I tried to get it out of my mind, but I couldn't. When the coach hit me the first fly ball to me I took two steps in as the ball sailed over my head. I was livid! How the fuck could I miss that?! What should have been an easy play turned into a disaster! I caught the second ball he hit but sailed the throw way over the third baseman's head. I was so distraught I don't even remember what I did on the third one. As livid as I was with myself I knew I could still impress them with my speed as the run was next.

I thought that they would individually time us around the bases and to first base, which is what I practiced in the weeks leading up to the tryout. According to my current coach, my times were already at the Major League level, which is why I was disappointed when they told us that we would just race each other. I was still mad at myself for missing that easy fly ball, and the thought of the drug paraphernalia in my bag still bothered me. But this was my time to shine and I wasn't going to blow it. The coaches put us in groups of three and had each group race. They would then take the winners and have them race, and so on until there was one left. I was hell bent on being that one guy left. As I lined up with my group ready for the short ninety-foot race, I took a deep breath as I looked at my opponents who were both to my left. The coach yelled "Go!" and as I took off I noticed the guy in the middle get a huge jump. He was immediately out in front. I turned on the afterburners and was running so fast that everything was blurry as I crossed the finish line. The coach yelled out the winner, "Number two!" I was number three.

What was supposed to be the greatest day of my life was a total nightmare, far worse than talking to a dying Joe Milo. We still had the hitting portion to complete, but as far as I was concerned the tryout was over. I hadn't lost a race since grade school and was still in shock that I had been eliminated. When it was time for my group to hit we were told we could only use the wooden bats that they provided. I hadn't used a wooden bat since I was eight and proceeded to miss the first four pitches thrown to me. I did hit a few hard line drives, but when it's batting practice you're not supposed to swing and miss. When the tryout was over they announced that if they were interested in anyone that they would be contacted by phone. As I dejectedly packed my glove into my bag of paraphernalia, I came to the realization that I would never become a professional baseball player.

I was so upset about everything that happened that day that I started crying hysterically as soon as I got into my car. Having my dream ripped from me in a matter of hours was difficult to digest, but the worst part was that I blamed the base pipe flying out of my bag for my poor performance. The truth was that I just wasn't good enough. I may have been the "fastest guy in Canarsie," but on that day I wasn't the fastest in Flushing. As I drove home I tortured myself thinking about what I could have accomplished had I stayed in school and stayed away from drugs. As I pondered my future I thought about enrolling in college or possibly joining the military. It was either that or working for my father. As I pulled into Canarsie I decided to stop at Mario's house to tell him about the tryout. As I was leaving he asked me what I was doing that night. I said, "Party at my house, bring me a fifty."

I broke my sobriety that night and smoked cocaine until five in the morning before drinking a fifth of vodka to help me pass out. I didn't tell anyone except Mario what had happened to me that day. I didn't want to have to rehash my Mets tryout fiasco. After that night we resumed our weekly freebase parties. I kept my father happy by going to work every day, as I didn't go out during the week, but within no time I began smoking pot morning, noon, and night. These cocaine parties continued for months until my parents announced they'd had enough of Canarsie and decided to sell the house and move to New Jersey full time.

My father had originally planned to stay in Brooklyn for a few more years but was becoming increasingly frustrated with all the car thefts in Canarsie. Brooklyn was saturated with Mafia-owned collision shops which fueled the thefts of radios, bumpers, and many times the entire car. Mob-connected window repair shops would send out guys to break car windows hoping to drum up business. In two years my father had four windows broken, two radios and a bumper stolen, and all four rims taken off the white Cadillac. The last straw was when they stole his Eldorado that was parked in our driveway.

In the Spring of 1984, my parents sold the house in Canarsie and moved into their condominium in Monmouth Beach. They wanted very badly for me to come with them to New Jersey, and I did briefly entertain the idea. My father offered for me to live rent-free in the unit that he and Warren had purchased in the same building. It was a first floor, oceanfront one-bedroom condo completely furnished to include a plush suede couch, a king-size waterbed, and a big screen projection television. The building also had an Olympic size swimming pool, sauna, gym, and two large tennis courts. It was the perfect bachelor pad, and nobody in their right mind would turn down such a generous offer. But without my friends there to enjoy it with me it meant nothing. I decided to stay in Canarsie.

My parents rented a one-bedroom apartment for me on the other side of the neighborhood. It was downstairs from the landlord and connected to houses on each side, so I had to worry about noise. They would pay my rent if I showed up for work, as I now had to take the subway every day. Without missing a beat my friends and I continued our Friday night freebasing sessions at my new apartment. It was a good thing that smoking cocaine made you quiet, as I had six or seven guys over on any given Friday and never once did my landlord complain. It was the same crew and same routine with Mario still supplying the cocaine. Within a few months, it wasn't the same anymore as the drug began to affect us all in different ways. It soon became outright strange.

After everyone did their first hit it, an odd silence would settle in the house with the only sounds now coming from the television. One of my friends would do a hit and immediately mute the volume then head straight to the window and start peeking through the blinds. When we'd ask him what he was looking at he'd look at you like a frightened child, placing his finger over his lips and quietly shushing. He was convinced that there was somebody coming in the house, and sometimes saw imaginary police through the window. "Badges, I see badges," he whispered one time, running through the apartment demanding that everyone put their drugs away. Mario screwed with him all the time and yelled loudly when he would tell us to be quiet. Naturally, it freaked him out. Each week he got more and more paranoid until finally he would just lock himself in the bathroom for hours. Eventually, I had to remove the lock so the rest of us could use it.

Usually, everyone blew through their dope long before Mario. He always had his personal batch which was triple the amount of everyone else's. He'd never share while everyone was scraping out the resin from our pipes trying to get one more hit. Once the last speck of brown residue was smoked from my pipe I'd start drinking to come down. A couple of my other friends wouldn't give up so easily. They'd search the sink where we cooled down the freshly cooked coke, or they got on all fours searching the floor for "rocks." They went so far as to put foreign objects in the pipe thinking it was coke, only to light it and find out it was food or plastic. I watched in horror as one of my friends lit something that wasn't cocaine but continued to inhale it. Another friend even suggested that I paint my kitchen floor black to make it easier to see any dropped rocks.

On one night, rather morning, Mario didn't finish all his coke but wrapped up the remaining piece and put it in his pocket. My friend Dave saw him and immediately started begging for some. Mario adamantly rebuffed him so Dave began more desperately pleading. "Please, please," he kept saying. He must have said "please" twenty times, but Mario said "no" just as many. "I don't understand," Dave reasoned. "You have all the coke you want, and I'm asking you for one hit. I thought we were friends and you're gonna make me *beg* you?" Mario became arrogant and replied, "I'm doing you a favor by not giving you any more. You're just gonna keep asking for another hit." Dave was furious, "What are you, my mother? I'll pay you if that's what you want. Just put it on my bill." Mario refused. Dave wouldn't relent and for over an hour continued to beg him for just one hit. My friend Armando, who was also Mario's cousin, got angry at Mario for making Dave beg. "What the fuck Mario, give the kid a fuckin' hit. Is it gonna kill you with all the money you make?" Armando barked. Mario didn't respond and still refused to waiver. I didn't want to take sides so I stayed quiet but was bothered that Mario would make our good friend beg like a junkie. The drug was beginning to control us.

As word spread throughout the neighborhood that I had my own place things quickly got out of control. Instead of six people freebasing in my apartment, there were soon ten or eleven. People were smoking cocaine in all three rooms in my apartment including the bathroom. Within no time various people that I knew from the neighborhood began knocking on my door asking me if I wanted to get high with them. Obviously, they just wanted to use my apartment, but since I wasn't paying for anything I didn't care. I continued my Friday night freebasing parties and found myself getting high whenever someone came banging on my door. In the beginning, I turned people away, especially on work nights. After a while, I never said no.

I was doing cocaine three and four days a week, and smoking pot daily. I was coming in late to work every day and called out once or twice a week. When I did come in I smoked weed nonstop and did as little work as possible. My father told me that if I didn't start coming in every day, he'd stop paying my bills and leave me to fend for myself. I thought he was bluffing at first, but when my landlord came down to tell me that she hadn't received a rent check I knew my father was serious. I was out of control and realized that if I continued my current path I would end up dead. I had two options. I could move to New Jersey and continue to work for my father, but with Canarsie only sixty miles away I knew I'd be there every weekend. Or I could join the military and get as far away from Canarsie as possible.

# Chapter 10
# Escape From New York

When I was seventeen I tried to join the United States Marines with two friends from high school. The plan was to enter on the "buddy system," meaning the three of us would be guaranteed to stay together during training. We all passed the entrance test, and it was time for our physicals. All three of us were underage so we'd need our parents' signatures to enlist at seventeen. Both of my friends backed out when their parents refused to sign, but I stalled my recruiter telling him I'd get the signatures before my scheduled physical. I had already talked my mother into signing the paper, but also needed my father's signature. On the night before my physical, I approached my father and told him what I wanted to do. Without hesitation, he laughed sarcastically and said, "Are you fuckin' serious? You won't last a fuckin' week. You'll end up in jail."

Over the next three years I thought about the military on many occasions, but never went through with it. Now that I was twenty I knew I had to leave Canarsie because I blamed the neighborhood for all my problems. My mother paid my rent and gave me food money, but I was spending it on drugs. Luckily, my Aunt Linda owned a small deli in Canarsie so I never went hungry. When my mother threatened to cut off my funds I knew I was at the end of my rope. On August 9, 1984, also my parents' wedding anniversary, I enlisted in the United States Army for a three-year stint. My mother was relieved because I'd finally confided in her about my drug use. I had toned it down to spare her distress but was afraid to tell my father because I knew how disappointed he'd be. I took the subway to the City and finally met him for lunch at the deli near his shop. I told him I had enlisted, and he just shook his head and said, "You're gonna end up in jail."

I was determined to prove my father wrong. Knowing I'd need time to pass the drug test, I opted for the delayed entry program and was scheduled to leave for training in six weeks. The physical would take place two weeks prior to shipping out, and included a urinalysis that tested for marijuana, cocaine, and opiates. I had done my research and found out that a urinalysis detects cocaine for up to forty-eight hours after using, and marijuana for up to three weeks. That gave me a month to clean out my system which would be a lot easier now that I was out of the apartment and living in back in New Jersey. My parents wouldn't allow me to use their cars knowing I would end up in Canarsie, so I spent most of my time working out trying to keep my mind off drugs. I was told that the closest place to purchase drugs was a section of Long Branch that was much too dangerous for a white guy to be walking in at night. Soon I found a bar down the road in Sea Bright, and instead of cocaine and marijuana, I got high on beer and vodka with the few dollars my mother would give me to go out on the weekends.

I had to report to Fort Hamilton in Brooklyn for my physical so the night before I drove to Canarsie to stay with my grandmother. I had been clean for over three weeks and had no desire to get high so I wasn't worried about being back in the neighborhood. My father's prediction of inevitable incarceration rattled me, but I was determined to succeed. Three days after taking the drug test I got a call from my recruiter. "You're good to go. You leave on the sixteenth. I'll pick you up at your grandmother's house at 4 am." I fucking did it! I was starting fresh in the Army. It was going to be the first step to doing something great with my life. I had a week before my departure date so I still needed to steer clear of drugs. The recruiter had mentioned that once on active duty the Army could randomly drug test you at any time. To play it safe I stayed in New Jersey the entire week and came back into Canarsie the day before I was to leave.

I arrived at my grandmother's house in the late afternoon. She wanted to cook me a big Italian dinner for my "last meal." My close friends wanted to have a sendoff for me and assured me they wouldn't keep me out late. I was hesitant since I had to be up rather early, and I didn't want to be hung over. I also knew that other things could happen when alcohol is involved. Although I had refrained from pot and coke for a month, I still didn't trust myself when I drank. Mario called the house and assured me that nobody would offer me drugs, and half-jokingly said he'd kick anyone's ass who did. He told me he'd pick me up at seven, and we'd meet the others at Ned's Bar. Before he hung up Mario said, "I have something important to talk to you about."

I was so curious that as soon as I closed the door to his BMW, I asked, "So what did you want to talk to me about?" Without hesitation, he replied, "We need to talk about your bill." "My what?" I shot back with irritation. "Yeah Cuc, you owe me four thousand dollars." I started laughing, thinking he was pulling my leg and said, "You're funny pal, you had me scared there for a second." The moment I looked at his face I realized he wasn't kidding. "Four thousand? That's impossible. I only owed you about a thousand when you stopped asking me for money. Where did you get four thousand from?" I couldn't believe the conversation was happening.

"Look…I have it all written down." He showed me a small black notebook. "Bro, you stopped asking me for money two years ago. C'mon, Mario…we're best friends," I said, realizing that maybe we weren't. "I got to pay for that shit, I don't get it for free," he argued. "So you're telling me that you charged me for all those times we partied in my house?" I asked in amazement. "Yeah but I only charged you cost," he said in a way that tried to soften the blow.

As we pulled up in front of the bar I asked to see his black book, and Mario turned to the page with my name on it. He had an itemized list dating back three years complete with how much he gave me and on what date. I also noticed that he had the names of our close friends in his book with amounts all in the thousands. According to his records, between the six or seven regular guys who partied at my house, we collectively owed Mario about $20,000. As I was looking at the dates and amounts he'd written down I thought to myself, "He could have written anything down and charged me whatever he wanted." I was seething in anger but didn't show it. I couldn't get tough with Mario as he was stronger than I was. Frustrated I just said, "I don't have any money to give you." He acted as if he was doing me a favor when he said, "Don't worry Cuc, you can send me a little money every month." With no intention of doing so, I calmly replied, "Yeah sure, no problem." We exited the vehicle and walked into the bar.

I felt betrayed by someone I thought was my best friend. Here was a guy who in three years had become the biggest cocaine dealer in Canarsie and was taking in thousands of dollars a month. He was also fortunate that the mob hadn't come looking for money, as Mario was supplying two wannabes who were dealing for themselves. Instead of sharing his good fortune with his "best friend," he had unknowingly charged me for every drop he ever gave me, even when he was using my house to get high. Not letting on that I was angry we soon changed the conversation. As we were about to order our first drink a few of my other friends showed up. There were other people in the bar that I knew, and everyone wanted to buy me a shot. I was still fuming over what had happened, and I found myself pounding shot after shot, almost forgetting I was leaving for the Army in six hours. I soon started getting the cocaine itch. True to their word none of my friends offered me any coke even though I knew they were doing it in the bathroom. It was now after 11 pm, and I knew I had to get home. As I was about to leave the bar with Mario, my friend Randy walked in.

"You can't leave without letting me buy you a drink," Randy said knowing I was leaving in the morning. "I appreciate it, but I gotta be up in four hours, and Mario's my ride home," I replied. "C'mon Cuc, I'll take you home. Just one drink, I promise," Randy said convincingly. With that, Mario turned to me and said, "What do you wanna do Cuc? I gotta leave." After I said I would stay, Mario gave me a big hug and wished me luck. As he was leaving he added, "You can send me a hundred a month, that'll work" I was so buzzed that I had forgotten about the "bill," and as soon as he reminded me I became angry all over again. One drink turned into three, and I was now very drunk and struggling to stand up. When I stumbled to the bathroom Randy followed me in.

"You need something to straighten you out," as Randy said as he handed me his vile of cocaine. Without hesitation, I took it from him and tried to scoop some out with the tiny spoon but was too drunk and was spilling it on the floor. "Here, let me do that." He took out a scoop of cocaine and held it under my nostril. I snorted it up. He gave me another one, and we went back to the bar to finish our drinks. "Did something happen between you and Mario? You looked mad before," he inquired. When I told him the story he said with a disgusted look on his face, "That's fucked up, aren't you guys best friends?" "I thought so," I replied. Then he casually asked, "What time do you have to leave?" With that, I looked up at the clock and freaked out when I saw that it was 3 am! "Holy fuck!" I yelled out, "I gotta leave in an hour!" When I walked into my grandmother's house it was 3:15. I had forty-five minutes before my recruiter would be there to pick me up. I was no longer drunk, but I was wired out of my mind.

As I showered the reality of what was transpiring hit me like a ton of bricks. I started crying and thought, "How could I be so fucking stupid?" I kept saying "Why? Why?" over and over. As much as I had wanted to leave this godforsaken neighborhood, in my current state of mind I contemplated not going. I wasn't in the Army yet, what could they possibly do to me? Maybe I could say I got the dates wrong and get a new ship date. So many crazy thoughts were running through my head. I just wanted to go to bed and hide under the covers. My grandmother woke up to make me breakfast and say her goodbyes. I nibbled on some toast but barely touched the eggs. I watched the clock while internally begging it to stop, wanting nothing more than one more day of freedom. The doorbell rang at 3:57 am. It was time to go.

As soon as the recruiter saw me he knew I wasn't in my right mind. "Are you okay?" he asked, "You don't look so good." I started getting paranoid thinking he might have me drug tested. "I didn't sleep at all Sergeant, I'm just nervous," I said as my voice cracked. "You'll get to sleep on the bus. It's a twenty-hour ride. It's natural to be nervous, you'll be fine," he tried to assure me. He drove me to the reception station at Fort Hamilton where I spent six of the most miserable hours in my life. I was crashing from the cocaine, had been up for over twenty-four hours, and was now forced to stand all day as we were processed into the Army. Luckily, they didn't administer another drug test. Finally, we boarded the bus for the long ride to Fort Leonard Wood, Missouri where I would complete eight weeks of basic training, and then five more weeks of Combat Engineer training. I found a seat in the back corner and got as comfortable as I could. I didn't fall asleep right away, but once I did I slept the entire way.

I awoke to the bus driver announcing on the intercom "We'll be arriving at Fort Leonard Wood in thirty minutes." I looked at my watch and noticed it was 11:00 pm, then dozed back off to sleep. I felt someone kick my feet, and when I opened my eyes there was a large man with a huge nose in a drill sergeant's hat standing directly over me. "Hey, sleeping beauty…you have exactly five seconds to get the fuck off my bus before I stick my foot up your ass!" he ordered in a heavy Southern accent. I froze in fear afraid to say anything, and before I could get out of my seat, he screamed even louder, "Get the fuck off my bus now!" I got off the bus as fast as I could, grabbing my bag as I stumbled out the door and into the formation. While I stood in line with the other recruits as the drill sergeants went around screaming insults at us, I thought, "I don't wanna be here."

For the first time in my life, I was out of Canarsie for a significant amount of time and began to experience a little culture shock. As soon as I opened my mouth my thick Brooklyn accent caught the attention of everyone, and many of the soldiers were soon referring to me as a Yankee. I took that as an insult, and I responded by calling them rednecks or goobers. I wasn't making too many friends except with a few fellow New Yorkers: Chris, an Italian kid from Queens, and two Puerto Rican guys from the Bronx, Izzy and Alex.

After three days at the reception station where we were fitted with uniforms and had our heads shaved, we began our training. If your last name was long or hard to pronounce the drill sergeants would call you "alphabet," which was what they called me the first few days. One drill sergeant asked me my name, and when I told him he said, "That sounds like a fucking disease. What kind of name is that?" When I told him it was Italian, he replied in his thick southern drawl, "An Eye-talian from New York, you must be in the

Mafia." I yelled out, "No sergeant!" What I really wanted to say was, "You must be married to your cousin," but I thought better of it. After a few weeks I'd gotten used to the drill sergeants yelling and insulting me, realizing that it wasn't personal and just part of the game.

We woke up every morning at 0500 to the sound of crashing metal pails being hurled across the barracks by the drill sergeants. After the entire platoon cleaned the barracks, we had about five minutes to make our bunks, get dressed, and be downstairs in formation. We would start every morning with calisthenics, tons of pushups, and then go on a company run. They started us off with two miles, but within weeks we were running up to six and seven miles every morning. After physical training or PT, we would have fifteen minutes to shower, shave, and get dressed for breakfast. After we ate we spent all morning training until lunch and then trained some more until dinner time. Following dinner, we spent time in class, or we shined our boots and wrote letters home. Mail call was my favorite part of the day, as I cherished any news from family and friends. "Lights out" was at 2100, and everyone had to be in their bunks unless you were on fireguard. After the lights went out and things got quiet I would lie in my bunk and think about home. As much as I cursed Canarsie and couldn't wait to leave, I was homesick and started questioning my decision to join the Army.

I seemed to get along with most of the African-American and Hispanic soldiers but always seemed to have problems with many of the white Southern guys who seemed to like calling me "Dago" and "Wop." One guy from Louisiana gave me flak because my roommate was black, even though we didn't get to choose. Whenever they would call me names or harass me, I'd break into my best Gomer Pyle impression and say something derogatory usually to the effect of rednecks being gun-toting illiterate drunks. Most of them took it in good fun, but a few of them hated my guts and would do anything to get me in trouble. Whenever I tried to smoke a cigarette or sneak out to use the phone, they would love to snitch on me to the drill sergeants. In Canarsie, if someone snitched or "ratted" on you they usually got beat up. In the military, I couldn't do anything about it unless I was willing to risk going to jail. The last thing I wanted was my father's prediction coming true.

Three weeks into training I started to experience nightmares that I thought had long passed. On several occasions, my roommate would tell me I was yelling things in my sleep but couldn't make out what I was saying. One morning he asked me who Joe Milo was. I freaked out. I'd been experiencing a recurring dream where I was having a normal conversation with Joe Milo as he sat there bleeding with four bullets in his chest. In the dream, just as in real life, he said, "I can't believe I'm going to die." That's when I would wake up. I even had a strange dream about Crazy Sal being with me on the shooting range. It was during training that I realized for the first time that I had more nightmares whenever I stopped smoking pot for long periods of time. As the nightmares became more frequent, I wrote to my friend Richie and asked him to mail me a Playboy magazine and place a joint in the centerfold. I wasn't worried about a drug test as they only do that during training, or following leave or pass. I thought even if I smoked once it might hold off the nightmares for a while.

About ten days later they called out my name at mail call, and I noticed the drill sergeant holding a magazine-sized envelope. When I came up to retrieve it from him, he said, "Don't pull your pud too hard," as I noticed the envelope was opened, and he saw that it was Playboy Magazine. For an instant, I got nervous that they might have found the joint but was relieved when he just handed to me. I waited until I was back in my room to open the magazine. As soon as I opened it to the centerfold I saw the joint taped in the middle. I'm not sure what got me more excited, the pot or the smoking hot naked woman with the large breasts.

I was extremely nervous just having it, but the thought of sneaking out to smoke it was very exciting. Since I didn't want to smoke it alone I went to the only two people I trusted, Izzy and Alex from the Bronx. We came up with a plan to sneak out of the window after lights out, and smoke behind one of the storage buildings across from the barracks. We had about seven minutes to pull this off before the fire guards would come around for a bed check. We also had to worry about of one the rednecks ratting us out. Izzy and Alex shared a room on the first floor, so we climbed out their window and ran about fifty feet to the building. I lit the joint and took a huge inhale and held it in. When I started coughing it out, Izzy and Alex started laughing hysterically, making me nervous that someone would hear us. We passed the joint around looking at our watches the entire time. With about two minutes to bed check, we finished the joint and ran back to the barracks. As I was running I tossed the marijuana roach into the sewer, then one by one we climbed back in through the window. We all managed to get back without getting caught, and when I arrived at my room I was so high that I felt like I had smoked for the first time. I slept peacefully that night.

After the first month, I had become so miserable and homesick that I began contemplating ways to get out of the Army. There was a guy in my platoon who had received an entry-level discharge for stealing a candy bar from the Post Exchange. Another recruit was discharged for failure to adapt to military life. I wanted out but not at the expense of going to jail. One way was to fail your physical fitness test three times, but my ego wouldn't allow me to do that. Also, I was one of the better athletes in my platoon, so it would have been too obvious. Another way out of the Army was to fail to qualify with your rifle. To graduate basic training, you had to achieve the level of Marksman which meant hitting at least twenty-three of forty targets. As we came closer to the qualifying date I began to miss targets to make it look like I couldn't shoot.

After the first day of practice my drill sergeant, Sergeant Pitman, pulled me to the side and began reaming me out. "How the fuck did you bollo out there?" using a term that meant failing the course. "Mister New York tough guy can't shoot straight? I don't think so." He stared at me as if he knew I failed on purpose and said, "You don't look like a bollo," whatever that meant. The next day on the range Sergeant Pitman stood over me the entire time I was practicing. I was too afraid to miss on purpose and ended up hitting twenty-eight targets. Three days later my ego got the best of me again and I couldn't go through with it. I qualified as a sharpshooter, hitting thirty-one targets.

I made one last feeble attempt at trying to get out of the Army, but it was what my drill sergeant said that made me want to reverse course. I went to his office door and stood at the position of attention and in a loud voice said, "Sergeant, Private Cuccurullo requests permission to speak." "Speak," Sergeant Pitman barked. "The private requests permission to enter." Looking annoyed, he broke from military protocol and said, "What the fuck do you want?" I asked to speak to him about a problem and he instructed me to come in and close the door. "What's your problem, Private?" he asked in a calm voice. I pulled out a candy bar, which we weren't allowed to have, and placed it on his desk. "I stole this from the PX. I think I have a problem and need help." He looked me straight in the eye and said, "Son, are you trying to get out of the Army?" Embarrassed that he called my bluff I replied, "Yes sergeant, I don't feel like I belong here." "What do you mean?" he said with some surprise. "You're a squared away troop." It was the first nice thing he ever said to me. He opened the candy bar, began to eat it, and said with a full mouth, "You graduate basic in two weeks. Finish up and when you get to your next duty station you can take care of those sticky fingers of yours. Dismissed!"

For the first time since I got there I left his office feeling good about being a soldier. I thought, "Wow, Sergeant Pitman said I was squared away." It was high praise. As I reflected on the past six weeks I realized that maybe I *was* squared away. I always passed inspection, aced the obstacle course, and did well on my PT test. I also exceled on the rifle range and was the best grenade thrower in my platoon. I began to look at the Army in a different light. "Do I really want out?" I pondered. I'd come this far and we had less than three weeks left of basic training. We also had Christmas break coming up, and I was going home for ten days before coming back to complete the final month of training. Somehow, I managed to make it through the eight weeks and graduated basic training in mid-December. I was thrilled to be standing in my dress greens at the graduation ceremony and thankful that I'd failed in my attempt to get discharged. I was excited to be going home to see my family, but I nervous about going to Canarsie.

My plan was to spend most of my leave at my parents' condominium in New Jersey and then spend the New Year's holiday with my friends. I had only been gone for about sixty days, but I felt like a completely different person. I was in great physical shape, and except for the joint I smoked in basic training I was drug-free. The first few days home were spent sleeping and getting fat on my mother's cooking. Both of my brothers had come home for the holidays, along with my sister, and it was the first time in six years we all sat down together for Christmas Eve dinner. After a glorious week of spending quality time with my family, I borrowed my father's new Mercedes and headed for Canarsie to see my friends for the first time in two months.

I was still angry at Mario about the money. I didn't send him a dime while I was away and had no intention of paying him. I still felt betrayed, but for some reason continued to be friendly with him. Mario could be intimidating at times, and I was afraid to speak my mind, but I also knew I'd be stationed in Kentucky after training and he couldn't do anything even if he wanted to. It was just easier to act like nothing had happened. Instead of going to Mario's as I usually did, I went to my close friend Armando's house. After picking up my friends Richie and Dave we headed to a New Year's Eve party at some girl's house.

It was as if I had never left. Within five minutes of my arrival in Canarsie I had a joint in my hand, and soon Armando was breaking up some lines on a small mirror. When it was my turn he held the mirror for me. I snorted two lines with a rolled-up bill as I drove to the party. I was so thrilled to be home and among my friends that I forgot I was in the Army. As soon as we arrived at the party I saw throngs of familiar faces from Canarsie. Within minutes people were offering the returning "hero" all sorts of drugs. I had at least seven different people offer me cocaine, and I obliged every one of them. Before I knew it was past 2 am, and the hostess was kicking everyone out of her house. I was still wired out of my mind, and with no alcohol to come down on, I had no intentions of going back to my grandmother's house to stare at the ceiling. The guys I came with all split up, either hooking up with a girl or just going home. The bars were all charging a fortune since it was New Year's Eve, and the dive bars were all closed. I wanted the party to continue, so I went to the person I knew would still be getting high.

When I pulled up to Randy's house I noticed there were no lights on in his basement where he hung out. I saw his car in front, so I knew he was there. I parked the car and went into his yard toward the basement door. Since I wasn't sure if his parents were home, I began to tap lightly on the glass door. There was no answer. I tapped a little harder and whispered, "Hey Randy, its Cuc, are you there?" There was still no response, so I decided to give up and leave. As I began to walk away I heard the glass door open slightly, and heard Randy whisper, "Cuc, is that you?" As I walked into his basement I noticed immediately that Randy had that paranoid look in his eyes. I assumed that he was being quiet so we wouldn't wake his parents.

When I asked him if they were home he told me they went away for the weekend. I thought to myself, "Then why the fuck are we whispering?"

The basement was pitch black except for a fluorescent black light on the table. It was almost impossible to see Randy's two friends who were sitting on the couch. When Randy went upstairs for the umpteenth time to "check" on things, the guys told me that Randy had been freebasing all night and kept imagining people trying to get into the house. They said when I tapped on the door he almost had a heart attack and wouldn't have opened the door if I hadn't whispered my name. When I asked them if they had any coke for me, they said that Randy had some but wasn't sharing. When I asked them for a beer they told me they were out. Desperate for some blow, I went upstairs to ask Randy for a hit.

The rest of the house was just as dark as the basement. Not whispering anymore, I called out, "Randy, where are you?" All I heard in response was "Shhhhh." I followed the sound to the staircase which led to the upstairs bedrooms. When I got closer I saw Randy sitting on the top of the steps holding his freebase pipe in one hand and the torch in his other. He whispered to me to keep my voice down and asked me to stand guard by his front door while he took his hit. Knowing that I wouldn't get to do a hit until he was done, I humored him and went to the door acting as if I was really watching. He lit the torch and then I heard the crackling of the cocaine while I waited impatiently for him to finish.

As I was standing by the door I noticed that Randy had put books on the top of the window shades in a pointless effort to keep someone out. When he was done I asked him for a hit, but he kept telling me to wait. He continued to sit at the top of the stairs with his eyes wide open and his head moving in eight different directions. After about an hour when I realized that he was never going to let me do a hit, I finally decided to leave and go to my grandmother's house. I sat in her kitchen still feeling the effects of the cocaine, eerily reminiscent of the morning I left for training. It was almost as if the last sixty days were all a dream, and nothing had changed at all. I was up for two hours staring at her ceiling feeling guilty and hating myself for what I had done that night.

Although I enjoyed seeing my family I was happy to be leaving again. On the plane ride back to Missouri I had the chance to think about why I had joined the Army in the first place. That last night in Canarsie made me realize that I didn't have the willpower to resist drugs and that I needed to be as far away as possible. The thought of ending up a paranoid junkie with books holding down my window shades scared the living shit out of me and made me look forward to finishing up my training and being assigned to my first unit at Fort Campbell, Kentucky. I tried desperately to forget about Canarsie and kept telling myself that I was a squared away troop.

# Chapter 11
# AWOL

The last four weeks of training sailed by, and we were now into the Combat Engineer portion of our training. The drill sergeants treated us a lot better, although they still liked to mock us. We were now able to go bowling or to the movies in the evening and were given weekend passes to go off post. It seemed that everyone had come back refreshed and reinvigorated, and the tensions between some of us had subsided. I found myself drinking at the bar with the same guys I had had problems with earlier in training. The Army didn't seem that bad anymore, and I was excited to go to Fort Campbell. After a month of learning how to plant and defuse landmines and how to build and blow up bridges, I was now officially a Combat Engineer in the United States Army.

Fort Campbell, Kentucky, home of the 101st Airborne Division, was located directly on the Kentucky-Tennessee border. The day we left Missouri there was a major snowstorm, and the drill sergeants instructed us to wear our combat boots with our dress green uniforms. Technically, it was against Army regulations. About seven of us from the Company who were assigned to the same post boarded a bus for the scheduled eight-hour trip to Fort Campbell.

Because of the snow, the trip took close to eleven hours. As we waited inside the bus depot for transportation to our new unit, a soldier with the rank of Specialist began yelling at us demanding to know why we were wearing combat boots with our dress greens. When we tried to explain the circumstances, he continued to berate us and ordered us all to drop which meant to do push-ups. "Y'all need to give me twenty-five each," he yelled. Since we were all privates and fresh out of training, we had no idea that we weren't required to do pushups for someone with a rank below sergeant. With the entire bus station laughing hysterically at us, the Specialist sarcastically said when we finished our pushups, "Welcome to Fort Campbell."

The Army assigned me to the 20th Engineer Battalion which was attached to the 101st Airborne Division. As soon as we arrived at headquarters another soldier with the rank of Specialist began chastising us for wearing our combat boots. "Who the hell gave you "'cruits" permission to dress out of uniform," he said, using a shortened version of the word recruit. I was now completely frustrated, and I blurted out, "How many fuckin' times do we have to tell everyone, we left in a snowstorm, and the drill sergeants told us to wear combat boots. Why is that so difficult to understand?" Taking offense to how I said it, the Specialist stood up and said, "I don't like your attitude boy." As soon as he said the word "boy" I wanted to punch him in the face. I can recall thinking to myself, "Why is everyone here such an asshole?" After receiving my assignment to Bravo Company, a private who was working in the office came to me and said, "I'm not sure if you guys know, but you don't have to take shit from anyone with the rank below Sergeant." "You mean I could've told that guy to go fuck himself?" "Yeah," he said. I was glad he told me that because when I arrived at my new Company, I would soon be put to the test.

They assigned me to a room with another private who had been there for about six months. The room had to remain completely military including the furniture, blankets, and wall lockers. Soldiers were allowed a television and a small refrigerator where you could keep one six-pack of beer at a time, but no hard liquor. The bathrooms, or latrines as they were called, were shared by everyone on the floor except the sergeants who had their own. Every morning at 0500 the platoon sergeants would start banging on the doors waking everyone up to clean the common areas of the barracks. PT formation was at 0600 usually ending with a three- or four-mile run. After breakfast and a shower, we would report to work formation at 0900. If the company wasn't in training, we normally worked until 1700 maintaining vehicles and equipment or attending classes on various military subjects. At the end of the day, we were free to do what we wanted. Occasionally we worked a half day on Saturdays if the First Sergeant was pissed off, but we usually had weekends off. Sometimes the privates got stuck working weekends as fire guard or in the mess hall. The "'cruits" were also given the worst work details, such as cleaning toilets, raking leaves and walking around the post for hours picking up cigarette butts, which the Army referred to as "Police Call."

The company was an equal mix of white, black, and Hispanic soldiers. Just like in basic training most of the white guys seemed to be from the South and Midwest. Some of the African-American soldiers were from various small towns around the country, but like myself most of the black guys were from big cities. Most of the Hispanic soldiers were of Mexican descent with many coming from California. There were a few guys who were from the northeast and one guy from upstate New York, but I was the only guy from New York City in the company. Some of the non-commissioned officers were black or Hispanic, but all the commissioned officers were white with generic Anglo names such as Smith, Parker, Jones, and Johnson.

I'm not sure if it was my Brooklyn accent, my Italian last name, or just the fact that I was a brash cocky short guy, but I seemed to rub a lot of people the wrong way when I first arrived at my unit. I tried to impress some of the other soldiers by telling them that my brother was in the band Missing Persons, but most of them didn't seem to know who they were. Every day someone would pass me by and make a derogatory comment, whether it was Yankee, dago, wop, or shorty. Remembering what the soldier in the battalion office told me about not taking grief from lower ranking guys, I began to defend myself. I would either mock their southern accents or I would just say "Eat shit" or "Fuck you." Most of them took it in good fun and seemed glad to see the new guy stick up for himself. One day a soldier who was constantly bragging about being from Texas, whom I had never spoken to, called me a dago in front of the entire platoon. With a smile on my face, I told him to go fuck himself. He didn't think it was funny.

He wasn't very big, but he was still three or four inches taller than me. Trying to intimidate me he got in my face and said, "What did you say 'cruit?" Feeling threatened I took a step back, slammed my gloves on the ground and said, "C'mon, let's go." The look on his face told me that he fully expected me to back down. "Do you really want to fight me, little man," he said with a change of heart in his voice. I was so amped up I could barely answer, instead motioning with my hands as if to say, "Let's go." He just waved his hand at me and said, "I'm not going to get court-martialed over you." That guy may have very well kicked my ass, but I was able to send a message to everyone that I wouldn't be intimidated.

This seemed to endear me to some of the other soldiers in the platoon. Many of them came up to me and patted me on the back for standing up to that guy. I was eating dinner at the mess hall with a fellow Private I knew from basic training when two guys from another platoon sat down at our table. "Nice job standing up to that asshole," one of them said. "Thanks," I said humbly. "Everyone in the company hates him. I wouldn't worry about him," the other soldier said. Trying to sound tough I proudly declared, "I don't worry about anybody. I'm from Brooklyn." After talking for about a half hour they invited me to hang out with some of the guys after dinner. As we were leaving the mess hall one of them asked me my first name. "My name is Rob," I said, "but my friends at home call me Cuc." "Alright Cuc, see you later." It was the first time in three weeks that someone referred to me as something other than 'cruit.

When I got to his room there were four or five other guys already there drinking beer. They seemed skeptical about me and appeared to be hiding something. They handed me a beer and started asking me all sorts of questions about where I was from and what I did before I went into the Army. I could tell they were leading up to something, and after about a half hour of them feeling me out one of them blurted out, "Have you ever smoked pot?" Lying through my teeth I said, "Yeah, a couple of times." With that, one of the guys rolled up a towel and sealed off the opening at the bottom of the door. They turned on a fan and pointed it towards the window. They all gathered under the windowsill as one of them lit a joint. After passing it around to everyone they motioned for me to come by the window and handed it to me. Wanting desperately to fit in, and trying to please my newfound friends, I took a few tokes on the joint and passed it. After we finished one of them saturated the room with air freshener. After a few minutes and well after the fact, I asked one of them, "Don't we get drug tested?" They all laughed.

The Army conducted random drug testing twice a month. When directed by the Battalion commander each company would draw three single digit numbers from a hat. If your social security number ended in any of those three numbers, you had to submit to a urinalysis. A non-commissioned officer, usually a Staff Sergeant, would knock on your door and escort you to the latrine, and literally stand directly over you as you peed. According to some of the soldiers in the Company there were countless ways to beat an Army piss test, considering the military tested thousands of soldiers and used the cheapest testing methods.

One way was to drink an excessive amount of water. When the sergeant knocked on your door to pee, you'd tell him that you already went and that you can't go right away. Ironically, they would sit you in a room and allow you to drink all the water you wanted so you could finally go. If you drank enough water the amount of THC, the ingredient for which they tested, would be minimal and therefore come back as negative. Another way was to dip your wet finger in laundry detergent, and then pee on that same finger as you filled up the cup. This caused the test to come back as void which would then constitute another test. Since this process took several weeks it gave you plenty of time to clean out your system before the next test. You had to be careful because if your tests continually came back as void the Army would administer a blood test, which is virtually impossible to alter.

With test results no longer an issue, before I knew it I was regularly smoking with these guys. A few of us would meet in a friend's room and burn a joint before we went running in the morning. This was risky because the officers were on the first floor during the workday. At night it was easier to smoke because there was only one sergeant on duty as CQ, or Charge of Quarters. Buying pot was another story. I was too afraid to go into town and buy it myself because the Army had undercover officers posing as dealers. Usually, I'd just throw the guys a few bucks when they got me high. Once word spread that I was willing to buy if they'd "fly," I had countless offers to smoke. Within weeks as I began to meet more of the soldiers in other platoons, I realized that almost half of the guys in my company were smoking pot. I was told there was a soldier who lived in the barracks that was also shooting heroin. The very thing I desperately wanted to get away from had now followed me to the Army. I was becoming a pothead all over again, and this time I couldn't blame Canarsie.

I started feeling guilty about smoking pot, but it made it bearable to be there. Even though I'd made many friends in the barracks, some of the sergeants would harass and ridicule me and I couldn't say anything. Being insubordinate to a non-commissioned officer earned you an Article 15, a company level punishment that usually came with a fine, barracks restriction, or a loss of rank. One sergeant kept mispronouncing my last name inserting the word "cock" at the beginning. Another sergeant who wasn't even my supervisor would wait for me as I came to formation just to make sure that everything from my haircut down to my boots were within regulations. One time he claimed I missed one hair on my neck, and not only did he make me do fifty pushups, he slapped me with guard duty over the weekend. Every day I had to hear him say that tired old Army cliché, "You ain't back on the block, boy." I hated that fucking guy with a passion.

Some of the newer soldiers were occasionally harassed, but I was clearly a favorite target. Although I understood it was a hazing for new soldiers, not all the sergeants harassed the privates, so I knew that the others were just being sadistic assholes. The worst part was that they laughed behind your back after humiliating you in front of everyone. After six weeks of dealing with the constant berating, and considering the fact that I was smoking pot daily, I thought, "What the hell am I doing here"? I wanted out of the Army again.

I went to see my platoon sergeant who seemed to be a good person. He was a decorated Vietnam veteran who had about a year until retirement and was extremely laid back. I told him that I was miserable and asked him if there was any way out of the Army without getting a dishonorable discharge or going to jail. He told me that there was an entry-level discharge for soldiers who had less than six months in, but you needed to be deemed "unable to adjust to military life." I only had five months of service, but there was nothing in my record that would indicate a failure to adapt. He encouraged me to stick it out, but he also said that if I was that miserable I should do what I thought was best. Then he surprised me when he bluntly said, "Fuck up enough and they'll kick you out eventually. Just don't get your ass thrown in jail." I knew my performance would have to suffer if I had any shot at an entry-level discharge. I decided that was my way out of the Army.

I had to be very careful about how and when I decided to "screw up" so as not to violate the Uniform Code of Military Justice, or USMJ, and possibly risk a bad conduct discharge. It wasn't as drastic as a dishonorable discharge, but it was still something that would follow you the rest of your life. I wanted out, but not that way. The first thing I started to do was fall out of the morning runs. After falling out for the third time my platoon leader ordered me to meet him after work to run with him. He would yell at me to keep going, but I'd stop halfway. "Are you kidding me?" You just came from basic training and you can't run two miles," the Lieutenant said in disbelief. "Shin splints sir," I replied, acting as if I were in pain. It had become more of a hassle to fake it, but I knew I had to keep up the act.

I began falling out or missing the company road marches they conducted once a week. We'd hike about twenty kilometers wearing full combat gear, and occasionally we would be "ambushed" by another platoon. As a private, I was responsible for carrying the M60 machine gun which weighed over twenty pounds. Halfway through the march, I would complain about shin splints, and the medic would have me ride in the jeep with him. My squad leader knew I was faking but couldn't do shit about it. I had a history of shin splints on my medical records. Other times I would go on "sick call" in the morning and report to the doctor instead of training. I began going on sick call two and three days a week lying about my shins and complaining of other imaginary ailments. If the doctors released me from sick call before lunch, instead of reporting to work I'd sneak into my barracks room and take a nap.

Knowing that the First Sergeant would randomly inspect our rooms while we were working, I snoozed under the bed in case he came in. One morning while I was lying under the bed still awake, I heard someone outside the door and froze in terror as I heard the door open. It was the First Sergeant and the company commander doing an inspection. I could see their feet as I laid there motionless, convinced they would find me. What I was doing constituted a violation of the UCMJ because I was required to report directly to work following sick call. They only stayed for a moment since the room was in order, but when the commander asked the First Sergeant whose room it was he mentioned my roommate's name and then referred to me as the "fucking new guy from New York." He then added, "He's starting to piss me off," as I heard the door close. I was afraid to get caught walking out, so I laid there for another hour until it was time for lunch.

The following day some of the guys invited me to go to Nashville, Tennessee for the weekend. Amazingly, I wasn't assigned any weekend duties, so I was free to join them. We got there on Friday night and the four of us checked into the motel. After smoking some weed we set out for the bars. Since we were in Nashville and my friends were into country music I was stuck listening to what I called "redneck" music all weekend. On Saturday night we hooked up with some girls and brought them back to the hotel room to party with us. The girl I was with asked me if I had my own room. When I told her I didn't, she asked me if I wanted to go to her place which was about an hour away. I decided to go only after she assured me a ride back to Nashville before my friends checked out the next morning. After having sex, we started drinking again until the early morning hours, and eventually, both of us passed out.

As soon as I opened my eyes I knew I had overslept. "What fuckin' time is it?" I screamed out. It was three in the afternoon! I jumped out of bed, waking up the girl who was still passed out.

Not only did I not remember her name I had no idea where I was. I began screaming, "Sweetheart you gotta take me back to Nashville immediately!" Still half asleep she muttered in her Tennessee drawl, "I told you I'd take you back, but I doubt your friends are still there." After calling the motel to confirm what she'd already predicted, I asked her to drive me back to Fort Campbell. With the look of dread on her face, she said, "Oh, that's far." I was in the town of Bell Buckle, Tennessee, an hour south of Nashville and two hours from Fort Campbell. She told me she had no money for gas. When I checked my wallet all I had was a five dollar bill and a useless maxed-out credit card. I gave her the five, and she drove me back to Nashville as promised. I'd then need to call my friends and have them pick me up.

She drove me back to the motel where I'd stayed the night before. I asked the clerk if he remembered my friends checking out, and he told me they waited around for a couple of hours before leaving. He let me use the phone to the call the barracks so I could get someone to fetch me. Since soldiers didn't have their own phones in their room you had to call the CQ, and then they would try to locate who you wanted. When I called the first time the CQ told me that none of the soldiers I was asking for were answering their doors and to call back later. The clerk was nice and let me sit in the lobby while I waited. After about an hour I tried again, but the CQ told me that no one had come back yet. Finally, at about 7:00 pm I was able to contact one of the soldiers who had come with me to Nashville.

He told me that he didn't have a car, and the person we drove with wasn't around. I told him that if he could find someone to pick me up I'd pay for their gas and throw in an extra ten dollars. He said he'd make the rounds and to call back in about an hour. When I called him back he told me he couldn't find anyone who was willing to drive to Nashville. It was now about 9:00 pm, and I had to be back at Fort Campbell by 0500 or I would be considered AWOL, absent without leave. I had no money and was stranded in Nashville, and I knew that there was only one person who could help me.

I went to a payphone and called my mother collect. I didn't give her all the details but told her I needed money to get back to my unit. I gave her the number to the pay phone and waited for her to call me back. After about twenty minutes she called and said there were no Western Union locations open until tomorrow, but she called the credit card company and had them add a hundred dollars to the credit line. As soon as I hung up I went back to the hotel to call the bus station to see if there were any buses going to Fort Campbell that evening. The woman at the station told me that there were no buses leaving that night, but that two were heading to Fort Campbell at 11 am and 5 pm the following day. I wasn't going to get back in time.

After checking back into the motel, I called the CQ to let him know I was stranded and would miss morning formation. Unfortunately, the Sergeant that was now on duty was the one who relentlessly harassed me. When he got on the phone he seemed to revel in the fact I couldn't get back to base. "It ain't my problem boy. If you're not back by 0500, your ass is AWOL." He sarcastically said, "Good luck," then hung up on me. For the first time since I had joined the Army, I was scared to death of going to jail. I was too afraid to return to my unit during the duty day when everyone would be there, so I decided to take the later bus and get to Fort Campbell at night. I thought to myself, "I'm already AWOL, what's another few hours." After successfully sneaking in past the sergeant on duty I went straight to my room and laid in my bed, worried to death about what was going to happen to me the next day.

The knock on my door came at 0430, a half hour earlier than usual. It was my platoon sergeant who very calmly and without mentioning the fact that I had been gone for a day, told me that I needed to report to the commander ASAP. After getting dressed

I hustled down to the commander's office on the first floor where a couple of the sergeants were hanging around waiting for PT formation. "Where the fuck were you, boy?" asked one of the sergeants. I didn't say a word. "You're toast 'cruit," another sneered as I entered the commander's office. I had rehearsed a few dozen different excuses the night before but decided to just tell the truth hoping he would understand. The company commander was Captain Jones who had a good reputation with the men and was considered a fair and reasonable officer.

After officially reporting he asked me to sit down and tell him what happened. I told him the entire story minus the weed. I must have sounded contrite because he seemed to believe me. Then my platoon sergeant intervened and said, "Sir, the Private is miserable here. He wants out of the Army." I was caught off guard when he brought it up and even more surprised when I heard the commander's response. "I don't want you here against your will son. If you want out, I'll get you out, but you had better keep your shit together until you leave." Raising his voice he then asked me, "You got that Private?" "Yes sir," I responded. As I was leaving the office I asked the commander what would become of the AWOL charge. "Talk to your platoon sergeant," he said.

I was ecstatic! I was getting out of this hellhole and going back to my life. It seemed that although I didn't plan it, going AWOL was the fast track out. Now I just had to deal with the punishment. I was a buck private with no rank to take, so I assumed I would get a fine or be put on barracks restriction, which wouldn't be much of a punishment with my friends bringing me weed every night. When I walked into the platoon sergeant's office I thanked him for talking to the commander about my situation. He then handed me a form and told me to sign it. "What's this?" I asked. "It's your leave form," he said. Confused I asked, "When am I going on leave?" He replied sarcastically, "You already did. The commander didn't want you to ruin the company's streak of consecutive AWOL-free days and put you on leave for three days." I couldn't believe it! Not only was I free and clear of the AWOL charge, I was getting out of the Army without going to jail!

As word spread of my entry level discharge I started to get harassed even more by some of the sergeants, especially my squad leader. He told me right to my face, "You're getting out early is bullshit. You signed a contract. Be a man and honor it." I tried to defend myself, but he was having none of it. "You don't know me, Sarge, you have no idea who I am." He got even angrier when he responded, "And how the fuck did you not get an Article 15 for going AWOL? That's fucking bullshit." I just smiled and said, "Yes, Sergeant," thinking to myself that it was only a matter of time before I was gone. Not happy with the sarcastic response he threatened me and said in a low angry voice, "I'm gonna make your life a living hell as long as you're here. You're getting every shit detail I can come up with," I just smiled and again replied, "Yes, Sergeant." I couldn't let him get to me. I just had to grin and bear it.

True to his word my squad leader had me scrubbing toilets and picking up cigarette butts, and assigned me to fire watch almost every night. He also assigned me morning mess duty which required me to be up at 0300. Normally, if you had morning mess duty you would be exempt from PT, but my squad leader pulled me out of duty just so I could run with the platoon. I would piss him off even more when I refused to finish the run. He had me on main gate duty on the weekends, so I didn't have a day off for three weeks straight. He kept saying repeatedly that I'd better pray I get out of the Army before the Company went to the field sixty days' training. That was only three weeks away, and I was starting to get nervous as I hadn't heard anything about my discharge. When I asked my platoon sergeant when he thought I might be getting out, he just said, "These things take time."

Ten days had passed and I still hadn't heard a word about my discharge. We were to leave for training in about a week, and I was dreading the thought of having to go. I went to one of my pot-smoking friends who worked in the battalion office and asked him if he could check on my discharge papers to see when I might be getting out. I was shocked to hear that my commander had never even begun the paperwork. The next day I used the commander's open-door policy to ask him about my discharge without letting on what I knew. He was furious and began screaming, "I don't give a fuck about your discharge. I have a company to run and we're going to the field in nine days! I suggest you stop your fucking whining and get ready to leave for training! You get out of the Army when I say you do! Now get the fuck out private!"

It was now apparent that my superiors were all lying to me just to shut me up. It occurred to me that since they wouldn't discharge me during training, two more months in the Army would make me ineligible for an entry-level discharge. The thought of spending three years here was bad enough, but the thought of spending sixty days in the field with my squad leader making my life a living hell was too much for me to bear. I was embarrassed, humiliated, and scared to death. More than anything I was livid for everyone lying to me. I refused to give them the satisfaction and decided there was no way I was going to the field. I packed my things and left Fort Campbell, eventually finding a bus to take me on the fifteen-hour ride to New Jersey. Now, I *was* AWOL.

From the moment I left I knew that I had to return or the Army could classify me as a deserter. That could mean jail time. Embarrassed by what I did I told my family and friends that my discharge papers had come through early, but my father immediately called my bluff. "Three days ago, you didn't mention a goddamn thing about your discharge, and then all of a sudden you're home? There's something you're not telling us," my father said in a calm voice. Knowing I wasn't going to fool him, I changed my tune and tried another lie, "One of the sergeants told me I was discharged, so I left." The second I finished that sentence I realized how ridiculous it sounded. "You better hope so pal," my father retorted. He wasn't buying a word of it.

The following day my mother received a call from my First Sergeant who told her that I was AWOL and that I needed to return immediately. She was angry that I would pull such a stunt, but she remained calm and supportive. "What were you thinking Robert?" she said dejectedly. "I'll try and help you through this, but you need to get your act together. You're getting too old for this nonsense." As soon as she told my father he started screaming like a lunatic, "I told you that you were going to end up in jail! You're a fuck up! Why can't you be more like your brother Warren?" Those words hurt more than anything my father had ever said to me. I knew that I had fucked up but being compared to Warren struck me to the core. Why would he say that to me? My brother was a Rock Star. What the fuck could I possibly do to compete with that? I was always happy for Warren's success, but when my father said that to me I couldn't help but feel jealous. I cried in my room all night.

The next day I packed my things to head back to Fort Campbell to face the music. My father bought me a plane ticket to Kentucky and drove me to the airport. We didn't talk much during the hour car ride to Newark, and all I could think about was having to deal with the consequences when I returned to my unit. He handed me a fifty-dollar bill, gave me a hug, and wished me luck. In case the need arose, my mother had already begun searching for lawyers who specialized in military law. I was hoping that since I was only gone for four days the Army would just take my pay and have me make up those days. That was wishful thinking on my part. My gut instinct knew they'd make it hard on me.

When I arrived back at the barracks I reported to the CQ. Because my company was in the field he then promptly contacted the Battalion Sergeant Major who arrived with a couple of other sergeants and ordered me to empty my duffel bag, taking all my civilian clothes. He then instructed me to remove the clothes I was wearing and took them as well. As I was standing there in my underwear, the Sergeant Major instructed the CQ, "This man is on barracks restriction. He can only leave to report for work and go to the mess hall. If he tries to leave the barracks at any other time, you're to call the MPs and have him arrested." I was terrified of going to jail so I decided not to cause any more problems and simply comply.

Two days later I was instructed to report to the battalion commander's office to find out what type of punishment I was to receive. I was told by some of the other soldiers that I could either get an Article 15, which comes with barracks restriction and a fine, or a Summary Court Martial which can come with a maximum of thirty days in jail. My heart sunk as I was told I was getting a Summary Court Martial, thinking immediately I would end up in jail as my father predicted. As I left the office they reminded me that I was still on barracks restriction, which wasn't bad because I could get stoned every night. They assigned me an Army lawyer who informed me that even with a Summary Court Martial, jail time was not mandatory. He told me it was up to the officer hearing your case, and if you make a good impression and show contrition you could receive a lighter sentence. The thought of jail consumed me while I waited three weeks before the Army would hear my case. I didn't mind that they were working me like a dog because I got to stay in the rear while my Company trained, far away from my squad leader. After twenty-one straight days of cutting lawns, buffing floors, and tackling every other shit work detail they could find for me it was finally time for my hearing.

A Summary Court Martial is decided by one officer, and in my case, it was a Colonel who looked like a hard-ass. He was wearing combat patches on his uniform, meaning he had been in Vietnam and was in great physical shape. While I was waiting to go in I decided that I was going to act as remorseful as possible and take full responsibility. Seeing the Colonel made me nervous, and I started rambling when he started asking me questions. "Why did you want out of the Army so bad?" the Colonel asked. "Uh…uh, I don't like it here, sir," I stuttered. "What don't you like about it?" he asked. What came out of my mouth even shocked me when I said, "There's a lot of drug use going on in the barracks, and I'm uncomfortable around it." I don't know what possessed me to say that, but I'm guessing I was trying to get some sympathy. "And you don't do drugs?" he asked. I replied, "No sir." "What if I have you drug tested right now Private, would you pass?" Calling his bluff, I replied, "Yes sir." The Colonel was having none of it and promptly gave me the maximum punishment. He sentenced me to thirty days in an Army correctional facility. I had proved my father right.

It was basic training all over again. From the moment I arrived in shackles, a screaming sergeant ordered me to dump all my belongings on the floor. Worried that I would say something stupid to piss them off even more I decided that I would stay silent. When he saw my Walkman and music cassettes, he began to laugh and said to the other sergeant, "Confiscate that, sergeant. This dumb fuck thinks he's back on the block." He then began to bark out rule after rule. "You will refer to yourself as prisoner at all times. In here, you have no rank. You will ask permission to do anything, even to speak. You will march everywhere you go and not speak to the other prisoners unless in the mess hall or inside your cell. Any questions prisoner?" I shook my head "no" so he screamed in my face, "I didn't fucking hear you!" I refused to give in and just stared straight ahead and said nothing. He got in my face again and said, "I'm the last guy you want to piss off. Move out, prisoner!"

After three days in a six by nine cell by myself for twenty-three hours a day, they moved me to a larger cell with three other soldiers and I was given a work detail. My assignment was in the kitchen, which was dirty work but kept you busy and made the time go by faster. After about a week I had settled in and accepted the fact that I would be there for another three weeks. I wasn't sure what would happen once I got out of jail, but I was hoping I would still be discharged which was still not a guarantee. The Army had every right to make me stay and fulfill my enlistment contract which called for three years' active duty and five more years on ready reserve status. The only upside was that a Summary Court Martial could not result in a bad conduct or dishonorable discharge. I had no phone privileges, but they allowed me to send and receive mail which the correctional officers monitored. After about two weeks I received the first letter from my mother who told me that she had hired an attorney to help me get out.

On the eighteenth day of my incarceration with only twelve more to go, I was informed that one of the sergeants from my unit was there to see me. He told me that he had orders to process me out of the Army by the end of the day. I was shocked and thrilled at the same time. When I asked him why I was getting out early he just said, "All I know is that the commander told me to process you out of the Army and drop you off outside of the main gate when we're done." I got my things packed and left the correctional facility for good. As we drove away I asked the sergeant if he could stop by a phone booth. I had to call my mother to find out what happened.

It seems it was all the work of my mother who had hired an attorney to get me out of the stockade. He was a high-priced retired military lawyer who knew the UCMJ like the back of his hand. According to my mother, he was relentless with his phone calls to various officers in my unit including the one who sentenced me. My attorney argued that a Summary Court Martial comes with a thirty-day maximum sentence and that my three weeks on barracks restriction should have counted as time served. My lawyer had found a loophole and the authorities decided not only to release me from jail but also to get rid of me completely. He was able to get me the entry-level discharge, but with the provision that I complete my eight-year military contract in the Instant Ready Reserve or IRR. Since that meant the Army could only bring me back in the event of a war I wasn't that concerned. I was going home, and that's all that mattered.

The sergeant hurried me around so that we could complete the out-processing by the end of the day. Since it was Friday we had to wrap it up by close of business or I'd have to stay the weekend. Luckily, we got everything done and I was discharged out of the Army in eight hours. As happy as I was to be leaving Fort Campbell, I was also steaming mad. I thought if it was this easy to get someone out of the Army, why the fuck did they make me wait so long. I couldn't help but think how this could've all been avoided. As ordered, the sergeant dropped me off right outside the main gate where I took a cab to the airport and then caught a flight to New Jersey. I was thrilled to be going home with the summer set to begin and my 21st birthday just around the corner.

# Chapter 12
# Wiseguys and Wannabes

My friend Albert was shot and killed in front of a Brooklyn bar two months prior to me leaving for the Army. We'd been close friends since the age of fourteen when we'd hang out at 114 Park. We continued to stay friends as we got older before finally heading our separate ways. Not surprisingly, after we outgrew the schoolyard Albert began hanging out with guys associated with Little Nicky's crew. And his stepfather had ties to organized crime. The rumor in the neighborhood was that it was Albert's stepfather who murdered Joe Milo, but I knew otherwise. Albert's death weighed heavily on me while I was in basic training, but it wasn't until I went home for Christmas that I found out who killed him.

While I was back in Canarsie for New Year's Eve I found out through friends that a guy named Todd Avito shot my friend Albert following an argument over a girl. Todd was a small-time associate of a rival mob crew that was part of the Lucchese crime family. I'd only met him a few times through mutual friends and Albert thought he was an asshole even before he was murdered. Todd had disappeared for a while in fear for his life but brazenly returned to the neighborhood a few months later. I had just arrived at Fort

Campbell when I heard the news that Todd was found shot to death in his car near the Le Parc nightclub in Canarsie, formerly the Bamboo Lounge. The police would charge Albert's stepfather with the murder, but word around Canarsie put the blame elsewhere.

Following my discharge, I decided that living in Canarsie full time would not be a smart move. To remain in the good graces of my father I would stay in New Jersey during the week and go to work with my parents every morning. On the weekends I would drive to Canarsie in the used Camaro I had just purchased with the help of my mother. She gave me $1000 for the down payment, then my father took the payments right from my check. Not wanting to disturb my grandmother when I came home late, I began staying with my Aunt Dee and cousins in nearby Starrett City. I got back into my pot routine almost immediately but for the most part stayed away from cocaine.

After being back for a few weeks I noticed that many of the people I grew up with in Canarsie, including some of my close friends, had become involved with Organized Crime. For those less fortunate, the Mafia was a way to make a name for yourself. In Canarsie, as in other Italian-American areas in New York, people in the neighborhood looked up to "wiseguys," as we called them, and many felt it was a badge of honor to be associated with the mob. The best perk was that if people thought you were a mob associate or a "wannabe," nobody would mess with you. Many of the guys who got involved did so because they had very few choices. Either they didn't finish school or were just dumb as bricks, and some of them were born into the life. I was friendly with many of the neighborhood wannabes, having known most of them from junior high. On occasion, I'd hang out with them but had no desire to get involved with the mob.

Some of the guys in my immediate circle had begun to venture into criminal activities although not directly connected to Organized

Crime. My friend Mario was still dealing cocaine and continued to avoid paying the mob, as he was supplying two wannabes in Little Nicky's crew. Our friendship was slowly on the mend as Mario was now making thousands of dollars a week and had stopped asking me for money. My other friend, Jambo, along with Mario and my longtime friend Richie, got involved with a stolen credit card scam which made them thousands of dollars. Jambo paid a local Canarsie girl who worked in the post office to intercept letters that contained pre-approved credit cards that the companies would mail to their customers. She would then give them to my friends who would then max them out, usually buying clothes, jewelry, and eating at fancy restaurants. The scam worked because the credit card companies sent out the cards without the customer's knowledge who then didn't find out they were victims of fraud until receiving the bill a month later. They offered me the opportunity to join them in their scam, but I chickened out at the last minute. I really had no reason to steal because I was doing well working for my father again and living rent-free in my parents' second condo. I had more than enough money and couldn't risk going to jail again.

With the Memorial Day holiday approaching, eight of my friends rented a house in Seaside Heights on the Jersey Shore for the entire summer. The house was an old single-level beach house with three small bedrooms, a kitchen, a tiny bathroom, and an outdoor shower. The house was fully furnished with cheap furniture and had yellow and green wallpaper from the seventies plastered all over the kitchen. The house was only twenty miles from the condo so instead of driving to Canarsie, I'd meet them at the beach house every weekend. What I didn't realize until that first weekend was that my friends were still freebasing on Friday nights.

After I left Canarsie the regular crew of guys who freebased at my house continued to smoke but in different locations. Mario would smoke with Randy in his basement, Dave and a few guys would party at his girlfriend's house, and Armando would go wherever he wanted. Richie was the only one in our immediate crew who didn't smoke cocaine but got high on everything else.

There were about eight or nine of us at the beach the first weekend, but that number grew every week. From the moment we got there Mario began cooking the cocaine with the rest of us preparing our pipes. At first, the thought of smoking cocaine for the first time in seven months scared me, but after a few shots of vodka, I was game. Just like back in my old house there were people freebasing in every room. Once everyone got started you could hear a pin drop, and you could never tell from the outside that there were almost a dozen people getting high in the house. It was contrary to Saturday nights when the place turned into a raucous party house with all of us drunk on beer and vodka. This went on for the first few weeks of the summer until the night that we all experienced the scare of a lifetime.

It was a Friday night in late June, the day before my twenty-first birthday. About nine of us arrived at the house in Seaside that evening and immediately began to prepare our pipes, getting ready to smoke. After Mario finished cooking the batch we all took our share and dispersed to different rooms in the house. I was in one of the bedrooms with my friend Armando and two of my other friends. The four of us all had our own pipes so we all began smoking at the same time. Just as I exhaled my first hit I noticed that Armando, who had also just done a hit, was staring at the lightbulb on the ceiling for about a minute. I tried to ask him if he was okay, but I was unable to speak. At that moment Armando began to start shaking and fell to the floor. My other friend yelled out, "Oh my God, help!" and the rest of the guys came running into the room.

I stood there completely frozen and watched in horror as Armando seemed to be having an epileptic fit, convulsing on the floor with his eyes rolling up into his head. Someone yelled out, "Grab his tongue so he doesn't swallow it!" Mario kneeled next to

Armando and grabbed his tongue with his fingers. A few of my other friends held his arms and legs as he shook uncontrollably for about two minutes. I kept saying to myself repeatedly, "Please don't die, please don't die." When he finally stopped shaking and started to come to, he looked confused and said, "What happened?" When Mario told him he replied, "All I remember is doing a hit, and then saw you guys standing over me." We wanted to take him to the emergency room, but he was adamant about not going. The incident traumatized us so much that everyone put their cocaine away and started drinking. I was thankful that my friends were able to help because I felt horrible guilt that I was too high to do anything.

Watching my friend almost die smoking cocaine was a wake up call and made me realize how dangerous this drug was. I didn't smoke the shit for seven months, and now I found myself freebasing every Friday all over again. I remembered how fast the cocaine got out of control before the Army and knew if I didn't stop it would happen all over again. I'm not sure how that night scared my other friends, because nobody wanted to talk about it, but I know I didn't want to be anywhere near that house. I decided that I needed a change of scenery and a break from my regular crew. A good friend of mine from 114 Park invited me to spend the July 4th weekend at his house in the Hamptons on Long Island. It was just what I needed.

My friend Anthony was part of a group of about a dozen people who rented a huge waterfront house right on Hampton Bay in the summer of 1985. I knew many of them from junior high school and a few of them from my days hanging out at 114 Park. All of them were mob connected, with most working for Little Nicky. These were the same guys that my friend Albert was with on the night he was murdered. They had reputations for being some of the craziest guys in Canarsie, and I was glad I was friendly with them. I drove to the Hamptons with Anthony and another friend who we called Sally Lip who I had known since the seventh grade.

These guys were involved in all sorts of different criminal activities, but most of them with stolen cars. As soon as I picked up Sally Lip in my Camaro he began eyeing my hatchback and asked Anthony, "Do you think we can fit a bumper back there," referring to the rash of Cadillac bumpers being stolen by his crew. When we arrived at the house I was greeted warmly as they knew I was returning from the Army, and the fact I hadn't seen some of them in quite a while. Another wannabe at the house that weekend was an old friend from 114 Park, Tommy Red. The only time that I was ever in a stolen car was one that Tommy Red stole back in 1980 when we were still hanging out together. Tommy didn't run with Little Nicky's crew as he was the cousin of a Lucchese wiseguy and part of a major stolen car ring. The guy with the craziest reputation at the house that weekend was Anthony's cousin Michael, better known in the neighborhood as Mikey Y.

Mikey Y started making a name for himself at an early age. When we were in junior high, Mikey Y and a couple of his friends tried to beat up a New York City cop named Officer Lark who used to patrol the school every day. Although the officer eventually subdued him, the story was that Mikey Y beat up a cop at the age of thirteen, and the legend of Mikey Y had begun. Mikey Y wasn't very big, but soon gained a reputation for being one of the toughest guys in Canarsie. After getting involved in various illegal activities he soon caught the attention of Little Nicky, who brought Mikey Y into his crew and took him under his wing. Now twenty-two, Mikey Y was working as an enforcer for Nicky, collecting debts and busting heads. The rumor in Canarsie was that Mikey Y killed Todd Avito in retaliation for the murder of my friend Albert. Mikey Y was never charged with Todd's murder because they charged Albert's stepfather with the crime. It didn't matter to me if Mikey Y did do it since Albert was my close friend, and Todd was a scumbag who deserved what he got.

I was having the time of my life. Instead of freebasing like a junkie I was jet skiing, playing naked volleyball, and going out to the clubs. All the guys from the house were at the club including Albert's younger brother Tony. He was angry at the world following his brother's death and had become a loose cannon. As I was talking with him at the bar he looked down, put his hand on my chest, and said, "What is that, a wire?" When I showed him that it was my dog tags, he just played it off and said, "You could never be too careful." As much as I was insulted that he would think I was a "rat," I just laughed it off. All weekend dozens of people came through that house with everyone drinking beer, doing shots, and smoking weed. Nobody did cocaine.

As much as I loved their hospitality and the fact that they weren't doing coke, they were just a little too much for me. The entire time all they talked about was who had the biggest balls, always trying to top each other. It was like a competition between wannabe wiseguys trying to prove who was crazier. Caught up in their bravado, Sally Lip somehow convinced me to cross Hampton Bay in a small rubber raft. Without wearing any life jackets, we paddled mid-way through the bay before realizing how far it was. Knowing we couldn't make it round trip we decided to continue to the other side. When a woman on a passing boat asked if we needed help, I had Sally Lip in stitches when I replied in a stern military voice, "No ma'am, we do this for a living."

We made it to the other side and realized we were stranded, and dreaded the thought of having to paddle back. As we laid on the sand in total exhaustion, we looked up and saw a motorboat coming toward the shore. A few of the guys from the house thought we may have drowned and had come looking for us. Sally Lip and I came back to the house as heroes. "I thought you guys were dead for sure," someone said as we got off the boat. "You guys are fucking nuts," Mikey Y said. "That took big balls." Sally would later tell me that many guys tried to cross the bay that summer, but all of them turned back. I realized later that we could have very easily drowned that day, but having those guys thinking I was the crazy one was great for my reputation in Canarsie.

I had a love-hate relationship with Canarsie. As much as I blamed all my troubles on the neighborhood, I couldn't seem to break away. I compared Canarsie to a line in Godfather III when Michael Corleone says, "Just when I think I'm out, they pull me back in." As much as I tried to make friends in New Jersey, I always felt out of place anywhere else and was only comfortable and trusted the guys in my immediate crew. As much fun as I had in the Hamptons I knew that I couldn't hang out with those guys on a regular basis, either. I knew it would only lead to one thing, and I wasn't cut out to be a wannabe, much less a wiseguy. I spent the rest of the summer back at the house in Seaside. After the incident with Armando we were so freaked out that we stopped freebasing cocaine, but we continued to snort it and do other drugs.

Every weekend we would spend the entire day on the beach and boardwalk, then hit the clubs at night. Every Saturday morning after we awakened from our drunken stupor we would head to the local supermarket to stock up on food for the house. Surprisingly, Mario began stealing items from the store by stuffing items down his pants, even though he was making thousands of dollars dealing cocaine. After realizing that there was absolutely no security we decided to get brazen. We would walk in the store and Armando, with his charm and good looks, would politely ask one of the female cashiers for empty plastic bags. They never hesitated to give them to him. We went around the store filling up the bags with anything and everything and put them in the cart. I was too afraid to steal anything, so I acted as the decoy.

While I was in line paying for a few items, Mario and Armando would bring the packed cart to the front of the store and stand in front of the line acting as if they had paid already. To make it even more convincing Mario would start a friendly conversation with the cashier acting as if he were just waiting for his friend. We would then calmly walk out of the supermarket with hundreds of dollars of stolen groceries without anyone noticing. This went on for several weeks until one day one of the employees yelled out, "Hey, you guys didn't pay," and started walking towards Mario. As the employee got within a few feet of him Mario pushed the cart full of groceries into the man, knocking him down as we ran out of the store and into our car to get away.

As much as I didn't have the stomach or the nerve to ever rob anyone, I got a rush from acting as an accomplice in a planned scheme. After the summer ended my friend Jambo told me about a scam that involved traveler's checks. Jambo had been the ringleader in the stolen credit card scam involving the girl at the post office, which I wanted no part of at the time. The previous year Jambo and a few of my close friends went to the Summer Olympics in Los Angeles and paid for everything with the stolen cards. They bought first-class airline tickets, stayed in four-star hotels, and went home with expensive jewelry. After Jambo explained how the traveler check scam worked it seemed relatively safe so I decided to get in on it.

Mario, Dave, Richie, and Armando were all in on the scam along with me and Jambo. The plan was to go to Disneyland in California, which made me happy as I'd be able to visit Warren. The scam was quite simple. Jambo would act as the customer and legitimately purchase five thousand dollars in traveler's checks which was all the money we had. The company requires the customer to sign each one of the checks in the presence of an employee. When a person uses a traveler's check to make a purchase they are required to sign the check a second time, so the proprietor can match the signatures. After Jambo used and signed a few of the checks legitimately he would give the rest of them to us to use before reporting them stolen. It was imperative that someone other than Jambo sign the checks so that a handwriting expert could never match the signatures, but it was equally important that the signatures looked identical as to fool the salesperson.

It seems that I had re-found my expertise in forgery. When I was in school I used to forge my mother's signature on all sorts of fake notes and was also able to fool dozens of teachers by forging the school dean's signature. I practiced Jambo's signature for about an hour until I had perfected it. We headed to the tourist area right outside of Disneyland that was rife with unsuspecting small businesses. The best part of using a traveler's check to pay was that you received your change in cash. We went up and down the streets using twenty-dollar checks to purchase items that cost a dollar. It took us almost the entire day, but we finally spent all the checks. After collecting about four thousand dollars in cash and about one thousand in souvenirs, Jambo reported the checks stolen and received another forty-nine hundred dollars' worth of new traveler's checks which we split up and spent "legitimately." We came home almost broke, but we paid for the entire trip using the traveler's checks. It seemed too easy.

The sad part was that I was oblivious to the fact that I had committed a felony which could've put me in jail for a long time. I didn't need the money at all, and I think I did it to show I wasn't afraid. I knew deep down what I did was wrong, but at the time it was more important to look cool and fit in. Reputation meant everything in Canarsie, and the last thing you wanted to be known as was a pussy. The neighborhood was like a giant high school and even at twenty-one I felt the need to be popular. It was also important to have a reputation for being a good fighter, or just outright crazy, so people wouldn't fuck with you. I was a good fighter but way too small to intimidate anyone, and I wasn't crazy, so I did what most guys like me in Canarsie did...hang out with ones who were.

# Chapter 13
# Bad Streets

On December 16, 1985, the boss of the Gambino crime family, Paul Castellano, was shot and killed outside of Sparks Steak House in midtown Manhattan as part of a takeover by fellow gangsters. John Gotti was now the new boss of the Gambino family and immediately changed how the mob operated as far as drugs were concerned. Under Castellano, drug dealing was forbidden by made members, although many were doing it behind his back. With Gotti at the helm, dealing drugs was permissible as long as he got his cut of the profits. This had a major impact on Canarsie as Little Nicky's crew saturated the neighborhood with wannabes shaking down every drug dealer they could find. Associates from the rival Lucchese crew began getting into the action and started competing with the Gambino associates for shakedown money. Wannabes were everywhere, and no dealer was safe. I knew it was only a matter of time before they approached Mario.

Prior to the swarm of wannabes shaking down everyone in Canarsie with a beeper, Mario was able to avoid paying the mob as he was supplying two associates from Little Nicky's crew who were making money on the side. Not having to keep low any longer these same two guys came to Mario looking to shake him down. They knew what kind of money he was making, and they demanded three hundred dollars per week. Since Mario didn't want to give these guys a dime, he told them that he would rather stop dealing. "You really gonna stop dealing?" I asked when Mario told me what had happened. "Fuck no," he said, "I'm gonna lay low and just deal with to immediate friends." As soon as he said that I recalled the little black book that had six names of close friends owing him thousands of dollars.

Mario had long ago stopped asking his immediate crew of friends for money, probably realizing we were never going to pay him. He did continue dealing with us, but everything was now cash only. I had begun snorting lines again on the weekends but gone were the days of smoking cocaine. The incident in Seaside when my friend almost died was deterrent enough.

When the "crack" epidemic hit New York it became a ghetto drug like heroin, and nobody wanted to be associated with it. Crack was the same as freebase but sold in smaller, more affordable amounts. The highly addictive drug saturated the areas of East New York and Brownsville which bordered Canarsie, and soon people we knew were now hooked on it. If you were trying to make a name for yourself in Canarsie the last thing you needed was to be known as a crackhead. The only person who I knew that was still doing it was my friend Randy who was now smoking it every day.

I was surprised that Mario continued to supply Randy with cocaine, knowing that he was out of control. When I left for the Army, Mario had begun getting high with Randy and they soon became friends. Mario even acted as Randy's "Godfather" when he went back to receive his Holy Confirmation to get married in a Catholic Church. When Randy's cocaine "bill" hit ten thousand dollars, Mario stopped giving him credit and eventually cut him off altogether. Randy became incensed, not just because he wouldn't sell him coke anymore, but because he felt that Mario was ripping him off, unknowingly charging him for all the times they'd smoked in Randy's basement. When Randy, who was a lot bigger than Mario, refused to pay him anything, Mario decided to enlist some help.

Unable to go to the guys in Little Nicky's crew, Mario went to a guy named Tony G, who was a wannabe who ran with the Lucchese wiseguys from Geffken's Bar. They cut a deal where they would collect the debt from Randy in exchange for half the money. Mario would later tell me that he went in offering them ten percent, and they laughed at him. I was stuck in the middle as both Randy and Mario were friends of mine, although I didn't let on I was pissed off at Mario for what he'd done. He could have just let this go, as he had already accumulated a few hundred thousand dollars, but his cheapness wouldn't allow it. When Tony G and his crew threatened to blow up Randy's family's restaurant if he didn't pay them, Randy enlisted some help of his own.

A few months prior, Randy had married the ex-wife of a made member in the Gambino crime family who was part of Little Nicky's crew. Randy went to him and asked if he could get the debt squashed. Randy also mentioned that Mario was still dealing. This infuriated the Gambino associates because Mario had lied to them. A sit-down was arranged between the Gambino and Lucchese contingents where the wiseguys decided that the debt belonged to the Gambinos as they had originally hit up Mario for protection money. Randy was now free and clear but Mario wasn't so lucky.

Mario and I were driving in his BMW when we decided to stop at the newsstand on Flatlands Avenue. As I sat in the car while Mario went to buy a drink, I noticed in the rearview mirror a car pulling up behind us but thought nothing of it. When the four guys simultaneously got out of the car, I immediately recognized them. When I turned to my right one of them was standing by my open window, blocking the door. He said, "Just sit there Cuc, this don't concern you." When I looked behind me I saw Mikey Y and the other two guys beating the shit out of Mario. When I reacted as if I wanted to get out and help, the guy put his hand on the door and said, "You don't wanna do that," and lifted his shirt with his other hand, showing me a gun. I sat there helplessly as they pummeled my friend until he lay motionless on the ground. Mikey Y stood over him and said, "Pay us or next time you won't be so lucky."

After they left I rushed out of the car to help Mario who was still conscious. As I helped him off the floor and saw his swollen, bloodied face, I said, "You gotta go to the hospital, I'm taking you to Brookdale." Hardly able to talk as his mouth was dripping with blood, he demanded, "Take me fucking home right now. I'm not sitting in that shithole for six hours," As much as I wanted to take him to the emergency room, I respected his wishes and drove him home. Within an hour he looked like Rocky Balboa after fighting Apollo Creed, with one of his eyes swollen shut and half of his face black and blue. "You gotta pay these guys. They'll fuckin' kill you," I said bluntly. He didn't respond. "With all the money you have, you're gonna risk your life over a few hundred dollars?" I asked rhetorically. "That's fuckin' nuts," I said as I looked l in his one open eye knowing that he was already scheming a way to get out of paying them.

Mario's little black book was filled with people who owed him money for cocaine. According to him he had over twenty-five thousand dollars on the streets owed to him by various people. Topping that list was Randy, who was now off limits, and about another ten thousand from our crew which we'd accumulated over that four-year period. The rest of the debts were comprised of dozens of other people who owed him much smaller amounts. When he went to meet with the guys who beat him up, Mario offered them a deal where instead of paying smaller amounts each week he would stop dealing and give them his little black book so they could collect the debts for themselves. They agreed to the deal, and soon Little Nicky sent Mikey Y and his other goons to start collecting. I didn't find out that Mario had given his black book to the mob until my friend Jambo told me. As much as I wanted to believe that Mario would never betray me like that, I was nervous as hell thinking my name was still in that book.

Knowing I couldn't ask Mario, I went to my friend Jambo who was dating the sister of a wannabe in Little Nicky's crew, who ironically was one of the guys who beat Mario up. I had become good friends with Jambo as we were both big pot smokers and had bonded after our traveler's check scam in California. I was relieved when he told me that Mario didn't give them the names of his close friends. But he also added, "Mario better hope the people in that book pay up or they're gonna come back to him." Mario laid low after that and I found myself hanging with Jambo more often. Tired of traveling back and forth from New Jersey, I decided to move back to Canarsie as I was spending most of my free time there anyway.

Jambo had gotten involved with various scams with his girlfriend's brother and some of the other wannabes. He would pick me every day and we would buy weed and pull over by Canarsie High School to smoke it. All he talked about was finding ways to scam money, and he was currently involved in a con that preyed on degenerate gamblers. They would allow these guys to get thousands of dollars in debt and then force them to pay the tax every week knowing they would never be able to pay the full amount. Eventually, they would force the poor guy to sell everything he had just to pay them off. He offered me an opportunity to get in on the scam, but I wanted no part of it. I had no desire to hurt anyone or ruin their lives. "What's the matter, you're a pussy?" he teased me. Trying to look cool and impress him I replied, "That ain't my thing. I'm more into what we did in California," referring to the traveler's check scam. "Oh yeah?" he said. "I got a scam you might like."

Knowing I had an American Express card which didn't come with a credit limit, he wanted me to let him use it and then report it stolen. We would then split everything he bought, and I wouldn't be responsible for paying since the card was insured. The problem was that it wasn't really my card. It belonged to my father's business. My father gave it to me to use for business expenses as I was now working outside sales. My first response was, "I'm not gonna fucking steal from my father." Jambo was smooth and convincing when he said, "Your father doesn't lose a dime, those cards are insured. He's never gonna know it's you. I'm gonna get someone to forge your signature, so they could never trace it back to you." As much as I wanted no part of this, I was too afraid to say no. I didn't want to look like a pussy again. I was twenty-two years old and willing to commit credit card fraud against my father's business to impress a wannabe gangster just to keep my standing in Canarsie.

Jambo used the card to purchase gold jewelry which was easy to turn into cash. He claimed the card was declined after several purchases, but I had my doubts as my father's business had very high credit limits. We made eight hundred each, but I had a gut feeling he made a lot more and wasn't telling me. It didn't matter. I was too afraid to accuse him knowing his local ties. Maybe I was a pussy. I lied to my father and told him I lost my wallet and that he needed to report the card stolen. It was then that he found out about the purchases and immediately suspected my involvement.

"Did you buy any jewelry lately?" he asked suspiciously. Playing it cool I replied, "No…why would you ask me that?" With a slight anger in his voice, he said, "Someone charged two thousand dollars at Kay Jewelers in Kings Plaza. You know anything about that?" Without hesitation, I shot back, "Why would I know something? I have an account at Kay Jewelers, they'd know me." That part was true. It seemed to pacify him as he stopped asking me about it. I thought the plan had worked just as Jambo explained and was happy to know he didn't cheat me. I would find out months later that when American Express questioned the claim, my mother paid the bill saying it was a misunderstanding. She covered for me suspecting I was involved but obviously didn't want to tell my father. I could never figure out how I was stupid enough to be talked into all of this, and the guilt of stealing from my father weighed heavily on my mind for years.

I continued to hang out with Jambo, and as usual he kept looking for ways to create income. One day in September 1986, a money-making scheme dropped right into our laps. Jambo, Richie and me were all huge Mets fans. The team had done extremely well that season and were ready to clinch their first division title in thirteen years. They came home to play, the Cubs still needing only one more win to clinch, and we were hell bent on being there. Hoping to get tickets, we all called out of work and a few of us went to Shea Stadium the morning of the game to wait in line at the box office. We were surprised that there wasn't much of a line and didn't have to wait very long. As soon as the person at the ticket booth told us there were still plenty of tickets left, Jambo immediately saw an opportunity to make money.

Knowing that there would soon be a demand for tickets the three of us pooled our money together to purchase as many as we could afford. Between cash and the credit card I had, we came up with about four hundred and fifty dollars which was enough to purchase over one hundred general admission tickets at four dollars each. After going back to Canarsie, we returned to the stadium about two hours before the 7:30 pm start time, and to our delight the box office had sold all their tickets. Since none of us had scalped tickets before we went around asking other scalpers for tickets to gauge the going rate which turned out to be about twenty dollars per ticket. The three of us each took about thirty tickets and went into the parking lot to avoid the police who were now an obvious presence.

As soon as I got the nerve to announce aloud that I had tickets for sale, I was immediately bombarded by fans who didn't hesitate to give up twenty bucks. Within an hour the three of us sold all our tickets and made close to two thousand dollars in profit.

Not only did I make about a week's salary in just over an hour I was able to watch my beloved Mets clinch the division that night. Jambo was hoping they would lose so we could make more money the next night. As the game was ending, and it looked like the Mets would win, many of us tried to make our way down to the field level so that we could jump on the field after the last out was made. The security guards made a feeble attempt at keeping the fans from coming down from the upper levels and were soon overpowered by the throngs of people all looking to join the celebration. When Mets first baseman Keith Hernandez made the final out, Shea Stadium erupted and the fans began pouring onto the field.

The three of us pushed toward the centerfield area so we could smoke a joint. As I was rolling it, Richie reached down and pulled out some of the outfield grass and mixed it with the pot. As we were smoking it with thousands of people celebrating around us, I couldn't help but think about my Mets tryout and that easy fly ball that sailed over my head. Before the police on horseback cleared the fans off the field, I reached down and ripped up a large patch of outfield grass as a souvenir, just as I had my dreams of playing professional baseball ripped from me in that very same spot three years earlier.

# Chapter 14
# Hungry Like the Wolf

As I arrived at work and came into the office, my mother was sitting at her desk beaming, and I knew by the look on her face that she was dying to tell me something. "What are you so happy about?" I started to ask her. "Your brother is in Duran Duran!" she blurted out even before I could finish my sentence. "They hired him this weekend. He's going on tour with them in a few weeks," she said proudly. This was amazing news! Duran Duran had become one of the biggest pop groups in the world! They were also one of my favorite bands. They had just released the title track for the new James Bond movie, "A View to A Kill," and were still on top of the charts. I was in shock and kept asking, "Duran Duran? Are you serious?" This was like my family hitting the lottery, maybe even better. After the initial shock wore off I asked my mother, "How the hell did Warren hook up with Duran Duran?"

In the spring of 1986, Missing Persons broke up along with the marriage of Dale and Terry Bozzio. Following their Gold record in 1983, the band had released two more albums that didn't do nearly as well, and Capitol Records didn't re-sign them. Within weeks of the band's breakup, Warren found out that Duran Duran's lead guitarist Andy Taylor had asked Terry to work on his solo project. Soon after, Terry informed Warren that Andy wouldn't be returning to Duran Duran. Warren seized the opportunity and sent a tape of his work to the band with a note attached that read, "I'm your new guitarist." It caught them off guard because Andy had never told them he was leaving. After confirming Andy's departure, the band decided to give Warren an audition. They were in the middle of recording a new album and Warren's playing made an immediate impression on them. They hired him as a session musician to complete the album "Notorious," and to then join them on the upcoming tour.

I had always felt that my brother's success with both Frank Zappa and Missing Persons were met with little or no enthusiasm with my friends in Canarsie. Most people my age in the neighborhood didn't listen to that type of music, and neither band received much airplay, so they weren't exactly household names. Duran Duran was another animal, and my friends freaked out when I told them the news. Mario was the most excited. He'd followed Warren's career and was an aspiring drummer himself. Naturally, when I told Jambo, he tried to persuade me to scalp tickets. "We made a few thousand on those Mets tickets. Imagine what we could make on Duran Duran," he said trying to lure me in. It bothered me when he said "we." I thought, "Even if I did do it, why would I give you any money?" I was still feeling horribly guilty about the credit card scam and wasn't going to be stupid enough to let him talk me into this.

It became the greatest pickup line, "My brother is in Duran Duran," and I used it every chance I got. It worked a lot better than telling girls I was a swatch card salesman working for daddy. It soon became my identity whenever I went out, and even my friends got into the act. I would see them talking to girls and pointing at me knowing exactly what they were telling them. It worked on many girls, but some would accuse me of lying because it sounded too unbelievable given the fact that the band was British. I remember trying to impress a girl one night, and she sarcastically responded, "Yeah and my brother is in the Rolling Stones." Some of the diehard Duran Duran fans got angry with me when I told them because they were upset that Warren had replaced Andy Taylor. Some of them became so mad you'd have thought Warren killed Andy. It didn't bother me a bit. I was loving all the attention.

The tour was scheduled to begin in two weeks and everyone I knew wanted me to get them tickets, even offering me money and drugs. With the help of my mother who was now acting as Warren's manager, I was able to get ten tickets for the Madison Square Garden show and invited my closest friends and some of their girlfriends. I had no intention of bringing a date as I knew there would be thousands of girls who wouldn't mind hanging out with a relative of a band member. We all chipped in for a stretch limousine, and the second we got in the car Mario began breaking up lines and Richie began rolling joints. Along with the liquor that came with the car, we were flying high by the time we got to the City.

Unlike the Missing Persons concerts that were held in small venues and drew crowds of a few thousand people, Duran Duran would pack arenas with screaming girls everywhere they played. It was reminiscent of the Beatles, and the press even dubbed them the "Fab Five." It had been a couple of years since their peak, but they were still drawing twenty thousand fans every concert. When we pulled up to the Garden about two hours before showtime, West 33rd Street was already closed off with thousands of fans standing behind barricades waiting for the gates to open. I was told by my parents to pick up my tickets at the Will Call window and meet them at the backstage entrance. As I made my way to the backstage area my father was standing outside the door waiting for me. He handed me some backstage After Show stickers for my friends, and then with a huge smile on his face placed a laminated pass around my neck that said "Family Member, Access All Areas." We went backstage to wish Warren good luck and then proceed to our seats.

Within minutes I had dozens of girls asking me who I was, and how I got the pass. One girl grabbed at it, and I had to push her away from me. It was all happening so fast that I barely responded to any of them. I was just grinning from ear to ear waiting for the show to start. We had excellent seats about seven rows from the stage on the right side where Warren would be playing. When we got to our seats there were a bunch of girls sitting in front of us who noticed my pass. One girl marched right up to me and said, "If you take me backstage after the show I'll give you a blowjob." Knowing there would be much hotter girls turning up, I turned down her offer.

As the lights went down a deafening roar came from the crowd, unlike anything I had ever heard. With thousands of girls screaming at the top of their lungs the band opened with the song "Hungry Like the Wolf." It made them scream even louder. With people screaming and dancing all around me, chills ran through my body as I looked up at my brother on the stage, wondering if this was really happening. I'd heard this song a hundred times, and now my brother was playing it live in front of twenty thousand people. He was playing lead guitar and supplying the backup vocals to Simon LeBon's lead. During the song "Rio," they turned down the lights except for the spotlight on Warren as he played the guitar solo. When the lights came back up I turned to my right where my parents were sitting and noticed my father crying.

As I tried to make my way to my friends who were sitting a few rows behind my family, I was surrounded by a group of girls who had also noticed my pass. I was eating up the attention as they asked who I was, but then one of them, a twenty-something overweight girl, grabbed my arm and pleaded, "Please take me with you, please!" A couple of my friends saw me and swooped in to pull me away from her. All I could hear on the way backstage was girls begging us to take them with us as my friends were also wearing their backstage stickers. When Mario suggested I take mine off, I replied, "Are you fuckin' kidding me, I'm loving every minute of this." It was beyond anything I could ever imagine. I had been transported to an altered reality.

After dodging desperate Duranies, we finally made our way backstage. We were ushered into a VIP room complete with a full bar and huge buffet. There were about fifty or so people mingling around. As I had predicted, the room was brimming with gorgeous women. We stood out like sore thumbs looking like the Guidos from Brooklyn surrounded by snobby, stuck up Manhattan elites. My parents, siblings, other family members, and a small contingent of Warren's friends from Canarsie all gathered in one area as we waited for him to exit his dressing room. As soon as he came out he was his usual self, talking a mile a minute and cracking joke after joke. While Warren had all his family and friends engaged as only he could, I noticed the rest of the band entering the room. I stopped Warren in mid-sentence and asked, "Can you introduce me to the band?"

He brought me to where they were sitting and introduced me as his little brother Rob. Simon LeBon seemed uninterested and said, "Hello mate," before quickly turning back to the woman he was chatting up. Nick Rhodes, the band's founder, took a moment to say hello and gave me a delicate handshake. John Taylor was the friendliest of the three, taking time from the stunning woman he was with to stand up and shake my hand. John was tall and lanky and looked like a Calvin Klein model. "Hello Rob, a pleasure to meet you," he said in a soft-spoken English accent. I was a little starstruck and could only utter "Likewise." As John shook my hand and looked me in the eye I knew immediately that he was stoned on weed. His eyes were bloodshot and glassy, and he had that grin on his face that a pothead like me couldn't miss. As we were walking away I said to Warren, "Wow, John seems like a great guy. But what's up with Simon and Nick, are they assholes?" He replied, "No, they're British."

Following the after-show party, my friends and I left Madison Square Garden through the backstage door that led to the street. I was mesmerized as I walked into a sea of thousands of screaming girls waiting to get a glimpse of their favorite band, packed together seven or eight rows deep behind police barricades on both sides of the street. It was a like a scene from a "Hard Day's Night." I could hear girls screaming trying to get our attention "Take me with you," one girl begged. "Who are you?" another yelled out. I could have sworn I heard people calling out my name, but as I looked out at the crowd I didn't recognize anyone. The New York City police officer who was guarding the back door said to me, "You might want to take off that pass before heading into the crowd. Those girls will attack you for that thing." I took the pass off and stuck it in my pocket as I walked past the barricades and onto the street. Dozens of girls followed us as we made our way to the limo which was parked on Seventh Avenue. As the car pulled away and headed to the Four Seasons Hotel where the band was staying, my friend Richie screamed out, "That was fuckin' sick!" We began celebrating like we'd won the lottery.

When we arrived at the hotel there was a crowd of a few hundred people standing near the entrance. The hotel had security outside the door keeping out the persistent fans who were pleading with the guards to let them in. As we were giving our names to the security guard, girls were screaming at us to take them into the hotel. As I was walking in I noticed this sweet-looking fan who couldn't have been more than sixteen years old, standing behind the barricade holding an "I love John Taylor" sign. For some reason, I felt the urge to make that girl's day and decided to use my newfound "power" to arrange for her to meet John. I told the security guard she was with me. As I escorted her into the hotel I said to her, "Whatever you do don't make a scene." She looked at me and said "You are so nice, thank you so much. I won't…I promise." As we walked into the hotel lounge I saw John standing and talking to a few people. I walked over to him. He recognized me immediately and said, "Hey Rob." Before I could introduce her to him she began screaming at the top of her lungs. The entire room stopped and looked at us. Mortified, as I grabbed her hand and pulled her away, John now had a "What the fuck?" look on his face.

After I escorted her out of the hotel I was almost too embarrassed to go back into the lounge. When I did go back in Warren walked over to me and I asked him if John was mad. He smiled and said, "Nobody's mad bro, that shit happens all the time with these guys. Just don't be a schmuck and bring these groupies anywhere near the band." Feeling much better I assured him, "I'll never do that again, I swear." When I went over to John to apologize he was still as nice as could be and said, "No problem mate, just be careful who you bring in with you." With that off my mind, I set my sights on some of the beautiful women that were draped all over my brother.

Warren had about six or seven girls sitting around him at the table, each one prettier than the next. We sat there for about a half an hour as my brother held court, cracking everyone up. Warren then said his goodbyes to me and my friends and went upstairs to his room with two of the girls. My friends were looking to go home, but I had no intention of leaving as I was sitting next to five beautiful women. I didn't want this night to ever end. I told them to take the limo back to Canarsie and I'd find my way home. Soon after, three of the girls left, leaving me with two of them. The girl who was flirting with me asked me if I wanted to bring the party upstairs. Without hesitation, I followed them to their room, and within minutes all three of us were naked and rolling on the bed. It was my very first ménage-a-trois, courtesy of Duran Duran.

The following morning, I sat alone on the subway, disheveled and hungover. I closed my eyes and replayed the entire night in my head. It was easily the greatest experience to date, and all I could think about was going to another Duran Duran show. But as the train exited the tunnel and the bright sunshine brought me out of my dream world, reality set in. Looking out at the dilapidated buildings plastered with graffiti as the train made its way through the ghettos of Brooklyn, I was suddenly overcome with a feeling of frustration knowing I was going back to my regular life. I knew I would never be able to achieve what my brother had done, and I was convinced that the only way I was going to make my father proud of me was if I took over his business. As I walked out of the subway station at Rockaway Parkway in Canarsie and began the short walk to my apartment, I came to the realization that I was destined for an ordinary life.

# Chapter 15
# The Frozen Tavern

In 1987, Vittorio "Vic" Amuso was named boss of the Lucchese crime family following the conviction of eleven mob members in the famous Mafia Commission Trial of 1985. Vic, along with his brother Bobby, were lifelong Canarsie residents who had attended grade school with my mother at P.S. 242. She would later tell me that she and her classmates knew the Amuso brothers were destined for a life of crime. Now, Bobby co-owned a bar on Flatlands Avenue in Canarsie called the Walnut Tavern, along with his childhood friend James McBride. My mother would also later tell me that she dated Jimmy McBride when they were young teenagers. After Vic became boss of the Lucchese family, many of the made members settled in at the Walnut.

There was also a younger contingent of guys who hung out at the Walnut, including two of McBride's sons, Jimmy and Joey. I was already friendly with the McBride brothers. When we were all kids our families used to get together occasionally. One afternoon Mario and I bumped into Jimmy Jr. at the newsstand. Things were friendly and the bar was nearby so he invited us over for a drink. The only time I'd been in the Walnut before was a few years earlier when I went in to cop a bag from the old bartender who was selling speed. We walked into the near-empty bar on that mid-Saturday afternoon as the Bobby Darin song "Beyond the Sea" played on the jukebox. As we sat down at the bar, Tony, an old bald guy who didn't seem to like his job, took our order then poured the three of us a draft beer. We clicked glasses and offered up in unison, "Salute." I looked around and noticed the jukebox under the front window that didn't have a song recorded in the current decade. There was also the pay phone in the back corner of the bar which I found out later was used to take football bets. There was also a door leading to another room. When I asked Jimmy what was in that room he smiled and said, "off limits."

Within weeks, Mario and I started hanging out at the Walnut and became "regulars" along with my friends Armando and Dave. Being involved with the rival Gambino crew, Jambo would never come to the Walnut. Because of my relationship with the McBride family I was treated quite well at the bar, especially by Jimmy Sr. When he got drunk he'd say to me, "I loved your mother, I could have been your father." I also got in the good graces of Vic and Bobby Amuso when Jimmy Sr. told them I was Ellen Pavlatos' son. From that day on whenever I saw Vic Amuso at the Walnut, he'd always say, "Hey, Ellen's son." He never remembered my name, but I recall thinking how cool it was for the boss of a major crime family to know who I was and say hello to me. As time went by I soon knew every wiseguy and wannabe who walked into the Walnut.

There was Anthony "Gaspipe" Casso, who was Amuso's underboss, although many claimed he was more of a co-boss. Short and stocky, Gaspipe was a stone-cold gangster with a reputation for being a homicidal maniac. Whenever he would come into the Walnut, he'd order a drink, nod his head to everyone, then join Vic in the back room. Sometimes another guy named Frank Lastorino would join them. "Big Frank," as he was known because he was tall, was also raised in Canarsie and had built a reputation as one of the most notorious hitmen in the Lucchese crime family. Lastorino's daughter, Lana, was best friends with my girlfriend, Tracey, who I had met months earlier when they came into the Walnut for a drink. I was afraid to approach him myself, so I asked Lana to introduce me to her father, who couldn't have been nicer, taking a few minutes to ask me about my Italian roots. After that meeting, whenever he saw me in the bar he'd always buy me a drink.

The only two Lucchese made members that interacted with the younger guys at the Walnut were Joey Testa and Anthony Senter. They weren't much older than us. Born and raised in Canarsie, Testa and Senter started their criminal careers in their early teens stealing cars for Roy DeMeo, a Gambino family associate who operated out of the Gemini Bar just outside of Canarsie. Testa and Senter would soon become the core of the DeMeo crew, notorious for their ruthless violence. After murdering their victims, they would take the bodies to the upstairs apartment over the Gemini Bar and bleed out the corpses in the bathtub. Then they'd saw off the limbs and heads and dispose of the body parts in various dumpsters throughout the city. DeMeo's crew had gotten so out of control that Gambino boss Paul Castellano ordered his murder and gave the contract to Gaspipe Casso. They lured Roy DeMeo to the home of Joey Testa's younger brother Patty and fatally shot their old boss. After the murder, Casso brought Testa and Senter into the Lucchese crime family.

Senter came across as a psychopath and rarely had a smile on his face, but Joey Testa was charming and charismatic. Drinks were always "on Joey" whenever he came into the bar. Growing up in Canarsie, everyone knew about the Testa family. Ironically, the oldest brother was a New York City police officer but the other siblings were also involved in organized crime. Patty operated a used car lot that was a front for chopping up stolen cars. His brother Dennis lived across the street from my apartment and occasionally came over looking to do coke whenever he saw us there. Michael, aka Mikey T, was the youngest brother and hung out with our crew. We soon became friends.

After befriending Mikey T and gaining the trust of the guys in the bar, I had now gained entry into the "back room" of the Walnut. Occasionally, Joey and Anthony would come into the back room and join our poker games. Even though it was obvious that they were cheating, nobody had the balls to say anything to them. I was out of cash one particular night and attempted to leave the table. "I can lend you some money if you wanna stay in the game," Joey offered. "I'd rather cash this check," I replied as I pulled it out of my wallet. "How much and who's it from?" he asked. "It's a fifty dollar check my mother wrote me," I responded. Without hesitation, he reached into his pocket, took out a wad of bills, and while handing me the money said with a huge smile, "You know what happens if this check is no good." With that, the entire room started cracking up. I had some idea of what he was insinuating, but I was unaware at the time of his tenure with Roy DeMeo.

When we weren't hanging out at the bar, we were visiting upscale dance clubs on Long Island like Channel 80 or Sprats. We dressed in Italian silk suits with silk ties as if to announce to the world that we were wiseguys or wannabes at best. My father had been flying high following Warren's debut concert with Duran Duran and shortly afterwards surprised me with a new sports car. My white Nissan 300ZX with a personalized plate that read "CUC" was parked near the bar almost every night. Soon I was greeting other guys in silk suits with a kiss on the cheek and before long everyone in Canarsie knew I was connected to the Walnut crew. I was enjoying my new "celebrity."

I was also doing well at work, showing up every day and becoming a solid salesman. The only thing my father expected me to do was make the payments on the Nissan and he'd pay for the insurance. Although I was hanging out at the Walnut every night, I didn't always drink, and usually left at a decent hour. I still smoked pot every day but kept my hard-core partying relegated to Friday nights. I went out with my girlfriend Tracey on Saturday nights. She didn't do drugs but didn't mind that I smoked weed. I knew she'd never tolerate cocaine because a friend of hers almost died doing it. I was usually drunk and looking to have sex with her when I came home on Friday nights, so I was able to hide my coke use from her.

Although the old school wiseguys frowned upon cocaine, the younger guys at the Walnut were all doing it. Mario, Armando, and I had regular jobs, so we didn't do cocaine during the week. The rest of the crew, including the McBride brothers and Mikey T, never seemed to work, and would get high on any random night. Because Mario had stopped dealing to avoid paying anybody, and since many of the Canarsie drug dealers went out of business when the mass shakedowns started, it became harder to buy cocaine. The only other way to get it was to drive to East New York at night and buy it from the black dealers, risking your life every time you went there. Since I had a flashy white sports car with a personalized plate I would never take my car to buy drugs, and usually nobody ever asked. One early morning following a night of drinking and snorting lines, I was pressured by a wannabe who came stumbling into the bar looking for cocaine.

They called him "Fat Dom," and he was a Lucchese associate who hung out at Geffken's but would come to the Walnut occasionally to get high. Dom was fat, loud, and obnoxious, with a reputation in Canarsie as a loose cannon and someone you didn't want to piss off. One Friday night after the bar had closed a few of us were waiting for the bartender to finish cleaning when Dom started banging and yelling for us to open the door. The second he walked in he asked us if we had any coke. When we told him we didn't, he asked if one of us could drive him to East New York to get some. Before anyone could even answer, Dom looked at me and said, "You're the guy driving that 300ZX. I need you to give me a ride." I hardly knew this guy and here he was asking me to take him to buy drugs in one of the worst crime neighborhoods in the country.

In a very polite and calm tone I replied, "Sorry man, my car is too recognizable. I can't risk going there." He kept asking and I kept replying, "Sorry, I can't." He then started to get angry and scared the shit out of me when he said, "You don't have to go, I'll go myself. Nobody's gonna fuck with me," while pulling his jacket to the side, showing me the gun in his waistband. He managed to scare me enough that I finally caved and let him use my car. The McBride brothers kept assuring me that everything would be fine. As soon as I gave him the keys I sarcastically thought to myself, "A white wannabe gangster packing a .38 caliber pistol driving a brand new flashy white sports car to purchase drugs in East New York at 4 am. What could possibly go wrong?"

The drug spot was only about a twenty-minute ride from the Walnut, so when Dom was still gone after about an hour I started to worry. I couldn't believe that I was stupid enough to give that maniac my car. He finally came back about 5:30 am and we could hear him screech my tires as he slammed on the brakes right in front of the bar. He rushed into the bar sweating profusely, obviously wired out of his mind with his eyes wide open and his jaw moving uncontrollably. Out of breath and struggling to speak, Dom blurted out, "You might wanna get rid of your car, they might come looking for it." He handed me the keys and left without saying anything else. As I looked out the window and watched Dom get picked up by another car, I noticed there was a huge dent on the front right side of my car.

"What the fuck just happened!? What does he mean I gotta get rid of the car!?" I yelled while rushing outside with the McBride brothers to inspect my car. "I don't know but you better not take any chances. This car is way too easy to spot," Jimmy Jr. advised. When I asked Jimmy what I should do, he said, "Let me take care of it. I'll drive you home and take the car to someone I know. Wait about six hours or so before you report it stolen." With visions running through my head of the police knocking on my door, I reluctantly agreed. When he dropped me off in front of my apartment Jimmy Jr. told me again, "Remember...wait at least six hours before you report it. Not a minute less."

When I woke up later that day I had almost forgotten what had happened until I noticed the empty driveway outside my front door. After calling the police and reporting my car stolen, I sat at home thinking that the guys at the Walnut had swindled me. I would expect it from a person with Fat Dom's reputation, but I didn't want to believe that the McBride brothers were involved. Our parents had grown up together as we all knew each other as young kids. I'd been hanging out with them for over a year now and considered them good friends. I seemed to be more concerned about betrayal by the McBride brothers than I was about committing insurance fraud. After driving myself crazy wondering if I was the victim of a scam, I realized I'd get a new car with the insurance money and wouldn't lose a dime. I soon let the incident go and continued to hang out at the Walnut as if nothing had happened. Two weeks later I received the insurance money and purchased another Nissan 300ZX. It was almost the same exact car except that it was a 1988 model...fire engine red.

A few days later a New York City Police detective caught my attention while I was standing outside the Walnut and eventually called me over to his patrol car. He was a plainclothes detective named Bruce Kern who worked at the 69$^{th}$ Precinct in Canarsie. Although I had never seen him before he seemed to know me. "Are you Cuccurullo?" he asked. Before I could answer he said, "You're the guy who had that white 300ZX that was stolen." After I confirmed who I was, he sarcastically replied, "That's funny because your car was spotted in front of Geffken's bar on the day it was reported stolen. Is there something you want to tell me"? I was scared shitless but stayed calm and gave him the typical wiseguy line, "I don't know what you're talkin' about." Then he said, "I'll make a deal with you. I won't bring up your car anymore if you get me some weed."

He threw me completely off guard but I just laughed and said, "Yeah right, how stupid do I look?" His face turned very serious and he replied, "Get me some pot or I start looking into your car theft." I had no idea what to do especially since some of the wiseguys were hanging outside. I walked back over to the bar and told them that the detective just asked me for pot. Joey Testa calmly said to me, "So get him some pot," as if it were no big deal. I went to my car and took a small bag of weed that I had stashed in the glove compartment. Just to be a smartass, I wrapped it in an unpaid parking ticket, went back to the patrol car and nervously handed it to him. As soon as I did his partner started the car and he said, "Thanks, I'll be seeing you again soon." I had no idea what had just happened, but when I went back to the bar everyone was laughing hysterically. It turned out that this detective had done this before with other people who hung out there. According to Joey, Detective Kern knew that the wiseguys would never rat him out because he had incriminating information on all of them. Then he added with a smirk on his face, "Nobody would believe us anyway."

By 1988 many of the made members of the Lucchese crew began staying away from the Walnut for fear the Feds were watching. I recall Jimmy Jr. telling me that the police were filming us from the rooftop of the furniture store across the street. After Vic Amuso became boss he was rarely seen at the Walnut, and soon the wiseguys only used the bar during the day. The younger guys, myself included, were the only ones there at night, with the McBride brothers watching the bar for their father. With Jimmy Jr. and Joey in charge, our crew took over the place. We turned the back room of the Walnut into our own personal den of iniquity complete with gambling, women, and lots of cocaine.

It soon became the never-ending party with most of the guys having no clue how to stop the booze and drugs. Mario and I did our fair share of cocaine, but we'd eventually call it a night and go home. Mario still lived with his parents, and I was now living with my girlfriend Tracey, who I'd been dating for over a year. Some of them would hang out in the bar getting high until the next morning when the day bartender opened up. It had gotten so bad that the wiseguys from Geffken's, who still came in for a drink now and then, nicknamed the Walnut the "Frozen Tavern" because the cocaine gave you a certain look. Sometimes we wouldn't even pay for the drugs, as Mikey T would just take me to Bailey's bar outside of Canarsie to shake down drug dealers. Mikey T was smaller than me but he only needed to mention his last name for the dealer to hand over a fifty-dollar bag without hesitation. I began hanging out with Mikey T more often, and I was getting high on any given night. Not surprisingly, my cocaine use began to affect my relationship with my girlfriend.

I had stopped hanging out with her on Saturday nights, instead choosing to hang out at the bar. I'd come home at three and four in the morning two and three nights a week stoned out of my mind and looking for sex. After a while, she refused to sleep with me if I was high. Since I would get extremely horny when I was coming down from cocaine I needed to satisfy my lustful urges elsewhere. After drinking and doing lines all night at the Walnut, instead of going home I would go on the hunt. The only problem is that at 4 am, the bars were closed and the only girls up at that hour were the ones working the streets. I'd been with a couple of prostitutes in the past, but never really had to resort to them. Until now.

Not wanting to drive to the city where all the better-looking hookers were, I started cruising around the industrial area right outside of Canarsie looking for crack prostitutes. Even though it was in the black part of the neighborhood I'd see countless white girls turning tricks, even ones I'd known from Canarsie. Ten bucks would usually get you oral sex, which is all I would do with them. One night I met a cute Puerto Rican girl, who was about twenty years old, working the streets around Sunnydale Farms. When she got into the car she asked me if I wanted to go back to her motel room to get high. I told her I didn't have any coke, but I could give her some money if she knew where to get it. She told me she'd beep her dealer, and he would bring it to the motel which was nearby. Although I knew there was a possibility they'd rob me, I was horny and stoned enough to take my chances.

She took me back to a motel on Pennsylvania Avenue near Starrett City, which was known for drugs and prostitution. She beeped her dealer and he called back within minutes. When she came back in after meeting him outside she dropped four vials of crack on the bed and began to prepare her glass stem pipe. Annoyed I said, "I thought you were getting powdered coke." Even as high as I was I really didn't want to smoke it, as I hadn't smoked cocaine in close to two years. "I never said that," she replied. "Anyway, nobody sells powder anymore. You want a hit…yes or no?" She really didn't have to twist my arm. I immediately agreed. After I did that first hit I sat on the bed for a good ten minutes unable to talk. "Are you okay?," she kept asking me. I kept holding my finger up as if to say "give me a minute." I couldn't utter a word. She soon began to ignore me and continued smoking her share. I was so high after that one big hit that I couldn't get myself to do another. She gladly did the rest. After all the coke was gone I gave her another ten dollars for oral sex but was so high I couldn't get an erection. After about twenty minutes I gave up and went home.

When I finally got to the house at 8 am Tracey was already up waiting for me. Her friend Lana was also at the house. I told her I'd been at the Walnut the whole time and that my beeper had died so I never got her calls. I added that we were in a serious poker game and lost track of time. I'm not sure if she fell for it but she didn't press the issue. She seemed to be more upset about how high I looked rather than the time. "I know you're doing cocaine," she said as her eyes began to tear. "Lana told me what goes on in that bar. I swear if you come high on coke one more time I'm leaving you." Knowing she had me dead to rights I just stood there and meekly said, "I'm sorry. You're right. I need to stop." Crying hysterically now, she said, "I love you, Rob, I don't want you to die." After Tracey calmly left with Lana I took a shower, nibbled on some toast, then laid down in my bed. Still high from the crack, my mind was racing a mile a minute. All I could think about was me lying dead on a motel floor with a crack pipe in my hand.

I was desperate to reconcile with Tracey, who had ended up moving back with her parents. I was very much in love with her and thought about marriage. I was now twenty-four and except for the wannabes at the Walnut, most of my friends were married or engaged. Mario and Armando were hanging out more with their girlfriends and spending less time at the bar. I knew that I needed to do the same. I'd been with Tracey for close to two years now, and the thought of settling down and having children was something I often pondered. I'd always loved kids, and even volunteered to coach my cousin Paul's little league baseball team that season, looking to do something positive for a change. After envisioning Tracey and me starting a family with sons of my own to coach, I decided to propose to her. My mother gave me her grandmother's diamond engagement ring to use, and I took Tracey to a fancy restaurant in Manhattan. After dinner, I arranged for the waiter to bring the ring instead of dessert. He placed the covered dessert plate in front of Tracey, and as he lifted the cover revealing the diamond ring I asked, "Will you marry me?" She said yes.

There were some conditions that came with that yes answer, and I was fine with them. The first thing she wanted us to do was get a new apartment. She had moved into my existing one and wanted to get a fresh start. She expected me to be home during the week with her but didn't mind if I hung out with my friends occasionally. "I don't mind you going to the bar on Friday nights, as long as you're not coming home all coked up. Just come home when the bar closes," she requested. After a small pause, she stated flatly, "but there's no way you're going to that bar on Saturday nights." A short moment later, she calmly asked, "Not for nothing Rob, but why do you still go there?" I quickly replied, "To see my friends." Ironically, except for Mikey T I never felt that anyone I met from that bar was a true friend. I realized later that I went there because I loved the attention and respect I got in the neighborhood just for being associated with those guys. I was a wannabe.

Realizing there wasn't a future as a wannabe mafioso I kept up my end of the bargain with Tracey, and within months everything was going great. We hadn't set a wedding date, but my mother did throw us a small engagement party in New Jersey. My parents loved Tracey and were thrilled when I asked her to marry me. I stayed away from the bar during the week and soon wasn't going to work hungover anymore. My sales increased and I started getting into shape again. I lost twenty pounds in two months, was still playing competitive softball, and having the time of my life coaching a team in the Police Athletic League. I thought it was something I could do on a regular basis because I would always love the game and had acquired some pretty decent coaching skills. That summer I spent most of my free time at Canarsie Park running practices, umpiring, and helping the league President. My life had promise and direction again…if I could just stay away from the Walnut.

I was still hanging there on Friday nights and getting high behind Tracey's back. I'd come home when the bar closed but was usually so drunk by then Tracey didn't suspect my cocaine use. One night when I was sloshed and she started to complain about me hanging out at the bar again, she firmly declared, "I don't I want you going there anymore. That place has a bad reputation and I don't want my future husband associated with a bunch of coked up wannabe gangsters." I knew she was right…again. "Why don't you come to the bar with me?" I blurted out in my drunken state. She seemed just as shocked hearing it as I was saying it. I thought for sure she'd say no. Instead, she excitedly replied, "That's a great idea, now I can keep an eye on you." I immediately regretted my invitation.

Unable to renege on the offer, Tracey began coming with me to the bar on Friday nights. As you can imagine, that didn't go over well with some of the guys, especially the McBride brothers. They knew that Tracey's best friend Lana would also hang out, and nobody wanted the daughter of Frank Lastorino seeing what went on in the bar. It turned out to be a good thing since things stayed tame when Tracey and Lana were there. It really didn't matter because those guys did most of their coke when the bar closed and everyone was gone. This arrangement salvaged my relationship with Tracey for the time being, but it would soon backfire in a way I never expected.

Tracey and Lana began hanging out at the Walnut every weekend. I didn't mind in the beginning because I was able to hang out with my friends and keep my girlfriend happy. On one Saturday night, I left the bar to go pick up a friend. While I was out Joey McBride did some lines with Tracey and Lana. When I came back I knew something was different about Tracey. She claimed she was just drunk but I was highly suspicious. Tracey had never done cocaine and was deathly afraid of it since her friend's near overdose. When the bar was about to close Tracey shocked me when she said, "I wanna stay." She knew I used to stay in the bar for hours after it closed and was adamant about having a few more drinks. I wanted to get laid. I insisted that she come home with me and after arguing for about twenty minutes she finally agreed to leave.

During the drive home I could tell she wasn't herself. She had all the classic cocaine side effects. She was talkative and seemed excessively nervous. When I asked her bluntly, "Did you do coke tonight?" she vehemently denied it. "I would never do cocaine. Are you nuts? You know how I feel about it." Still unconvinced, I pressed her. "You were acting completely different after I came back to the bar. I'm not a fuckin' idiot. You can tell me if you did it. I won't get mad, I swear." She continued to deny it, and as we pulled into the driveway I decided to drop it. I had my mind on one thing and it didn't require talking. When we got inside the house I told her I was going to take a quick shower. When I was done, she was gone. So was my car.

I was in complete shock. Not only because she'd split, but because she was also deathly afraid to drive following a serious accident years earlier. To make matters worse I knew that she'd never driven a manual transmission. I immediately called the pay phone at the Walnut. Nobody answered. Since Tracey didn't have a beeper, I beeped both McBride brothers to see if she'd gone back to the bar. Jimmy Jr. got back to me to say he hadn't seen her but would call me right away if he did. I debated calling the police but didn't want Tracey arrested for driving without a license. So, I just waited... pacing back and forth while imagining the worst. Three hours later at about 7 am, she showed up.

From the second she walked into the apartment I knew that she was high on cocaine. Crying hysterically, she repeatedly sobbed, "I'm sorry, I'm sorry." I didn't know whether to console her or scream at her. When I finally got her to calm down, I angrily asked, "Where the fuck were you?" She started babbling about doing some coke at the Walnut, and that she just couldn't help herself and wanted to do more. I interrupted her and demanded to know where she had gone, and if she was with anyone. She started spinning some story about her and Lana going to another friend's house to do some more coke. I knew right away she was lying.

At that point, I had a strong feeling she had been with another man. I started to freak out while standing over her as if I was going to hit her. "You better fuckin tell me the truth," I screamed in a rage. I must have scared her because she finally blurted out, "I was with Joey McBride! But we didn't do anything." It felt like someone had just stuck a sword right through my heart. "Did you fuck him?" I yelled. "No, I swear," she insisted as she continued sobbing uncontrollably. I kept pressing her about whether they'd hooked up, but she stuck to her story and insisted that they only did coke. I didn't believe that, either.

Joey McBride was not very big, but he could be somewhat psychotic especially when he was high. Cocaine made him extremely paranoid and that made him become violent. I'd seen Joey throw a bar glass at our friend missing his head by inches just because he wanted to go home and call it a night. So I thought it best to approach him when he was sober because I knew he could turn on a friend in a heartbeat. I called him up and asked to meet at the diner so we'd be in a public place. After a few minutes of small talk at our table, I came right out in a calm, friendly manner and asked, "What happened that night with Tracey?" He replied, "Yeah, she came back with your car and said you knew she was there. Her and Lana wanted to do some lines, so we gave 'em some." He passed it off as no big deal, but immediately I knew that he was lying, too.

When I spoke to Jimmy that night he told me that Tracey was never there. I realized at that moment that he was covering for his brother. I was now fuming inside but stayed calm and asked Joey again, "Did you sleep with my girlfriend?" As soon as the words left my mouth I was afraid of his reaction. To my surprise, he calmly assured me, "Please Cuc, we're friends. I would never do that to you." Happy that he didn't go nuclear on me, I played it off as if I was sorry for accusing him. "I'm sorry, bro. I was just so freaked out that night." As we paid the check and left he said, "It's all good Cuc." He shook my hand and gave me a kiss on the check.

I still didn't believe him, but I was proud of myself for confronting him. We left the diner and returned to our cars. As I was just about to pull out from my spot, I noticed Joey coming back towards me smiling and signaling for me to open my window. As soon as I opened it he grabbed me by the jacket collar and pressed a set of brass knuckles to the side of my face. With the look of a crazed lunatic in his eyes, he said with clenched teeth, "I will break your fucking jaw if you ever question me again." I sat there frozen with fear. His demeanor then instantaneously changed as he smiled and said, "C'mon Cuc, don't make me do that to you, I like you." As he fixed my jacket collar then walked away I immediately knew I could no longer be friends with this psychopath. I also knew my days hanging out at the Walnut were over.

Several weeks after I stopped going there Bobby Amuso decided to close the Walnut Tavern. The cocaine parties had gotten out of control with some patrons doing blow for three days straight, not to mention that the bar was losing money since no one in our crew was paying for drinks anymore. Many of the wiseguys that used to hang out there were either dead, in jail or on the lam, so the Walnut Tavern had become just another bar for cokeheads. Once Mikey T took the party to a Knights of Columbus bar a few blocks away the McBride brothers were among the last Walnut Tavern diehards. I had no desire to go there because I wanted nothing to do with Joey McBride, even though Tracey still denied sleeping with him. I stayed friendly with Mikey T but he wanted to get high all the time and it became a struggle to hang out with him. The only true friend that I still hung out with was Armando, as the guys in my original crew were all involved in their relationships. With the Walnut days behind me, I decided to try and salvage my relationship with Tracey.

Although we both tried to put the incident behind us, things were never the same. I still loved her very much, but felt she was lying about sleeping with Joey McBride, even though I had no proof. I wanted to get the spark back in our relationship, so I decided to take her to the City for Saint Patrick's Day. We got there early and went to McSorley's for lunch and then watched the parade. We stayed in Manhattan and bar hopped, drinking green beer and Irish Whiskey. Tracey and I hadn't had a night out like that in months, and when we got home we tore each other's clothes off and made up for lost time. We sipped on some wine and smoked a joint before we both passed out on the couch. I awoke to my phone ringing at about 5 am and waited for the answering machine to pick it up. It was Jimmy McBride Jr. He called to tell me that my friend Michael Testa was found dead from a drug overdose. He was only twenty-seven.

I only knew Mikey T for about two years, but I considered him a good friend. It wasn't always about getting high. Mikey and I would cruise down 86th Street in Bensonhurst in my 300ZX looking for girls, or he'd take me to after-hours clubs all over Brooklyn. He was a charmer like his brother Joey, and the girls loved him. He may have used his name to shake down drug dealers, but I never saw him get mad or hit anyone. I found out later that Mikey T was smoking crack at someone's house the night he died and went into a room to lay down. When they went to wake him up a few hours later he was already dead. I had done lines with Mikey T many times but never smoked crack with him. I had never admitted to Mikey T that I had smoked crack out of embarrassment, and I had no idea he was smoking it. His death was a rude awakening and I knew I could be one cocaine binge away from the same fate.

I steered clear of the bars following Mikey T's death and spent most of my time with Tracey. We were getting along, but it felt like we were going through the motions again. We hadn't done much after our Saint Patrick's Day adventure, and I was looking to get out of Canarsie for the Fourth of July weekend. Mario invited Tracey and me to spend the weekend at a house on the Jersey Shore with some of my other friends. I thought it would be the perfect opportunity to rekindle the relationship with my fiancé and have a good time without drugs and alcohol. The only one of my close friends that didn't go with us that weekend was Armando, who chose to spend the holiday at his girlfriend's summerhouse. The weekend was going great until Mario got a phone call from his mother urging him to come home right away. The rest of us were sitting in the living room and intensely watched Mario, sensing something was wrong. She wouldn't tell him what happened and kept insisting he come home immediately. "Mom you have to tell me what happened," he insisted numerous times. When I saw Mario's face go blank I knew something bad had happened. Armando had been killed instantly when he drove a motorbike into a tree. I had now lost two friends in less than four months.

Armando was only twenty-eight, and I had known him since I was fourteen. Over the last few years, he had become one of my closest and most trusted friends. He was the one guy in my crew that I could confide in, and he always kept my secrets. He was the only one I had ever told about the recent crack prostitute, and I had confided in him about the Joe Milo murder and the nightmares that followed. After the initial shock on the way back to Brooklyn, I got home and cried for hours, wailing, "My friend, my friend, I lost my friend." Tracey tried to console me but I was completely numb over the next few days and during the funeral. I cried uncontrollably as I helped carry my friend's casket and place him in the ground. Too depressed to go back to work I sat in my apartment for a week straight drinking and smoking pot trying to kill the pain.

Following Armando's death, my relationship with Tracey got progressively worse. We fought constantly, usually ending up with me storming out of the house. With nowhere else to go I went back to hanging out with the guys from the Walnut who were now drinking and drugging at the Knights of Columbus bar. And, I was hanging out with the McBride brothers again. Whenever I saw Joey I played it off as if I was still his friend, but I hated his guts for what I was convinced he did. That bar became a mirror image of the Walnut, minus the wiseguys. My cocaine use once again spiraled out of control causing me to miss work and pissing off my father. I was coming home drunk and Tracey would scream at me calling me a junkie and a drug addict. One night I got so mad I screamed out, "You're a fuckin' cunt!" something I had never said to her. She froze for a second, then blurted out, "Oh yeah, well I fucked Jimmy McBride!"

# Chapter 16
# Certified Crackhead

Even though I had suspicions that Tracey had cheated on me, her admission absolutely devastated me, and a few days later she moved out of the apartment for good. I couldn't get myself to go back to the bar, as I wanted nothing to do with Joey McBride. With no girlfriend, no single friends, and no bar to hang out in I needed somewhere else to go. Mikey T had brought me to Bailey's bar a few times to shake down drug dealers so I knew the place. Bailey's was a dive bar with a jukebox, a pool table, and plenty of cocaine. Most of the Canarsie guys who hung out at Bailey's were a few years younger than me and two of them were the younger brothers of friends I had gone to school with. I soon became friendly with Robby and Henry and started hanging out at Bailey's every weekend drinking and snorting coke just as I'd done at the Walnut.

Without a girlfriend at home, I'd sometimes hook up at closing time with girls from the bar. After a while, I'd exhausted all my possibilities. One night after the bar closed I decided to look for the Puerto Rican crack prostitute. Baileys was located a stone's throw to the Sunnydale Farms area where I had picked her up months earlier. Within no time I saw her on the street and picked her up. Even though I lived alone now I would never take a crack prostitute to my apartment in fear that my neighbors would notice. Although she was pretty, she was dark-skinned and would stand out in my all-white neighborhood. I knew she'd want to smoke crack if I took her to the motel, so I had the money ready for her. She bought a few vials from her dealer and we went back to the room and smoked it. After I came down on the six-pack of beer I had brought with me, I gave her ten bucks and she gave me a blowjob.

After that night I'd go looking for her whenever I wanted sex. I would drink and snort lines all night, and when the bar closed I would go prowling for the Puerto Rican girl. At first, it was just Friday nights, but soon I was drinking and doing cocaine all weekend. At first, I would only buy enough crack to keep her content so I could have sex with her, but soon I was smoking just as much as she was. I went from spending thirty to forty dollars on a Friday night to spending a couple of hundred dollars each weekend, smoking crack until late the next morning. One Friday night I picked her up, and when I'd finally spent every last dime on drugs and alcohol it was Sunday afternoon. I had been up for over forty-eight hours, and when I finally came out of my crack stupor I'd basically lost an entire day of my life.

I slept straight through Monday morning, missing work. My father was infuriated because I'd missed a major sales meeting with a prospective account. He was able to close the deal in my place, and I was able to smooth it out with a lie that I got drunk watching the Jets on Sunday Night Football. I always woke up depressed and guilty following a crack binge swearing I was never going to do it again. A few days later I'd be back to my old tricks when Robby and Henry came knocking on my door. We started going to a bar in Canarsie called Le Parc. It was the old Bamboo Lounge that had been remade into an upscale mini nightclub. Every Wednesday they had a promotion where you paid a fifteen-dollar cover charge and drank at the open bar all night.

We drank there every Wednesday, and as soon as the bar closed, I'd head straight to the motel to smoke crack with the Puerto Rican prostitute. Occasionally I couldn't find her so I'd pick someone else, nothing terribly difficult given the area. I'd smoke crack up until the time I had to go to work and then call out at the last-minute further infuriating my father. Tired of hearing him scream at me, after a while I didn't even bother calling in. I was drinking, snorting lines, and smoking crack three nights a week, spending hundreds of dollars, missing work, and falling behind on my bills.

Although my mother had been secretly giving me money behind my father's back it was never enough. The more money I had the more I seemed to spend on drugs and alcohol, and less on life's necessities. When I ran out of money I'd use the Amoco gas credit card that my mother had given me for emergencies as a cash card. I made a deal with the gas attendant where he would swipe my card for forty dollars and give me the cash instead of putting gas in my car. I would have to give him half, but when I was desperate twenty dollars was enough to get two vials of crack. After a while, I stopped spending money on the motel and started bringing the Puerto Rican prostitute to my apartment. I had reached the point where I couldn't care less what my neighbors thought of me.

By the summer I had fallen three months behind on my car payments, and the finance people were calling me constantly, leaving messages that they were going to repossess the car. I started to park it a few blocks from my house so they couldn't find it, and sometimes I'd be so high when I came home that the next day I'd forgotten where I parked. I was also a month behind on the rent and had already exhausted all the money my mother had given me. I knew if I asked for more then she'd suspect the worst. I didn't dare ask my father for any money since he would've laughed in my face. I was considering having the car "stolen" with the help of the Geffken's crew who had made my other Nissan disappear but was also afraid that Detective Kern would be suspicious if I reported another car stolen. An incident after a night of drinking and snorting lines made my decision for me.

I went out with Robby on a Friday night, and as usual, spent the evening at Bailey's bar drinking and drugging. Before the bar closed we had snorted our last lines, and Robby and I wanted to get more since the both of us were still drunk. I foolishly got in my car and we drove to East New York to buy some. On the way back, as we entered Canarsie I started horsing around and began to knock down the orange safety cones used to cordon off an area of the street. Not realizing that one of them was placed in front of a gaping hole I swerved my car into the cone to knock it down. My front right tire immediately got stuck in the hole, violently jerking us forward while our seatbelts kept us from flying into the windshield. I was able to reverse the car out of the hole but soon noticed that there was major damage to the front axle and that the car was barely drivable. I knew I couldn't pay for the damages, and I couldn't ask my parents. If I tried to use my insurance to fix the car it would alert the finance company to the car's location and they'd quickly take it. I realized that unless I wanted to be without a vehicle for the long haul I would have to get rid of the car.

Robby and I were both very stupid-drunk and had just finished the bag of coke that we'd bought. Wired and freaking out about my car my first reaction was to try to contact somcone from the Geffken's crew. I then realized that it was already 3 am, and I wasn't about to go walking into Geffken's high as a kite asking them to "steal" my car for me. Then I blurted out to Robby, "Fuck it, let's torch it ourselves." He didn't bat an eyelash and simply replied, "Okay." Since Robby's house was only a few blocks from the accident we somehow managed to drive the car to his house on three wheels.

He took his father's car, and we drove to the gas station and bought two gallons of gas. We knew that once the fire went out the vultures would strip the car of all its parts long before I reported it stolen. We then took my car to a secluded area located near a known drug park next to my old school, P.S. 242.

While Robby waited in his father's car acting as a lookout I poured the gasoline all over the hood, the hatch, and then doused the front driver's seat. I lit a match and threw it in from about three feet away. It went out. With Robby whispering from the car, "Get closer," I moved in another foot or so and lit another match. It also went out. Now Robby was getting nervous and said as low as he could, "C'mon let's go." Getting a little frantic and worried about the police, I moved right up to the car and lit the third match. This time the car caught fire and I was close enough to feel the heat on my face as the flames shot out, singeing the hair on my mustache and eyebrows. I ran into the waiting car and we sped off back to Robby's house, sneaking in without his father ever knowing. With no car to get home or to see my Puerto Rican friend, I crashed at Robby's house for the night.

When I woke up I reported the car stolen at the 69$^{th}$ Precinct. When we went to see what had become of it, just as we expected the entire car was stripped down to its frame with not one removable part left to take. When I told my parents about the car they didn't get suspicious. Everyone knew that car theft was common in Canarsie. All my father told me was that I needed to rent a garage, and I don't believe he suspected I had anything to do with it. Surprisingly, he gave me his company van to bring home every night while I was waiting for the insurance money. It was his way of making sure I came to work because without the van his deliveries couldn't reach his customers, which in turn would ruin his business. He trusted me enough where he assumed I would never do that to him. There was no way I would let him down.

A few days following the car incident an unmarked police car pulled me over while I was driving my father's work van near my apartment. Although the papers on the van were in order I had a half joint sitting in the ashtray which I quickly hid. When the plainclothes detective got out of the car I noticed immediately in my rearview mirror that it was Detective Kern. He was the same cop who had made me get him pot at the Walnut, so I wasn't worried that the van smelled like marijuana. "What happened to that fancy car of yours?" he asked. Trying to look like I was upset about it I replied, "They stole it." In a sarcastic tone he replied, "Wow, you have bad luck, two cars stolen in a year's time." Instantly he went from friendly to deathly serious and flat out asked me, "Did you torch your car?" I obviously denied it, and although I was now terrified I tried to remain cool. Without saying anything else about the car Kern quickly changed the subject and said he needed me to do him a favor.

At that point, he could have asked me to do anything since I knew that he would have no problem proving that I had committed insurance fraud. Even though I knew Kern was corrupt he was still an NYPD detective, and he had the power to put me away. I was relieved when he told me that he just wanted to use my apartment to hang out with a girl. He said he needed it for Friday night from about 7 'til 11 pm. I figured I would just go out early that night and he'd be long gone by the time I came back. Before he left he made an expression as if he smelled something, referring to the pot smell coming from the van. "You got any of that left?" he asked. I reached for the half joint that I had hidden, and as I handed it to him he completely shocked me when he demanded, "Make sure you have at least a half gram of coke waiting for me when I get there." I just nodded without saying a word as he got back into his squad car and pulled away.

The night I was to let Detective Kern use my apartment I bought a half gram of coke from a neighborhood dealer and had it ready for him just as he asked. Even though he was holding two felonies over my head, I rather liked the idea of having a local detective on my side should I get into any trouble. He arrived a little after seven, and after I handed him the cocaine I left in my father's work van. After picking up Robby and Henry and smoking some weed we headed to Baileys without me telling either of them about the detective in my apartment. The night started out just like every other Friday night for the past six months. We got drunk, snorted cocaine, drank some more, and when the bar closed I went looking for my favorite Puerto Rican prostitute to smoke crack and get off.

Knowing my routine, she was waiting in her usual spot when I pulled up. At first, she didn't realize who I was since she had never seen the work van but jumped in once she saw my face. She told me her usual dealer was not around, so we had to drive to East New York to score. Without even caring that the name, address and phone number of my father's business were plastered on each side of the van we drove to the spot where she bought sixty dollars' worth of crack. It was all the money I had left. We drove back to Canarsie and pulled up in front of my apartment. There was a strange car in my driveway, and the lights in my apartment were on. I made some excuse that my friend might still be in there and for her to wait in the van while I checked it out.

When I walked in my apartment Detective Kern was sitting on my couch chopping up lines of coke with a razor blade on my glass table. He was wired out of his mind, and I knew that he had done a lot more than just the half gram that I had bought for him. When I asked him where the girl was he pointed to my bedroom and told me she had fallen asleep on my bed. Not only was I furious that some strange girl had crashed on my bed I was livid that Kern was still in my apartment at 5 am when he told me he would be gone by 11 pm. I told him that I had my own girl waiting in the van and that I needed him to leave as soon as possible. Knowing that he had overstayed his welcome he apologized and asked for about an hour to straighten up a bit, so he could get the girl out of my room and leave. I wanted him to leave immediately so I could smoke crack but knew I really didn't have a choice and went back out to the van.

When I told the Puerto Rican girl that we couldn't use my apartment for an hour she immediately suggested we go to the motel. When I told her that I was out of money she then suggested we drive to a secluded area and smoke in the van. At first, I was dead against it knowing I would get too paranoid, until she suggested we smoke in the back of the van where nobody could see us. Desperately wanting to do a hit, I agreed and parked the van in front of a weeded area behind the Starrett City apartment buildings.

We proceeded to smoke in the back of the van with the door closed and no windows for air. After an hour had passed I was too wired and paranoid to drive so we just continued to smoke in the van which had turned into a sauna as the sun began to rise. When we were finally done I opened the van door and was immediately blinded by the blaring sun. After my eyes adjusted to the daylight I noticed my reflection in the window of the car parked next to us. I was sweating profusely with my eyes bugging out of my head and my jaw moving in six different directions. For the first time in my life, I felt like a junkie. I was so embarrassed and disgusted with myself that if I'd had a gun I would have blown my brains out.

I was now a bona fide crackhead and had hit rock bottom. After that night I knew I desperately needed help but didn't know how to ask for it. I was deathly afraid of admitting to my father that I smoked crack and figured that my best bet was to try and explain my situation to my mother.

Two days passed, and I still couldn't get the nerve to tell her about my drug problem. I knew she would be understanding, but the thought of having to tell her that her "golden boy" was a drug addict who smoked crack with prostitutes was too difficult for me.

After I got the nerve to talk to her I finally admitted to her that I had a problem with cocaine, and I began to cry uncontrollably for about five minutes. She remained consoling and understanding and assured me that she would assist me in getting the help I needed. Until I could check into a rehab clinic, she thought that the best thing was for me to get the hell out of Canarsie and stay in New Jersey.

I told my friends that I was going to visit my brother who had moved to London when Duran Duran made him a permanent band member. My mother had found a rehab clinic in Long Island which had a twenty-eight day inpatient program but the open bed wasn't available until the following week. I'd have to stay in Jersey for a few days before being admitted. On the day I left Canarsie I picked up the newspaper in the front yard and read the headline which at the time meant absolutely nothing. The front page of the August 3, 1990 edition of the New York Daily News read, "IRAQ INVADES KUWAIT."

# Chapter 17
# 21 Days

One of the first things I learned at the rehab clinic was that each person's addiction was unique. Looking back, I realized that I never did cocaine when I wasn't drinking. The moment I got my alcohol buzz I would immediately get an urge to do coke. I had recalled several times during my worst days when I had turned it down when I wasn't drinking alcohol, so I felt that going twenty-eight days without cocaine would be easier with no booze around. The marijuana, on the other hand, was another story. I had been smoking pot almost every day for the past ten years, and I never really wanted to stop, but that wasn't an option in rehab. When I had stopped smoking to pass my Army induction physical a few years back I used alcohol as a replacement drug, but now I had to stop smoking weed cold turkey. My first night there I didn't get a wink of sleep as I stared at the ceiling all night wondering how I wound up here.

During the first week at the clinic, I spent a lot of time talking about my past in group sessions, and one on one with a psychologist. In my first solo session, I had to chronicle my drug use from my first joint right up until the day I arrived at rehab. I broke down crying on several occasions recalling the worst days of my addiction. I recalled the time when I almost overdosed on pills when I was fourteen, and smoking angel dust and not being able to remember my name. I cried thinking about all the cocaine and crack nightmares that followed, and I agonized over the credit card scam, and how I'd abused the gas card my mother entrusted to me. Looking back, I realized that except for coaching little league baseball, I had wasted ten years of my life getting high.

The counselors stressed that when you complete the program you can't expect to stay sober if you go back to hanging out with your old drug friends. I started to think about what I might do when I got out. During my sessions, I talked about how I really had no desire to work in my father's business. I wanted to do something on my own, preferably more exciting than selling swatch cards. I truly loved coaching baseball but knew I wasn't going to be able to make a living doing it. The counselor suggested that if I loved it so much that I might consider becoming a teacher and coach the school teams. The thought of that sounded glorious to me, but I knew that I didn't have the patience to complete four years of college considering that I'd only completed one year of high school.

Two weeks into rehab the psychologist began to dig into my childhood looking for clues as to why and how I went from an honor student and star athlete to a drug addict dropout. I'd always blamed Canarsie, but I knew now that it went much deeper. In retrospect, it seemed that everyone blamed their parents for all their childhood woes, but although my father hit us when we were little, I knew that I was fortunate to have the father I did. He wasn't perfect, but he worked hard to support his family and wanted nothing more than to give his children all the things he never had growing up in Italy. Like most sons I just wanted my father to be proud of me like he was of Warren. I loved my brother dearly, and I was thrilled for all his success, but I always felt that I lived in his shadow and would always be Warren's little brother. I wanted desperately to make a name for myself. I just wasn't sure where to start.

Three weeks into rehab I began having a recurring nightmare about Joe Milo. In the dream, he's sitting behind his counter when I enter his store to buy crack from him. As he's handing me the drugs, the guy who shot him in real life comes in and calmly shoots Joe four times in the chest. Before he leaves he turns and says to me, "I thought I told you to wait in the park." I then turn to Joe who's lying on the floor bleeding from his chest, and he says just as he did that day, "I can't believe I'm going to die." Then I suddenly wake up. After explaining the dream and the actual incident to the doctor during one of our private sessions, he said that it was common for people who witness traumatic events to turn to drugs and alcohol to help them suppress the memory. He said by me discussing it in depth it might help sort out the nightmares. When I asked him why the marijuana seemed to help, he had no answer

The recurring theme of most of the other addicts at the clinic was that they felt that marijuana wasn't the problem for them and still expressed a desire to smoke after they kicked the harder drugs. There was one guy at the clinic, a recovering heroin addict who talked about smoking pot constantly, that had entered about the same time as me. Whenever I'd see him during free time all he talked about was finding a way to sneak out and buy pot or have someone smuggle it in. I wanted no part of sneaking out of the clinic to buy weed, although I did have the urge to smoke. He then asked me if I knew anyone who could sneak some into the clinic. I told him that none of my friends even knew I was there. Two days later the heroin addict came up to me in the weight room and told me he was able to get a joint smuggled in. He invited to smoke it with him when the staff thinned out to just one for the night.

As much as I did want to smoke, I didn't want the doctors to kick me out of rehab with only seven days to go. He convinced me that if I never left the hospital grounds they wouldn't drug test me unless they had reasonable cause. Within a half hour of smoking the joint with him and another recovering addict in the shower stall, the three of us were called in to take a drug test. It seems that someone overheard us and ratted us out to the orderly on duty. An hour later they came back with the positive urine test, and promptly discharged all three of us, escorting us out the front door. Before we were discharged one of the counselors suggested that we check ourselves back in the program, but that we would have to start from day one. I had no intentions of checking back in as I felt that my twenty-one days in the program was sufficient. Besides, I had no desire to go back to my old lifestyle. The only thing I was worried about was what my father would say when I came back early.

My father was furious when my mother told him I had been kicked out for smoking pot, and he refused to talk to me for days. He told my mom that he had enough of my nonsense and that I wasn't welcome to work for him. When he finally did take my phone call, he didn't yell but said, "You're a fuck up. And as long as you keep doing that shit you're always gonna be a fuck up." I started crying which pissed him off. "Act like a fuckin' man," he said. "You're twenty-six fuckin' years old, when are you gonna grow up?" I tried desperately to convince him that I was a changed person, but he said I would have to prove it to him. "How?" I asked. I was ready to do anything to please him. "Go work for someone else," he said before he hung up.

My mother, on the other hand, noticed a difference in me even though I didn't complete the program. My sessions with the psychologist seemed to open my eyes about who I was and gave me new hope that I would do something special. My mother made me a deal. She said she would give me enough money to get me started, but if I screwed up again I would be on my own. My original plan was to leave Canarsie and move back to New Jersey following rehab but had no choice as my father wouldn't let me use the second condo. I knew that staying in Canarsie and returning to the same friends went against everything they counseled me about in rehab. I knew I finally had the strength to stay away from the drugs. I was now on a mission to earn my father's respect.

My mother helped me lease a new car. It wasn't a fancy sports car, but a moderately priced Acura Integra. I realized for the first time how fortunate I was that my family had the resources they did and that I had been taking advantage of them all these years. I knew that this might be my last chance to do something positive with my life, and I was determined not to screw it up. I found a job making deliveries for a local distributor and stayed away from the bars. I started running again and was looking forward to playing in the fall softball league. I did start smoking pot again, but regardless of what the experts said, I knew it kept me from drinking which in turn kept me away from cocaine.

After a few months of driving the delivery van and stocking shelves with beauty products I knew that I couldn't do it much longer. I didn't just want a job that paid the bills, I wanted to do something great with my life. I was watching the news and saw that President George H. W. Bush was sending more American troops to Saudi Arabia following Iraq's invasion of Kuwait two months earlier. They were sending thousands of troops each week with the news that the President was about to call up the reserves to help with the mission. It then dawned on me that I was still part of the military as an inactive member of the ready reserve. Inexplicably, I was overwhelmed with a sense of duty and the feeling that there was nothing greater than serving your country in time of war.

The next day I stopped at an Army recruiting station and told the recruiter my situation. He told me that the only soldiers the Army takes from the ready reserve are those removed from active duty for less than a year. He assured me I wouldn't be called back. When I told him that I was *interested* in going he said that I'd have to be part of a reserve unit, and then they would have to be called up. The thought of going into a possible war zone was scary, but I wanted redemption in the Army and was willing to take the risk. I never shook the guilt and embarrassment about how I got out of the service and thought that if I could somehow be called up in and go to the desert, I might erase the mistakes of my past.

After meeting with the recruiter again he informed me that since I had been off active duty for over five years I'd need to get three letters of recommendation from people other than my family to attest to my character. I laughed to myself about the thought of having some of the wiseguys from the Walnut write me a letter. I knew that I could get one from my father's business partner, and one from my current boss, but didn't know who else to ask. When the recruiter asked me if I had ever done any volunteer work I told him I had helped coach a local baseball team the past few years. He told me to have one of the league officials write a letter for me, and then he'd be able to get me processed back in the Army and assigned to a reserve unit.

I knew that if I had any chance of getting back in the service I was going to have to stop smoking pot because I'd be taking another physical. For the next month, I continued running to keep my mind off the weed, ramping up to five and six miles each day. Four weeks later the recruiter had finalized the paperwork, and the Army gave me a urine test during my physical. It came back clean as a whistle. Since there were no Combat Engineer units in my area, which was technically my military occupation, I was assigned to a supply unit at Fort Totten, Queens. I was issued my uniforms and gear, and my first weekend drills were scheduled for the week before Thanksgiving. I was now officially an Army Reservist with the rank of Private, and one step closer to my goal of being deployed to Saudi Arabia in support of Operation Desert Shield.

I had only served five months on active duty, so I didn't remember much of what the Army had taught me. I spent the next couple of days before my first drill re-learning Army rules and regulations. I practiced some military drill movements in the mirror so I wouldn't look like a moron on my first weekend back. I was glad that they assigned me to a supply unit because I remembered nothing about being a Combat Engineer. Before they released us for the weekend the company First Sergeant talked to the entire company about the possibility of deployment to the Gulf. He told us that although activation of our unit was unlikely, we should be ready regardless. That was a huge letdown because the main reason I re-joined the Army was to go to Saudi Arabia.

Before I left for the weekend I spoke with my new platoon sergeant and expressed my desire to go to the Gulf. He explained to me that our unit probably wouldn't deploy but said that from what he'd heard there was a shortage of drivers in the transportation units. The Army was seeking soldiers who could drive tractor trailers. Although I'd never driven anything bigger than a van, I lied and told him I'd driven military trucks when I was previously enlisted. He told me he'd see what he could do, but not to get my hopes up. Our next drill was right before Christmas and he said he'd have an answer by then.

On November 29, 1990, President Bush, along with leaders of thirty-four countries, passed a United Nations resolution which gave Iraqi President Saddam Hussein a deadline of January 15 to withdraw his troops from Kuwait or face a full-scale attack by the U.S.-led multinational force. The President also announced that he was sending more reservists to the region. Two weeks later I received a phone call from my platoon sergeant. "You still looking to go to Saudi Arabia?" he asked me. "Why? Is our unit being deployed?" I excitedly asked him. "No, the Army is looking for volunteers to help drive supply trucks." Before he could finish extending the offer to sleep on it, I blurted out "Hell yeah, I'll go!"

# Chapter 18
# The Highway of Death

I had less than three weeks to get my affairs in order before heading to Fort Benning, Georgia for a two week "refresher" course and then on to Saudi Arabia. I had a reporting date of January 7, 1991 so I'd be able to spend the Christmas holidays with my family. My mother was extremely worried as any mother would be, but I think that deep down she knew I needed to do this. Both of my brothers thought I was out of my mind and didn't want me to go. My sister told me that I had a death wish, but never understood what she meant as I wasn't suicidal. I also desperately needed my father's approval. He had mixed emotions about me going and told me I had big balls for volunteering, but he was concerned about my "adaptability." He felt once again that I wouldn't be able to handle the Army lifestyle. "Please, no jail this time," he said half-jokingly. I assured him it would be different this time, and joked back, "If I go AWOL during the war, they'll shoot me."

I arrived at Fort Benning on the evening of January 7. Although all the soldiers in my group were reservists on "active" duty, the Army sent us to basic re-training. From the moment we arrived at the facility, some of us were referred to as "prior service" to differentiate us from "new" recruits. The drill sergeants weren't used to training "prior service" and began treating us as if we were new to the Army. A couple of our assigned sergeants kindly reminded the drill sergeants not to treat us like recruits. Regardless of how I was spoken to or how I was treated, I promised myself that I would do what I was told, and not let my ego get me in trouble. I was going to be the perfect soldier.

The January 15 deadline for Saddam Hussein to leave Kuwait or face an attack came and went uneventfully. The following evening, we watched President Bush address the Nation, and announce that Operation Desert Shield was now Operation Desert Storm with the coalition bombings of targets in Baghdad and occupied Kuwait. The United States was officially at war. The stark reality began to sink in that I might not make it back home. I spent hours on the payphone during those last few days at Fort Benning, calling everyone I knew. On January 22 I boarded a 747-commercial airliner with over two hundred soldiers for the eighteen-hour trip from New York to Rome, and then Riyadh, Saudi Arabia.

As soon as I stepped off the plane I felt the heat punch me in the face. It was the middle of the winter, with afternoon temps of 95 degrees Fahrenheit. We were taken to an airplane hangar to wait for our company assignment orders. The soldiers who were on the plane with me were individual volunteers unattached to a unit. They told us in the briefing that most of us would be assigned to various transportation companies, and some of us would become personal drivers for Army brass. They lined us up in single file and one of the sergeants eyeballed each of us from head to toe then chose ten soldiers for duty as personal drivers. The rest of us waited another two hours before finally receiving our orders.

Prior to shipping out to our units the Army continued to In-Process us. We were put up in a Saudi apartment complex called Khobar Towers, complete with AC and hot showers. They told us not to get used to the accommodations because we'd soon be sleeping in a tent and taking ice cold showers. We had some downtime so I decided to catch some rays in the afternoon sun. It was the middle of winter, and I was extremely pale, so I grabbed some baby oil to help speed up the process. After about an hour of intense, desert heat I went back inside only to notice that I was already burned all over my body. I could barely move the next day but had to report for duty. I was told later that I could have received an Article 15 if I'd missed work due to my negligence. We left Khobar Towers two days later and headed to our units. Three weeks later the very same building I had stayed in was hit by a Scud missile, killing twenty-eight U.S. Army reservists from Pennsylvania.

They assigned about fifteen of us to the 915th Transportation Company and we boarded a bus to take us to our new unit. About twenty minutes into the ride one of the soldiers on the bus started freaking out screaming for everyone to "Get down!." Everyone on the bus immediately dove on the floor and under the seats. The soldier yelled out that he saw someone pointing a rifle at the bus, but the sergeant in charge dismissed it immediately and ordered us to get up. We were deep in Saudi Arabia a few hundred miles from the Iraqi border, and nowhere near anywhere dangerous. After the sergeant chastised the soldier for being paranoid and jeopardizing the safety of everyone else, we continued.

The 915th Transportation Company was a reserve unit out of Council Bluffs, Iowa that had been in Saudi Arabia since the end of August. The company consisted of men and women from Iowa and neighboring Nebraska, and many of them had known each other for years. The company commander and my platoon leader were both females. It was strange at first having never served alongside a woman, but they soon gained my respect as competent and caring leaders. The fifteen of us were from various parts of the country, and the other soldiers in the company immediately considered us outsiders. Some of them resented us at first, but many of them were happy we were there to help lighten their workload.

I shared a large tent with about twenty troops and slept on a foldable cot in my Army-issued sleeping bag. It was quite handy during the desert winter months when the temperatures would sometimes drop into the 30s. Even in February, daytime temperatures could soar over 90 degrees, and the brass reminded us every day to drink water. If not, you'd succumb to dehydration or heat exhaustion. No matter where we went, we were required to carry our M16 rifles and our M1A gas masks which were supposed to protect us in the event of a chemical attack. The military was confident that Saddam Hussein had chemical weapons, and everyone knew he had poisoned the Kurds. If you heard the command, "Gas, Gas, Gas," real or not, you were required to get your mask on within one minute, then put the rest of your chemical suit on, adding twenty degrees to your body temperature. Besides the threat of a chemical attack, we had to be cognizant of Scud missiles that Saddam had been firing into Saudi Arabia since the beginning of the Coalition bombing campaign weeks earlier.

Since many of the new additions to the Company had never driven a tractor-trailer before they trained us before being assigned a mission. Driving the vehicle was relatively easy; it was backing up with a large load attached to the cab that was extremely difficult for a new driver. After about a day and a half of training, although I still hadn't mastered backing up, they gave me my license and assigned me to a vehicle. Our job was to transport ammunition, which included surface to air missiles, to various locations inside Saudi Arabia in preparation for the inevitable ground war. Some of the missions only took a few hours, and you returned to base camp when you were done.

Other missions took you to the other side of the country which required you to sleep in your vehicle overnight. On my first overnight mission, I had just pulled over after ten hours of driving to get some shut-eye. As I fell asleep on the back of my empty trailer the sound of Islamic prayers blasted out from nearby speakers and immediately woke me up. Not realizing that my words could have serious diplomatic implications I screamed out, "Shut the fuck up!" I was soon quite glad that none of the Saudis had heard me.

When we weren't transporting ammunition, we were required to perform various work details inside the base camp. Besides guard duty detail, we occasionally worked in the mess tent helping with breakfast and dinner. It always meant a hot meal. During one shift I stood around for four straight hours with nothing to do. I finally picked up three oranges and taught myself how to juggle before the shift ended. For lunch, we ate MREs, which stands for "meals ready to eat" and are specifically made not to go spoil. I hated them all but was able to tolerate "number five," a passable spaghetti with meat sauce. Being Italian, I took a lot of flak from the guys for my culinary choice. My friend Pete would jokingly say, "The Wop has to have his spaghetti or he'll die."

However, the worst detail of them all when you were required to burn human feces. You had to pull the buckets of shit from the wooden latrine shacks and light them on fire using diesel fuel. To ensure that it burned correctly you had to stir the burning feces with a large pole while the thick black smoke and horrid stench went right up your nostrils. It was so nasty that soldiers would pay up to fifty bucks to get someone to do it for them. I pulled shit burning duty the most as I was the only Private in the entire company.

As our company hauled ammunition and other supplies around Saudi Arabia the coalition bombing of Iraq continued into February. The plan was simple; bomb them into submission until the time was right for a ground invasion into Iraq and Kuwait. Even with our missions and camp details, there was still plenty of downtime and not a whole lot to do in the desert. The two biggest vices of most soldiers are alcohol and pornography and both are banned in the Kingdom of Saudi Arabia so many of the soldiers had to find other things to occupy their free time. My buddy Pete was a hard-drinking Irishman from Boston who would polish off a case of non-alcoholic Mousy beer and then swear it gave him a buzz if he drank 'em fast enough. I even tried to get my friend Robby to send me pot in the mail since the Army wasn't drug testing during the war. I told him to roll a joint and place it in the middle of a magazine. Not knowing about the ban on pornography he sent the joint in the middle of a Playboy magazine. I never did receive it. The joke was that there was some soldier back in the mailroom smoking a joint and jerking off.

Another favorite pastime of many soldiers is gambling which was no exception and quite rampant in my company. Most of the soldiers played poker which was my game of choice. You could also find a game of craps in one of the enlisted tents on any given night. I made hundreds of dollars playing poker using my Canarsie skills to take advantage of some of the country bumpkins in my Company. We also gambled on Scorpion fights whenever we able to capture a couple of the "guys" crawling around in the desert. Occasionally, they'd just crawl right into your sleeping bag at night. The Army knew that gambling was a major problem within its ranks, so they only allowed us enlisted soldiers a fifty-dollar advance on our paycheck every two weeks. Other than gambling you really didn't need money in Saudi Arabia except for snacks at the exchange tent, or if you dared to purchase food from one of the roadside trucks that dotted the highways.

The favorite part of my day was mail call. Getting mail from home was better than gold especially if it was a care package full of goodies. My mother sent me several boxes filled with non-perishable food from home which I would always share with all the soldiers in my tent. My mother was great at writing me letters keeping me posted on everything that was going on in my family, and with public opinion about the war. I spent much of my free time writing letters home knowing that to get mail you had to write people. Since the government didn't charge postage for the soldiers' letters I sent out dozens each week in the hope of getting more responses. I wrote letters to the head coaches of all my favorite sports teams and would later receive a personal message from New York Rangers head coach Roger Neilson. The worst part was the waiting since it could take from three weeks to a month to receive a letter from home.

Other than writing letters we also could call home every few weeks using phone tents set up by AT&T. I remember thinking how nice it was for them to set up free phones for us to use until I found out that you had to call collect. The lines at the phone tents were so long that sometimes you waited for two hours. When you finally made it to a phone you only had ten minutes to call whoever you liked as long as they accepted the charges. I spent most of my time talking to family but would occasionally call a few of my close friends. Because of the eight-hour time difference, I would sometimes wake people up in the middle of the night with a "collect call from Saudi Arabia" which didn't go over well with my friend Dave. "Saudi Arabia are you kidding me?" he yelled at the operator. He eventually accepted my call.

With the ground war drawing near my phone calls to my parents became more somber. I apologized to them for all the heartache I caused over the years and promised my mother that "when" I made it home I would make it up to her in any way possible. I also had an extremely emotional phone call with my father. He told me for the first time in over ten years how proud he was of me, and that he supported my decision to go to war. I began crying and apologized repeatedly for acting like a child and missing work because of drugs and alcohol. Then he told me something that I never expected. He said that when I came home I would have a choice of either committing to the business, and eventually taking it over, or that if

I chose to do something else he would understand and not be angry with me. That was the first time my father talked to me man to man.

On the evening of February 23, my father's birthday, our platoon leader called us to a meeting and informed us that the ground war was to begin the next day. She said that we needed to start fortifying the bottom of our trucks with metal sheets and sandbags in the event we hit any landmines. She also ordered us to ensure that our gas masks and weapons were cleaned and functioning properly. The Lieutenant briefed us on how the attack would occur and how we were involved. We were to support the First Cavalry Division who would enter southern Iraq from Saudi Arabia, and then flank the enemy from the left, cutting off any Iraqi troops trying to escape back to Baghdad in the north. Each truck would have two soldiers who would alternate driving, and each trailer would carry a full load of ammunition. As the combat troops advanced into Iraq we would follow right behind them.

Knowing that the U.S. bombing missions had decimated the Iraqi Air Force was a major relief for our unit, as supply trucks packed with ammunition are usually the first to be bombed. The truck I was in was carrying dozens of surface to air missiles which were almost as big as me, making the trip into Iraq a little more nerve-racking. With a night invasion, the convoy of trucks had to drive without using headlights. They called it "blackout drive." You had to follow the truck in front of you using only the very small fluorescent lights that were located on each side of the back bumper. After a while your eyes played tricks on you making it difficult to see the truck in front. It was imperative to constantly rotate drivers.

Heavily armed combat troops in Abrams tanks escorted the convoy with Apache attack helicopters minutes away should we need additional support. Each soldier had an M16 rifle with four fully loaded magazines and a couple of explosive grenades. Although the odds of the Iraqis getting through our escorts were slim, they told us to be cognizant of snipers and those who separated from their unit and may be roaming the desert. To limit unnecessary noise, the commander ordered us to use our radios only in an emergency. In a light rain on a very cool evening at about 10 pm local time on February 24, 1991 the U.S.-led ground invasion of southern Iraq and occupied Kuwait began.

Our convoy of trucks moved into Iraq at a snail's pace driving about ten miles an hour at best. When word came over the radio that we'd passed across the border into southern Iraq a chill ran through my body as I locked and loaded my M16 rifle and clicked off the safety device. My partner in our vehicle was an ex-Marine who had served in a combat unit, so I felt safe with him. We knew that before any enemy troops got near our convoy they'd have to pass our escorts, giving us plenty of time to react accordingly. After driving for over an hour into Iraq the convoy came to a halt. We sat there for about twenty minutes before finding out why.

We were a part of the back end of the convoy and had gotten separated from the rest of the Company. The truck that was in front of us lost sight of the vehicle in front of him and got lost trying to catch up. Behind my vehicle were another three trucks and the rear escort which, was an armored personnel carrier with six combat troops and a mounted M50 machine gun. It seems we'd been driving the wrong way for close to an hour and were about ten kilometers from the rest of the convoy. The sergeant in the escort vehicle informed the rest of us that we would follow him to meet up with the rest of the company. After driving for about ten minutes the convoy stopped again. Within seconds a message came over the radio that ordered us to dismount our vehicles and take cover.

As I grabbed my Kevlar helmet and rifle and jumped out of the vehicle taking cover behind the huge front right tire of the vehicle, my partner did the same on the left side. Within minutes I began to hear what sounded like Arabic voices getting closer and closer. As my heart beat out of my chest and my trigger hand shook, I pointed my rifle into the pitch-dark night still unable to see more than two feet in front of me. I then heard a single shot fired and someone from the escort vehicle screamed, "Get down on the ground, put your hands on your head," then they repeated the command in Arabic.

One of the other combat soldiers came back and told the rest of us to follow him back to the escort vehicle and to remain locked and loaded. As we got closer to the vehicle I saw about ten Iraqi soldiers lying face down in the sand with their hands on their heads, while the other combat troops were searching their pockets. They were Iraqi soldiers who had deserted their unit and were looking for American soldiers so they could surrender. We assisted the combat soldiers in tying their hands behind their backs, then waited until the Military Police unit came to pick them up before driving back to meet up with the rest of the Company.

After returning to the convoy we proceeded to drive deeper into Iraq as the sun began to rise. Once it was light enough we saw hundreds of empty Iraqi foxholes that had been deserted within hours of the invasion. The convoy stopped so we could inspect them and take anything of importance. Each foxhole was big enough for one man and was about five feet deep. Empty water bottles and dozens of empty packets of processed cheese, which is probably all they ate, filled each space. A few of the foxholes contained Russian-made AK-47 rifles that the Iraqi soldiers had left behind which a few of the American soldiers tried to keep hoping to mail it home piece by piece. Our superiors immediately told us that anyone trying to steal one would be court-martialed. His mandate didn't deter everyone.

In one of the foxholes that I was searching I found a couple of pictures. One was of an elderly Arab couple, possibly the soldier's parents, and the other of a young Muslim woman who could have been his wife or girlfriend. It made me realize that the Iraqis were no different from us. I was about to take the photos as a souvenir, but as I went to put them in my pocket a strange feeling came over me about having another soldier's family pictures. I left them in the foxhole.

Over the next two days, we made our way north towards the Air Rumaylah Oil Field which was where the First Cavalry was supposed to position its troops and wait for further orders. It was initially thought that the coalition would have to invade from all sides to defeat the Iraqis, but after suffering massive losses Saddam Hussein ordered his troops, including the so-called elite Republican Guard unit, to retreat from Kuwait and return to Baghdad. When the first Cavalry unit got near the oil field they encountered thousands of Iraqi troops trying to escape. Although we were a mile away we clearly heard a firefight, and soon heard the roar of U.S. fighter jets flying overhead on their way to bomb the retreating enemy soldiers. Within an hour the Air Force had incinerated most of the Iraqis attempting to flee Kuwait. The next day, on February 28, President Bush announced that the liberation of Kuwait was complete and that the war was over.

Although we were excited that the war was over we knew that as a transportation company we would be one of the last units to leave Saudi Arabia and that it might be months before we went home. Our orders called for a six-month tour, but the government could change that in seconds, keeping us there for up to a year. I felt bad for many of the soldiers in the Company since they'd been in the country since August. I'd only been there for six weeks and although I missed home, I didn't mind staying to do my share, especially since the hostilities were over. After we had secured our equipment we were prepared to convoy back to Saudi Arabia to set up a new base camp when we received new orders. They ordered our platoon to drop off the unused ammunition at a nearby depot then proceed to Kuwait City to assist with the cleanup. At first, I was excited to be going to Kuwait, but as our convoy got closer to the tiny Arab country my excitement soon turned to horror.

As our convoy drove south along Highway 80 towards Kuwait City we witnessed death and destruction on an unimaginable scale. Bombed out Iraqi military vehicles and hundreds of dead Iraqi soldiers were scattered everywhere. The closer we got to Kuwait City the stench of burning vehicles mixed with the smell of mutilated dead bodies became unbearable. The highway became impassable at one point with dozens of military and civilian vehicles blocking the road in what looked like a desperate attempt to escape the coalition bombing. As we got out of our vehicles to get a closer look at the damage I instantly came upon a bombed-out military truck with the driver still in his seat burned to a crisp with no eyes, and his hands still on the steering wheel. What I thought was the worst thing I could possibly see was tame to what I would witness next.

Right in the middle of the pile of damaged and abandoned vehicles was the worst carnage imaginable. Body parts were everywhere including the severed head of a man with his eyes still open. Most of the victims who were still in their vehicles had been severely burned and many of the bodies that were outside of the vehicles were missing limbs. Many of them were bloated and covered with hundreds of flies. With temps already in the 90s, the desert heat intensified the putrid stench of the dead with everyone in the platoon puking at one point or another. I threw up three times.

As we sat on the side of the highway waiting for further orders other units and assorted Army officers traveling in Humvees began arriving at our location. Most of us in the platoon assumed that we would drive around the roadblock through the desert and make our way to Kuwait City, our original destination. We waited as our platoon leader met with one of the higher-ranking officers who had come to assess the scene. When she was done she met with our platoon sergeant who then informed us of the bad news. Our platoon was to stay and help the other unit bury the dead bodies, and to sufficiently clear the highway for vehicles to pass through.

They ordered us to wear our chemical suits and gloves to avoid contracting diseases while moving the bodies which made the heat even more unbearable.

Our platoon sergeant told us that he thought that the Army wanted us to clear away much of the carnage before the press came and took pictures to avoid the negative publicity and anti-war sentiment associated with such carnage. Picking up mutilated body parts is something that nobody should ever have to do. To make this unimaginable task more bearable I began making jokes using lines from my favorite movie "Goodfellas." In the movie, Joe Pesci's character jokes as he picks up body parts of a dead person they were digging up. Just as in the movie I would pick up a body part and say in my best Pesci impression, "Look I got a leg, I got an arm, I got a wing." It was morbid and in bad taste but my jokes were cracking everyone up which helped alleviate the horror of what we were doing. Just as we were finishing clearing out the bodies from the vehicles I came across a civilian vehicle that had the burnt corpses of a woman and her infant child, who she was holding against her chest. As another soldier and I attempted to move the bodies, they were so charred that they fell apart when we picked them up.

I couldn't help feel as if we had just cleaned up a crime scene. We were forbidden to take pictures and many who tried had their cameras confiscated. Weeks later there were guys selling pictures of the carnage for five dollars each. I didn't need any pictures of those images. They're ingrained in my head forever. I knew that all wars caused civilian deaths but growing up we were taught it was always the enemy doing it. I thought to myself, "America is not supposed to kill mothers holding their babies, what the fuck?" I was angry for what I had witnessed, but I also knew that we were by far the lesser of two evils, as Saddam Hussein had done worse things to his own people. Looking back, I think I was just angry because I felt that the Army didn't prepare me for what I was forced to do, especially since it wasn't our job in the first place. When the company commander found out that our platoon had been "hijacked" by another officer, she immediately called for our return. We never made it to Kuwait, and soon began the long drive back to base camp.

On April 20 our commander announced at evening formation that we were going home. The entire company erupted in a giant cheer. I'd only been there for four months, but most of the company had been in the desert close to eight. We packed up the entire base camp and headed to Dhahran, Saudi Arabia where we would stay in the barracks for a week before heading back to the United States. Eight days later we boarded a commercial airliner and flew into John F. Kennedy International Airport in New York. I was twenty minutes from Canarsie, but I still had to fly to Fort Benning to Out-Process. After spending three days in Georgia where I got drunk, had sex, and got a Desert Storm tattoo on my right forearm, I finally went home.

# Chapter 19
# Canyon of Heroes

I arrived at LaGuardia Airport in Queens to a hero's welcome with the receiving area plastered with American flags, welcome home signs, and yellow ribbons. As two of my fellow soldiers and I walked into the waiting area in desert fatigues, we were greeted with a loud cheer from the crowd of people inside the terminal standing behind police barricades. I noticed a girl who had ducked under the barricade and began running full speed towards me and as she got closer I realized it was my sister Stephanie. While crying uncontrollably she jumped on me and gave me a huge hug. As I made my way over to my parents and friends, my sister continued to cling to my neck, still crying. I hugged my mother first, and then my father as he kept saying, "You did it, Rob You did it."

For the first time since I was eleven, my father told me he was proud of me. He was impressed that I had the guts to volunteer and said, "Your brothers could have never done what you did." I had never heard my father put me "above" Warren. I had to admit, it made me feel pretty damn good as I'd never thought in a million years I could compete with the title of Rock Star. Apparently, in my father's eyes being a war veteran put me in Warren's league. He suggested that I take some time for myself, and when I was ready we could sit down and discuss the future. After spending the night in New Jersey, I went back to my apartment in Canarsie and saw my brother Jerry for the first time in four months. I was so excited to see him I tackled him on the bed. We both cried.

The weeks following my return from the war were something special. The country was on a patriotic high following our victory in the Gulf, and the public treated returning soldiers like kings. I loved all the attention and wore my desert fatigues every day for two weeks. A local charity group asked me to be a guest speaker at their dinner, and the American Legion selected me as one of three Grand Marshals for the annual Memorial Day Parade in Canarsie. The president of the Police Athletic League asked me to help organize and coach a travel baseball team made up of local Canarsie kids. I immediately agreed. When I went to Shea Stadium to see a Mets game I had complete strangers paying for my food whenever I tried to order something. I was in my glory and loving all the attention, but the best was yet to come.

On June 10, 1991, the country honored Desert Storm veterans with a ticker tape parade in downtown Manhattan. The unit I served with didn't come to New York, so the Army attached us to a makeshift group of reservists from Fort Hamilton. As we marched down Broadway it rained confetti from the skyscrapers as thousands of jubilant people dressed in patriotic garb and waving American flags lined each side of the street. As I looked up through the constant stream of confetti into the bright blue sky, I noticed people in every window of every building screaming and waving. I was being honored down the same parade route as heads of state, astronauts, and Olympic champions. Only five years earlier I was on the other side of the barricades as the World Champion New York Mets enjoyed their parade. In less than five months, I went from smoking crack in the back of a sweltering hot van to marching down the “Canyon of Heroes” to the cheers of thousands of grateful Americans.

When we came to the end of the parade route a few of us decided to walk back through the crowds of people to the starting point. When we stepped into the crowd and made our way up Broadway people immediately swarmed us. We couldn’t walk five feet without someone stopping us to shake our hands, take a picture, or have us sign an autograph. I was signing my name on Desert Storm banners, American flags, and on girls’ rear ends. One girl asked me to sign her chest and then requested that I also write my phone number. I was asked a hundred times if I was single and went home with a dozen phone numbers, most of them unsolicited. Every time we passed a bar someone wanted to buy us a beer or a shot. We had to start refusing or we wouldn’t have lasted ‘til dinner time. We ended the night at a concert on the bay and were again swarmed by folks wanting to meet us. As I signed autographs and took pictures with complete strangers, I thought, “This shit happens to Warren all the time.”

My brother had moved to England the previous year after Duran Duran made him a full member of the band in 1989. He bought Simon LeBon’s house in Battersea, London, and built a recording studio in his basement. Their last album didn’t chart well, and there was talk about the group breaking up. Warren convinced the rest of the band to record their next album at his house, far from the trappings of fame. In one of my phone calls to Warren while still in Saudi Arabia, the band was in the middle of recording the album when all the guys got on the phone to wish me well. Then Warren played me rough track of a song he was currently working on with Simon writing the lyrics. Although it was difficult to hear with soldiers talking all around me in a crowded phone tent, I said to Warren, “It’s great. If you guys do well, you better give me a job if I make it out of here.” I’ll never forget his response. “Absolutely.”

When all the excitement from the war started to wind down, I had to think about what I was going to do next. I sat down with my father and confided that I didn't want to take over his business. "What do you plan on doing then?," he asked. Following my experiences at the Duran Duran concerts and the Desert Storm parade, I yearned to do something exciting and be in the spotlight. I had seen an ad for a bartending school that taught you how to flip bottles. I thought, "Yeah, I can see me doing that." Following the success of the movie "Cocktail" with Tom Cruise, I envisioned myself working in popular nightclubs making hundreds of dollars a night. He encouraged me to go for it, but also reminded me that I could always return to the military. I used the money that I had saved while in the service and enrolled in the nine-week course at the American Bartending School in Manhattan.

Following graduation, my dreams of blending Margaritas in the tropics and performing flair bartending in front of adoring women were short-lived. My first job was working at a Chinese restaurant from 11 am until 11 pm with a two-hour break in between. I was paid sixty dollars a shift and made another thirty in tips. I stood around most of the time when not passing bottles of Chinese beer to the waiters who spoke no English. I was still living in Canarsie, so I took the subway every day. I had to travel through some sketchy neighborhoods late at night and carried a small metal pipe in my bag for protection. After about a week I got fed up and quit. A few days later the school got me a job working at another bar in the City.

My former bartending instructor had become the manager at a brand-new sports bar in midtown Manhattan and gave me a full-time position. It was an upscale establishment that catered to the advertising executives on Madison Avenue. The hours were great with the bar closing by midnight. I still had to take the subway through the ghetto, though, and continued to carry my "weapon." During one of my shifts, one of the bartenders said to me, "You should consider renting a room here in the City, it's only a matter of time before you get robbed on the subway." When I shot back, "Who's got the money to rent here in Manhattan?" he replied, "I know where you can rent two rooms for four hundred a month." It sounded too good to be true so I asked, "What's the catch?" He lowered his voice and said, "You have to share the kitchen and bathroom with a middle-aged Spanish couple."

The apartment on Columbus Avenue was in a nice area only a block away from Central Park. It was on the second floor directly above a jazz club with a bustling 24-hour grocery store on the corner. I wasn't too concerned about the jazz club because I used earplugs to sleep. But I did have reservations about sharing a bathroom with complete strangers. I'd always envisioned leaving Canarsie so after meeting the incredibly nice couple who'd lived there for twenty years, I decided to take the place. I'd only moved across the river but it was a start. My brother Jerry was pissed off after he was forced to move in with a friend when I gave up the apartment we shared. He was separated from his wife at the time. Robby and Henry helped me move, and except for the military, this was the only time I had lived outside of Canarsie.

Within weeks I felt I'd made a mistake. I didn't adjust well to living in Manhattan. The job was fine, but when I hung out with people from the City I always felt out of place. The people I worked with in the bar were cool, but most of them were doing coke and I needed to stay away from them. I had started smoking pot again to help me sleep, but it wasn't habitual this time. On my days off I tried to do things in the City and began running the reservoir in Central Park every day. I was in bars five days a week, nine hours a day, so I stayed away from them. I still had my car so occasionally I'd drive to my parents in New Jersey or stop in Canarsie to see family and friends. On one rare Friday night when I didn't work, I headed to Canarsie to hang out with Robby. We hadn't seen each other in a while and he knew about bar that had just opened in the neighborhood. We decided to check it out.

It was called Alaska, a strip bar across the street from Le Parc on Rockaway Parkway. It featured average-looking Spanish women dancing in bikinis who would flash you for a dollar. After a couple of drinks, Robby and I started talking to the random guy sitting next to us. When I came back from the bathroom two large men were arguing with him and threatened to beat the man up. Thinking that Robby and I were with him they added, "Yeah...and we'll beat up your two friends also." When I tried to explain to them that we weren't together he dismissed me and told me to "shut the fuck up." Without getting angry I tried to reason with these guys, but they didn't want to hear it. Without directly saying it, one of them implied that we'd better be careful when we leave the bar.

In case there was a fight and because these guys were a lot bigger than us, Robby called a close friend with mob ties. When Robby's friend and a couple of his *associates* showed up the other two clowns were now acting friendly, claiming it was just a misunderstanding. They knew immediately that Robby's friends were mob connected and realized their mistake. Soon after Robby's friends left the bar, the guys who started the trouble were now buying us drinks. They played stupid and kept saying, "You should have told us you weren't with that guy, we didn't know." We ALL knew that was bullshit. When they left the bar, they shook our hands and apologized for the umpteenth time. Robby and I exited a few minutes later. As we were getting in my car a rust-colored Cadillac pulled up alongside us. It was the two guys from the bar and one of them jumped out and started walking toward me. I still had a slight buzz but was far from intoxicated at that point. He got within two feet of me and I landed a right hook to the side of his face instantly knocking him to the ground. As he tried to get up Robby and I started kicking him unmercifully and mocking him about being a "tough guy" earlier at the bar. He was screaming, "Please stop! I was trying to apologize," but we continued to kick him as he covered up his face. We expected his friend to get out of the car and help, but he peeled away, leaving his friend lying in the street. We then realized that *we* needed to leave before the police showed up. Robby and I took off in my car and, foolishly, drove by the scene of the fight about twenty minutes later. The guy was gone.

I had had dozens of fights growing up in Brooklyn, but not since I was a teenager. I had never been violent in my life, and what I did to that guy scared me when I sobered up. As I played the incident over in my head, it was as if I was watching a completely different person kicking that man. I knew something had come over me, but at the time I dismissed it, and blamed the alcohol. When I returned to Manhattan the next day I sat in Central Park and pondered my future. I went through one hell to get away from another. I had no intentions of slipping backward. It had been months since the Desert Storm parade, and I missed the admiration of being a soldier. I was just another bartender in New York City, twenty-eight years old, and still caught up in the neighborhood nonsense. I was living across the river but it was still too close. I wanted to get as far away from Canarsie as possible and knew that the best place for me was back in the Army.

# Chapter 20
# Ordinary World

"I can send you to Korea or to Germany," the recruiter said as I completed my reenlistment paperwork. I called my father on the spot and requested his input. He said, "If you go to Korea, you're an idiot." That sealed my decision and I left for Fort Jackson, South Carolina on October 8, 1992, before leaving for Germany the following day. I was assigned to the 54th Engineer Battalion in Wildflecken, a small town of about three thousand people located in northwest Bavaria approximately one hundred miles east of Frankfurt. Camp Wildflecken, as it was once known, had been nicknamed "Top of the Rock" because of its high altitude and extreme weather conditions, making it an undesirable place to live and train. The soldiers on post called it "Wild Chicken," which made no sense but was good for a laugh. The camp was a former SS training post under Adolf Hitler during World War II that the Americans took over in 1951. When I arrived at my new unit they assigned me to Delta Company which was part of Allied Mobile Forces, a separate unit that trained jointly with soldiers from other countries in Europe.

Wildflecken was one of the smallest American posts in Germany. Like most military installations it had a medical center, a mess hall, a gymnasium, and multiple athletic fields. There was a small post exchange complete with a barbershop and a shoppette which sold snacks, alcohol, and cigarettes. The Army issued each soldier a ration card to prevent them from selling alcohol and cigarettes on the German black market. The post had an enlisted club where the soldiers could drink and dance on the weekends. On Friday nights, they'd play country music attracting every white person on post except me. On Saturdays, it was rap night which catered to the black soldiers. I tried going to the club on Saturdays, but since most of the German girls were there to meet black guys, they wouldn't give me the time of day. That turned out to be a blessing because the last place I needed to be in was in a bar.

The most pleasant surprise when I arrived at my unit was the new living conditions in the barracks. The Army had just instituted a program called Single Soldier Initiative which gave the unmarried soldiers the same privileges as their married counterparts. The soldiers could decorate their rooms within reason and could bring guests in anytime during non-duty hours. In each building, the highest-ranking soldier who lived there was in charge and responsible for organizing a clean-up, and alternating duties equally among all the residents regardless of rank. During my first stint in the Army single soldiers were only allowed one six-pack of beer at a time and no hard liquor. Under SSI, soldiers could bring in as much alcohol as they wanted, and things could get crazy on any given night.

Due to the lack of activities in and around the post, drinking was rampant in the barracks. Other than the enlisted club and a small bar in town that closed at midnight, there weren't many places to drink socially other than the barracks. The town of Fulda was only an hour away and included a legal red-light district, which we'd sometimes visit on payday. The problem was that most of the single enlisted soldiers didn't have cars, and public transportation in Wildflecken was nonexistent, so leaving post was difficult or expensive or both.

There was one soldier in my building who had spent his entire two-year tour without ever leaving Wildflecken. He spent all of his off time drinking in the barracks. I swore that was not going to be me.

With all the drinking going on I just assumed that there were people smoking pot, but I was wrong. Unlike at Fort Campbell when half the company was getting high, I never heard it mentioned in the Wildflecken barracks. The fact that we were in a remote area of Germany in tandem with the Army's stricter drug policy and improved testing methods meant marijuana was not an issue in my unit. With all the alcohol in the barracks, I managed to steer clear of it. To my surprise, I had no desire to drink. I think it had to do with the fact that I'd always associated alcohol with cocaine which still scared me although it was impossible to get given our desolate location. The saying in the barracks was that there were only two things to do in Wildflecken; drink or work out. I chose the gym.

Within months I got into the best shape of my life. I hit the gym every day, lifting weights, using the cardio machines, and playing racquetball. I found a public swimming pool right off the post and began swimming a few days a week. Even though we'd run as a platoon most mornings, I continued running on my own to tackle the steep hills of Wildflecken which gave me trouble at first. I played for both the company softball team and the post softball team which traveled all over Germany to play other American posts. When I wasn't playing softball, I was coaching a little league baseball team made up of the military kids who lived on post.

I also decided to use my free time to further my education which would help when it came to a promotion. I had returned to Active Duty with the rank of Specialist. The next rank up was Sergeant, a promotion based on a point system. You received points for your military accomplishments along with points for college and military correspondence courses. Central Texas College had an agreement with the Army and offered classes to soldiers in their off-time paid for by the government. The Army also offered courses by mail on various military subjects that counted as promotion points. I didn't have enough time on Active Duty to be eligible for promotion to Sergeant but was accumulating as many points as possible for when that time came.

I had become a completely different person, living the clean life I had always envisioned for myself. I was obsessed with becoming the perfect soldier, clearly trying to make up for all the years I had wasted. I pressed my uniforms, my boots shined like mirrors, and my haircut was always high and tight. I hadn't been in a Combat Engineer unit in over five years but my squad leader worked with me for countless hours helping me catch up on job skills. If I wasn't training or working out, I'd spend my downtime listening to the radio in my room or watching TV. The only English-speaking station we got was Armed Forces Network, which broadcast various American shows, including sitcoms, movies, and sporting events.

On Sunday mornings Armed Forces Radio would simulcast Casey Kasem's American Top 40, counting down the top songs of each week. In one of my calls back home, my mother told me that Duran Duran had just released their new single, Ordinary World. It was the first single off the album they'd recorded at Warren's house, self-titled "Duran Duran." It was also the same song that Warren had played for me over the phone while I was in Saudi Arabia. The cover art for the album featured the wedding photos of each of the band members' parents. Soon after the album's release fans and media alike began referring to the LP as "The Wedding Album." Ordinary World debuted on the charts at number eighty-eight, and I would listen every week waiting and hoping the song would make Casey Kasem's Top 40.

Each week Ordinary World made its way up the charts. In February 1993 it cracked the Top Forty, and back in the States the song was getting massive airplay and heavy rotation on all the pop stations. I had to wait a week just to hear it once on the military station but made up for it by constantly listening to the CD. During each show, Kasem would read a letter from a fan who had some sort of connection or story about a song in the countdown and were usually reserved for songs in the Top Ten. When Ordinary World entered the countdown I decided to write a letter hoping the track would continue to rise. I looked at it as a challenge to see if I could get my letter read from among the thousands they probably received. I know now that it was a way of seeking the attention I so desperately missed.

A month later the song reached the Top Ten but I still hadn't heard my letter. The following week Ordinary World made it to #5, but Kasem read a different entry. The next week I'd already known from my mother that the song had moved to #3 on the charts and thought that this might be my last chance. As I was listening to the show they had just played the #4 song, and I knew that Ordinary World was next. As they were about to go to a commercial break I heard Casey Kasem say, "Up next, a letter from a relative of Duran Duran." I jumped out of my bed and yelled out "Holy shit!" I went into the hallway dying to tell someone but quickly saw that everyone was passed out drunk. I went back to my room, and when the show returned from break, Kasem began to read my letter. He mentioned that I was Warren's brother stationed in Wildflecken, Germany with the 54th Engineer Battalion. As the song began to play, Kasem said, "We dedicate this song to Specialist Rob Cuccurullo, and all the brave men and women serving our country overseas and listening to American Top 40 on Armed Forces Radio."

I thought I was the only one who was listening until Monday morning formation when dozens of guys in my company came over to tell me they'd heard it. The company First Sergeant even made an announcement during morning formation. In his thick Panamanian accent, he yelled, "Seems we have a celebrity in our ranks. Cuccurullo has a brother in Duran Duran." I got exactly what I was looking for when I wrote that letter, but as soon as made the announcement I realized that maybe I'd made a mistake. I had come back in the Army to find my own identity, and to be recognized for my accomplishments, and now through my own doing I was once again Warren Cuccurullo's brother. Then the First Sergeant cracked everyone up when he said, "If you got a brother in Duran Duran, why the fuck aren't you working for him?" I wish a had a dollar for every time someone asked me that over the years.

As much as I loved being a soldier again, I couldn't help but think that if the album had been released earlier, or if I had waited a few more months, it may have changed my decision to come back in the Army. I had always wanted to work for Warren, but now that would be impossible as I had enlisted for three years. Deep down I knew that being in the Army and away from Canarsie was the best thing for me, but I wanted badly to be a part of my brother's success. Duran Duran released their next single Come Undone in March, and the song soon rocketed up the charts, peaking at number seven. The band had consecutive back-to-back Top Ten singles for the first time since their "Fab Five" days, and both singles occupied the Top 40 charts simultaneously for three weeks in May. My brother was experiencing the most successful year of his musical career, and I was three thousand miles away on the top of a mountain missing most of it. I had to go home.

I had put in for leave so I could go home for two weeks in the summer. Duran Duran had begun their 1993 tour and was scheduled to play the New York area in July. I intended to be at every show. I had been to many Duran Duran concerts when my brother was a hired guitarist, but I had never experienced a concert with Warren as a full member and with two major hits to boot. The first show was at Jones Beach on Long Island, and my mother made sure that I had enough tickets and passes for my entire entourage.

Warren had given me two All-Access passes which allowed me to go anywhere I wanted to including the band's dressing room which Simon LeBon stocked with a never-ending supply of Corona beer. I gave the other pass to my pal Robby, and we walked around the Jones Beach Amphitheater like kings. We had a bevy of girls at our side once they saw the passes around our necks, but I reminded Robby that there would be plenty of girls to meet backstage. After the show, my family and friends all gathered in a large VIP area where Warren and the rest of the band came out to socialize, take pictures and sign autographs. I was having the time of my life, and this was only the first night.

I didn't trust myself going to the shows with just my friends. I had no intentions of jeopardizing my Army career by failing a drug test so I brought a girl I had dated before leaving Germany with me to the shows in Boston and Connecticut, a decision that didn't go over well with Robby and my friend Jose. I had known Jose since the seventh grade when we used to cut class and smoke pot together. I also played baseball with him and his brother for many years. A year earlier he had completed eighteen months of rehab for a crack addiction much worse than mine. Jose had worked in Patty Testa's auto shop for years, and it was Patty and his brother Joey who told Jose that he "either goes to rehab or they'll kill him." A few months following his return from rehab Jose was standing ten feet from Patty Testa when Patty was murdered in his auto shop in an apparent mob hit. Jose was a loyal friend who always had your back, but he was a loose cannon. Watching his boss get shot in the head probably didn't help.

The last show before I had to return to Germany was at Radio City Music Hall. Robby and Jose once again joined me and my date, Dawn. We met my parents at the show who were there with my Aunt Nancy and Uncle Bob. After meeting Warren in his dressing room before the show, we made our way into the audience to find our seats while my family stayed back to watch the show from the stage. Dawn and I found our seats about seven rows from the stage and noticed Robby and Jose's two empty seats as they wandered around the venue. Towards the end of the concert, I noticed a commotion going on about four or five rows behind us. I was unable to see through the crowd at first, but soon noticed my parents in the middle of it. I jumped over the seats to get to them as fast as I could.

My mother, aunt, and uncle were all standing behind my father as he was arguing with a Radio City security guard when I stepped in to intervene. They had gotten tired of standing on stage and decided to take their seats. Realizing they didn't have tickets but each of them was wearing an All-Access pass, they sat in an empty row. All in their early sixties and dressed to the nines, they stood out like sore thumbs in a crowd filled with people half their age. The security guard asked to see their tickets, and when my father showed him the All-Access pass and explained who he was the security guard dismissed him and kept asking them to leave. My father began to get angry and told the security guard he wasn't moving. The security guard went to grab my father by the arm, and I stepped in between them. Before I could say a word, someone grabbed the security guard around the neck and pulled him to the ground. It was my friend Jose.

Jose began beating the security guard, and screaming "I'll kill you, you mother fucker! That's my friend's father, you fuckin' asshole!" Jose was strangely hitting this guy with his open hand front and back several times, and kept screaming, "You mother fucker!" Within thirty seconds there were security guards all over us and it took three of them to get Jose off the guy. Two of them got in front me and Robby as I was yelling. "My brother is in the band you fuckin' idiots, we're his family, can't you see the fucking passes!" My father continued to scream so loud that you could hear him over the music while the rest of my family stood there in shock. With that, a few more security guards came over to escort all of us to a side area backstage as Jose and my father continued screaming at them.

The show had now ended and the commotion had caught the band's attention. They came over to see what was happening and immediately Nick Rhodes got a mortified look on his face as if he couldn't believe what was happening. At the same time, Jose was still yelling at the security guard who had started the whole incident and threatening to beat him up. Nick was pleading for everyone to calm down, and to stop screaming. He looked deathly afraid while Warren stepped in front of my father to try and calm him down. As they were trying to sort everything out, Robby and I, along with my date, snuck Jose out of there as fast as we could. On the way home when I asked Jose why he was hitting that guy with an open hand, he said, "It's more humiliating when you slap them like a bitch." I was thankful to Jose for protecting my father, but this was exactly the kind of Canarsie nonsense I wanted to leave behind.

As much as I enjoyed sharing my brother's success, I couldn't get back to Germany fast enough. I was almost glad that this incident happened because it made me realize why I had returned to the military. I had to concentrate on making something of my life, instead of trying to live vicariously through my brother. The fantasy was over, and it was time to get real. I picked up where I left off and was now committed to making Sergeant. Within a few months, I caught the attention of the Battalion Sergeant Major who recommended me for the promotion board. I went in front of the board in September, and after grilling me for an hour on various military subjects they recommended me for promotion to Sergeant and scheduled me for the Army's Primary Leadership Development Course. I was one step closer to becoming a non-commissioned officer in the United States Army, something I would never have fathomed only a year ago.

After graduating from the 30-day course, I was now eligible for promotion to Sergeant and just needed to make the cutoff score which came out each month. When I returned to my unit back in

Wildflecken, most of the soldiers had already left the post which was scheduled to permanently close at the end of the year. It was sad because I knew I'd probably never see some of them again. Most of them went stateside and were assigned to various Combat Engineer units all over the country. I left Germany in December 1993, eight months earlier than originally expected. Following a few weeks at home during the holidays I had orders to report to my new duty station at Fort Knox, Kentucky.

# Chapter 21
# Kentucky Woman

When I returned home I learned from my mother that Frank Zappa had died from prostate cancer on December 4th, at the age of 52. Two days later his family put out an announcement that read, "Composer Frank Zappa left for his final tour just before 6:00 pm on Saturday." Warren was stricken with grief but Duran Duran was still on tour and he had to perform. In a tribute to his idol and mentor, Warren performed a solo during the concert and played "Watermelon in Easter Hay," a signature song that Zappa regarded as the best song on the Joe's Garage album. Someone would later tell me that if you closed your eyes during the song you would swear that Frank Zappa was playing it.

I arrived at Fort Knox, Kentucky in late January 1994, and was assigned to the 19th Engineer Battalion. When I arrived at my new unit I met my friend Wayne from Germany who had gotten there a few days earlier. Purely by coincidence, the Army assigned us to the same company, and later we'd be assigned to the same platoon. When my new First Sergeant found out that I was promotable to Sergeant based on the Army promotion system, he placed me in a leadership position as an Assistant Squad Leader. Each month the Army would put out a point total based on how many Sergeant positions were available. Soldiers received points for education, training, and physical fitness tests. It fluctuated each month, so it was always a guessing game, which made it nerve-racking every time the cut off scores came out.

Fort Knox is in the town of Radcliff, about forty miles south of Louisville, Kentucky. When I asked Wayne if there were any good clubs or bars off the post, he replied, "Yeah, but you have to go to Louisville, they can't sell alcohol in this county." Kentucky had "dry counties" which prohibited the sale of alcohol. Hardin County, home of Fort Knox, was "dry." It didn't affect the soldiers who drank because all posts have a Class 6 store where you can purchase beer, wine, and alcohol. Fort Knox also had an enlisted club for the lower ranking soldiers, and a club for the NCOs ("non-commissioned officers") with the rank of Corporal or above. Although I was promotable, my rank was Specialist, so I had no access. The enlisted club had too many teenagers, so I'd sneak into the NCO club while my friends distracted the woman checking IDs. The only problem with clubs on the post was that they were swarming with BAQ bandits, woman who wanted nothing more than to marry a soldier and enjoy the benefits that come with wedded military bliss. BAQ was an Army acronym for Basic Allowance for Quarters, which was an extra stipend paid to married soldiers living off post.

Wayne and I soon found out about a club called Sparky's located just outside the county line about thirty minutes from post. On Friday nights Sparky's hosted a "Weenie Roast" when they brought in male strippers to entertain the women. The best part was that when the show was over there were dozens of horny women all over the place looking to hook up with a guy. Every week I was having sex with random girls either at their place or sometimes right in the parking lot. There was one night where I got oral sex from a girl in my car and then left with another girl at closing. Most of my sexual liaisons were fueled by alcohol and the desire to impress my new friends as I was approaching thirty years old and most of the guys were in their early twenties. I often felt guilty the next day because I knew what I was doing had consequences, and deep down I knew I was searching for a relationship. I was just going about it the wrong way.

In May of '94, I still hadn't made the cutoff score for promotion to Sergeant, missing it by one point. In August I went home on "leave" to attend the wedding of my friend Henry. Following the extended weekend, I flew back to Kentucky and landed at Louisville Airport where my friend Wayne was there to pick me up. As soon as I saw him he said, "What's up, Sergeant." I thought he was joking until he said, "Congratulations, you made the cutoff score." I froze for a second, then said with a smile, "You better not be fuckin' with me, Wayne." He wasn't. I'd made the cutoff score for August, and on September 1st, less than two years back on active duty, I was promoted to the rank of Sergeant. As soon as I got back to Fort Knox I called my father to tell him I was now a non-commissioned officer in the United States Army. He was beside himself, and said, "I can't tell you how proud I am of you. You've come a long way, Robert. Wow, my son is a Sergeant in the Army. I love the sound of that." Tears were now rolling down my face. When I hung up I wept uncontrollably after realizing what I'd accomplished.

In two years my life had completed changed. I was drinking on the weekends but was drug-free except for the few tokes of pot I took in between duty stations. Now that I was a Sergeant not only did I get a pay raise, I was also given an NCO room which was much larger than the enlisted rooms, including a private bathroom. The Army had instituted the Single Soldier Initiative here in the States, allowing us to furnish our rooms as we pleased. I broke my room into four sections, with a living room and a makeshift kitchen complete with a microwave and a hotplate. We were permitted to have cable television and a personal phone line which made it feel like an apartment and not an Army barracks. My life couldn't have been better except that I was missing one thing.

After attending Henry's wedding, I started thinking more about marriage. I was now thirty years old, and most of my close friends were married and starting families. I was tired of the bar scene and wanted nothing more than to settle down and start my own family. The problem was that I wasn't going to meet my future wife at Sparky's and certainly didn't want to hook up with any of the BAQ bandits who hung at the NCO club. Now that I had my own car I could go where I wanted and started going further away from the base to get away from the GI bars. On a freezing cold night in early February a bunch of us decided to go to downtown Louisville to look for a new bar. As we drove around the city one of my friends noticed a bar called Shooters, so we decided to try it. Within minutes of sitting down at our table, I knew that we had made the right decision.

As soon as I saw her I was smitten. She had short blonde hair, beautiful blue eyes, and a prominent nose that made her even more attractive. She was wearing tight turquoise stretch pants that perfectly accentuated her backside, and although she wasn't our server, she was working the table next to us and I couldn't keep my eyes off her. She looked like she was in her late teens or early twenties, so I was a little self-conscious about being thirty. After a few drinks, I got up the nerve to go talk to her when I noticed she wasn't busy. Her name was Toni, and her bubbly personality was magnetic. After a few minutes I asked her how old she was, and to my surprise, she told me she was twenty-three. When she asked me my age I replied, "I'm a very young thirty years old." She smiled and said, "You look great for your age." I asked her for her phone number and she obliged.

I took her out the very next night and picked her up at her family's house in Louisville. After meeting her mother and stepfather

I took her out to eat at an Italian restaurant, and spent the entire dinner staring into her mesmerizing blue eyes. She had the most adorable Southern accent and couldn't stop commenting on mine. She made fun of every other word I said, but it didn't bother me in the least bit. After dinner and a few cocktails, we decided to go back to Fort Knox and hang out in my barracks room. From the moment I kissed her I knew that there was something special about her. I liked her so much that I promised myself I wouldn't try to have sex with her on the first date. What started out as kissing soon turned to heavy petting, and eventually, we did sleep together that night. I didn't think any less of her and knew this wasn't going to be a one-night stand.

The next day I went to Louisville to hang out with Toni. I was about to leave on a two-week training mission in California but it couldn't have come at a worse time. That day she admitted to me that she wasn't twenty-three, but a month away from turning twenty-one. She had to lie about her age to serve alcohol so she told everyone at work she was twenty-three. Fine by me. I spent the evening hanging out at her house with her mom and stepdad, who were super nice to me. I also met one of her three sisters who still lived at home. I immediately felt comfortable around her family, especially her mom who was only twelve years older than me, which was a little weird at first. When the night was over it was difficult to leave knowing I wouldn't get to see Toni again for two weeks. It had only been two days and I was already falling in love with her.

I spent every minute of those two weeks thinking about her, wondering what she was doing and hoping she wouldn't meet someone else while I was gone. When I finally got to a phone to call I was thrilled and she told me that she missed me. My plan was that as soon as I got back to Fort Knox and released from duty, I'd head straight to Louisville to see Toni. When the bus pulled up in the parking lot next to our barracks, Toni was already there waiting for me, leaning against her car with the biggest smile on her face. The second the commander released us from duty, we went straight to my barracks room and made love. It was then that I told her how I felt. Thankfully, the feeling was mutual.

Over the next few weeks, Toni and I spent all our free time together, and she frequently spent the night with me in the barracks. Her twenty-first birthday was two weeks away, and I wanted to do something special for her. She had told me that she always wanted to see New York City, and I thought who better to take her there than me. Once my Commander approved my four-day pass, I told Toni that I was taking her to New York and she was ecstatic. Toni's mother was nice enough to let us use her car for the twelve-hour drive to New Jersey since mine was a little old. The plan was to stay in New Jersey the first day, and then drive to Canarsie to meet up with Robby and his girlfriend before heading to New York City for Toni's birthday on March 11.

My parents absolutely loved Toni, and my father couldn't stop flirting with her. We spent the day at my parents' condo in Monmouth Beach where my mother cooked a huge meal, giving Toni her first taste of real Italian food. After dinner, my mother gave Toni a tour of the place, including the room where she hung all of Warren's Platinum and Gold records. It was then that Toni admitted that she thought I was lying when I told her my brother was in Duran Duran. She was a little overwhelmed at first by my loud, boisterous Italian family, but soon relaxed and fit right in. As I watched her laughing and talking as if she had known my family for years, I remember thinking to myself, "This is perfect."

On the morning of Toni's 21st birthday while she showered and got ready, I told her I had to go out and run a few errands before we left for Brooklyn. I drove to the Monmouth Mall in Eatontown and went to the jewelry store where I had purchased my gold crucifix. I asked the girl at the counter to show me some moderately priced engagement rings. I was going to do it! I had only known her for six weeks, but I was madly in love, and I was certain that I wanted to marry her. With about two thousand dollars in my savings account, I plucked down twelve hundred and walked out with a shiny new diamond engagement ring. Now I just had to find the right moment to give it to her.

Toni and I drove to Canarsie to meet up with Robby and his girlfriend. As we made our way into Brooklyn, Toni couldn't help commenting on how crazy people in New York drive. While we were stopped at a traffic light she almost jumped out of her seat as a taxicab suddenly stopped next to us a foot away from her window. After picking up Robby and Jennifer, we proceeded to give Toni the Canarsie tour, showing her my old house and some of my old hangouts. We passed by 114 Park, and I showed her where Joe Milo was killed, although I didn't tell her the entire story. We passed by the Walnut Bar and told her about some of the characters that used to hang out there. I also showed her the corner where Crazy Sal murdered Officer Sledge. I could tell that Toni seemed a bit overwhelmed by the stories Robby and I told her that day, and I was a little worried that I might scare her into saying "no" to a proposal.

We parked in downtown Manhattan and went to Battery Park, which gave you a perfect view of the Statue of Liberty. Since none of us had ever been there we decided to take the ferry ride to Liberty Island. We took some great pictures on the ferry with the Manhattan skyline in the background highlighted by the World Trade Center. The whole day I was trying to figure out when and where I would propose to Toni but couldn't find the right moment. After returning to our car we decided to head uptown to Rockefeller Center to eat and see the sites. When my friends said they were ready to leave, I knew I had to act fast if I planned to ask her while we were still in the City. I grabbed Toni by the hand and took her to the spot where they place the giant Christmas tree in December, directly over the ice skating rink. As soon as I got down on one knee, her gorgeous blue eyes opened wide in anticipation. "Toni, will you marry me?" I proudly asked. She began to shake with excitement, and with a huge smile on her face blurted out, "Yes!."

My family was excited for me, although they were concerned that I was moving too fast. I explained to them that I had never felt this way about a woman before and knew that Toni was my soulmate. My father was delighted because he now loved Toni as well and thought it would be the best thing for me. My mother gave me her blessing, but I had a feeling she wasn't completely sure I was doing the right thing, although she didn't come out and say it. My sister was extremely negative as usual, and said, "You're making a big mistake." I immediately dismissed her. My brother Jerry was fully supportive, and Warren's response was, "You sure you want to fuck one woman the rest of your life?" When we returned to Kentucky we broke the news to her family. Her family seemed to like me, and my future in-laws couldn't have been more generous offering to pay for the wedding. We set a date for August 19, giving us over four months to plan the wedding and for my family and friends to arrange to come to Kentucky.

Now that I was getting married I had to decide about staying in the Army. My three-year enlistment was up in seven months, and I had a three-month window to reenlist for three or four years. I was perfectly content with pursuing my military career as I had just made Sergeant and continued to excel at work. A few months earlier I had been named head coach of the Fort Knox Women's Softball Team, a position usually reserved for higher ranking soldiers. Once Toni told me that she had no problem being a military wife and traveling around the world, I re-enlisted for four more years. I just had to complete a routine physical before making it official. As part of the physical, I was required to take a chest x-ray.

A few days after my physical the doctors found some irregularities on my x-ray and told me that I would have to see a specialist. I wasn't overly worried because I felt fine physically, but the fact that I had smoked cigarettes and pot for the past ten years did make me a little apprehensive about the upcoming exam. The Army sent me to Wright Patterson Medical Center in Ohio, and after examining my x-ray and conducting various breathing tests, the doctors were still baffled. They decided to send me to the Walter Reed Army Medical Center in Bethesda, Maryland, home of some of the finest military doctors.

It was at Walter Reed that the doctors began inquiring about my service in the Gulf War. It seems that many soldiers who served in the desert were experiencing respiratory problems and other ailments such as fatigue, muscle pain, cognitive problems, rashes and post-traumatic stress disorder. The Army couldn't pinpoint a specific cause or explain why thousands of men who served in the Gulf were experiencing the same symptoms. I told them that I did experience unsettling dreams about the war after returning from Saudi Arabia, but other than that I felt fine. They decided to give me further breathing tests to compare them to the ones I took earlier. They also wanted to perform a biopsy, which meant they would have to stick a tube up my nose and down into my lungs to get a sample of my lung. I would have to be awake for the procedure, and I almost chickened out at the last minute. Wanting to get some answers I did go through with the biopsy and it was easily one of the worst experiences of my life.

The results of my biopsy turned up negative and the doctors diagnosed me as having an interstitial lung disease, which was another way of saying they didn't know what I had but I had something. When I asked the doctors what it meant for my military career, they told me that if I could pass my physical fitness test, my "illness" would not preclude me from staying on Active Duty. The doctor also warned me that my breathing capacity could diminish over time. She also suggested that I talk to a professional about my troubling dreams but I never did. I was more concerned with planning my wedding, which was now only a few weeks away.

Toni and I had discussed a few different options for the wedding ceremony. I wanted to have our wedding in a Catholic church, but Toni was Southern Baptist, so she would've had to convert which I thought was senseless. We settled on a traditional ceremony in a non-denominational chapel on Fort Knox, and her family rented a Knights of Columbus hall for the reception. We invited about a hundred or so people, which were mostly from her side of the family since the wedding was in Kentucky. The only family members that made it from my side were my parents and my Aunt Nancy and Uncle Bob. I invited about twenty people from my unit, two of whom were in my wedding party. My friend Henry was also in my wedding party, and Best Man Robby flew into Kentucky the day before the wedding. Naturally, they wanted to throw me a bachelor party.

Our families met for the first time at the rehearsal dinner we had in a restaurant near Fort Knox. It was a clash of two completely different cultures, but everyone got along great. Robby, who sounds like Joe Pesci, had everyone in stitches telling stories. Following the dinner and rehearsal at the chapel, Toni went back to her mother's house, and I took the guys in my wedding party back to the empty new apartment in Louisville that Toni and I had rented. Before we were about to leave for the bar, Henry pulled out an eight ball of cocaine and started making lines on the kitchen counter.

I hadn't done cocaine in over two years, and when I saw him chopping it up I still had no desire to do any. That changed quickly as I drank a few beers and did a couple of shots. Suddenly I was back in Canarsie. We each snorted a couple of lines, and my friend Matt who had never done cocaine in his life took a hit. I wasn't too worried about doing coke that night as it was a special occasion, and I was on leave so I wouldn't have to worry about a drug test. We drank a couple of more beers and did a few more lines before leaving to go to the club. I was excited as I had always imagined having a bachelor party, but when we pulled into the parking lot a strange feeling came over me as if I knew I shouldn't have come here.

I hadn't been to Sparky's in months since dating Toni, but it hadn't changed at all. They still had the "Weenie Roast" with the male strippers, and women packed the place. I ran into a few girls who I had previously hooked up with who wanted to know where I'd been. When I told one of them that I was getting married the next day, she still wanted to hang out with me. As tempting as it was, I hadn't cheated on Toni and didn't intend to. Throughout the evening we would go out to the car to do some more lines and then come back in and drink some more. After a few hours, I was high as a kite and found myself looking at every girl in the place. I thought I could control my urges until a girl I had never seen before approached me.

I could tell by the look in her eyes that she was trying to seduce me. She wasn't a beautiful girl but had a sexy look with an amazing body. The cleavage from her "D" cup size breasts was staring me in the face, and she had a large round rear end. Standing directly over me as I sat in my chair, she came right out and said, "I have to have you. You are so fucking cute." I was instantly aroused, but I pushed back my chair and told her flat out that I was getting married the next day. She didn't seem to care as she sat down next to me and started rubbing my leg eventually getting to my crouch.

Unable to resist my urges I started making out with her, and within minutes she grabbed my hand, pulled me out of the bar and asked where my car was. After performing oral sex on me for a few minutes, she pulled out a condom from her bag and said, "I want you to fuck me." I pulled the car to the edge of the parking lot where I opened the passenger side door and bent her over the front seat. With her big round ass sticking up in the air, I had sex with her while standing up outside the car with my pants around my ankles.

When the bar closed we went back to my apartment in Louisville and continued to do more lines. I was so high that the fact that I had just cheated on my fiancé the day before my wedding hadn't sunk in. We didn't get to sleep until about 6 am, had to be at the church by 9 am, and almost overslept because nobody bothered to set an alarm. We scrambled like crazy to get dressed and make the thirty-minute ride to Fort Knox.

It was during the car ride to the church that I remembered what had happened the night before. If Robby and Henry weren't in the car I probably would've broken down crying. The guilt of what I had done began to diminish what was supposed to be the happiest day of my life. I was madly in love with Toni and couldn't believe that I had cheated on her with some cheap bar slut. I knew I'd made a huge mistake allowing the life I desperately wanted to escape to mix with the life I had always dreamed of living. I was getting married in less than thirty minutes, and I knew I had to snap out of it. To feel better I told myself that once Canarsie left Louisville, I could go back to my dream life with my new beautiful bride. The moment I saw Toni in her wedding dress I instantly forgot about everything that had happened and was ready to start a new chapter in my life.

# Chapter 22
# Desert Storm Syndrome

As soon as I returned from leave I met with my doctor to discuss the results of the breathing tests I'd taken a few weeks earlier. Compared to the tests from a few months ago, the new tests showed that my lung capacity had decreased over time, and she was concerned it might continue. When I pressed the doctor for answers, she confided in me that there might be evidence that thousands of U.S. troops suffered exposure to a poison nerve agent called Sarin, which may have been in the Iraqi weapons destroyed by coalition forces. When I told her about some of the areas I'd been to in Saudi Arabia, she told me there was a possibility that I'd been exposed. They still couldn't pinpoint anything specific, and the government simply called it "Desert Storm Syndrome." When I asked what that meant for my military career, she told me that if my breathing capacity continued to decrease the Army would medically discharge me.

The last thing I wanted to do was to leave the Army since I'd just gotten married and re-upped for four more years. I insisted that I was fine and could still pass my physical fitness test. To prove it, I requested to take a new PT test well in advance of the next one scheduled. My time in the two-mile run had decreased since Germany, but I attributed it to the fact that I wasn't training as hard as I had months earlier. I passed the test, but my time in the two-mile run had dropped another two minutes. Over the next few weeks I was obsessed with improving my run times, but each day found it harder to breathe whenever I tried to run faster. As much as I tried to deny it, there was something wrong with me, and I began to start thinking about what I would do if I had to leave the Army.

I went back to the doctor and told her that I was having difficulty breathing when I tried to run, and she immediately scheduled a medical board to determine my military fitness. A week later I met with the panel who determined that based on my breathing tests, I had clearly lost some lung capacity. They claimed it wasn't enough to warrant a thirty percent disability rating which would have qualified me for a military retirement. They awarded me a ten percent disability, which came with a $25,000 payment, but no retirement. One of the doctors on the board did admit that he thought my lung capacity would continue to decrease, but until it did, they could not justify a claim of thirty percent. I had three days to appeal the board's decision.

My wife was enjoying the role of a military spouse. She was adamant that I try to stay on Active Duty but I told her that I since I was in a combat unit and needed to be in good shape, there was no way they'd allow me to stay in the Army. When she suggested I change jobs I told her that it was more economical for them to retire me than to retrain me. I called my father for advice who immediately told me to appeal. He told me that if I was retired I'd receive money and medical benefits for the rest of my life, as opposed to receiving twenty-five grand which my father joked would last me about three months. The next day I appealed the decision and retained a military lawyer to represent me. The attorney told me to wait about two weeks and then take another breathing test. Even if we could show a slight drop, she would be able to argue that my lung capacity would eventually drop to a level which constituted a thirty percent disability rating.

I loved being a soldier and knew that the military had saved my life. I really didn't want to leave. I went back in front of the medical review board in late September, and they awarded me a thirty percent disability rating with the medical retirement. Being retired meant that I'd receive a small pension every month, but more importantly, I'd receive free medical benefits for life. As much as I was upset about being discharged, I tried to look at the positive, and at only thirty years old had plenty of time to start a new career. Three weeks later I was honorably discharged and retired from the United States Army.

Toni and I were both upset about leaving the military, but our new life couldn't have been better. We were madly in love with each other and nearly inseparable. We did everything together, from going bar hopping in downtown Louisville to playing on a co-ed softball team. We also spent a lot of time at her family's house so we could eat her mother's delicious Southern cooking. Financially, we were doing great especially since the cost of living in Kentucky was much lower than the rest of the country. Toni was working at the UPS hub at Louisville Airport, while I was working part-time as a hotel bartender and figuring out what I'd do next. My father-in-law suggested a job in law enforcement since they preferred to hire ex-military. My only concern was that my disability might preclude me from being hired.

My disability turned out to be a positive because as a disabled veteran I received a ten-point preference on all civil service tests. I was told that if I could pass the physical fitness test, which varied by department, I'd be eligible for employment. To stay in shape I took up swimming, which didn't affect me as much as running. I took the written tests from several different departments including the Louisville Police Department. I was later told by some cops that they would never in a million years hire some Yankee from New York City. I also took the test for a State Corrections position, which was a much easier job to get since the pay was lower. With my disabled veteran status, I went to the top of the hiring list and was called in for an interview within weeks of passing the test. I wasn't crazy about the idea of working in a prison, but I figured I could do it until another agency called me. After completing a background check and a psychological exam, they scheduled me to attend the Corrections Academy in January 1996.

I found it more than a little ironic that someone who used to do drugs and hung around gangsters could be working in law enforcement. Now that my start date was set for after the New Year, I was looking forward to the holidays, which Toni and I decided to spend in Kentucky. I enjoyed my first Thanksgiving with the new in-laws, and they immediately made me feel like a family member. Toni and I were excited to spend our very first Christmas together, and I remember how happy I was when we bought our first tree and went home to decorate it. A few days after we put up our Christmas tree, Toni surprised me and brought home a kitten. We would eventually adopt the last two of the litter and now had three kittens running around the apartment. I was living the life I'd always dreamed of and knew that it was only a matter of time before we started having children. Two weeks before Christmas I woke up to a note that Toni had written on the bulletin board we had in the kitchen. It read, "You're the greatest husband in the world! I love you! Toni." That evening I wanted to surprise her by cooking her a big dinner. She never came home.

I just assumed she had stopped by her mother's house, but when I called her sister she told me she hadn't seen Toni all day. I called a few of her friends, but they hadn't seen her either. Just as I was about to panic and call the police, Toni finally rang me. She told me that she needed some time to be by herself and that she would be staying at a girlfriend's house. When I asked her if I did anything to get her angry she gave me the "It's not you, it's me" line. I begged her to come home so we could talk but she refused. She started rambling on about how we got married too fast and that it might have been a mistake. I was devastated when she said that, thinking that we were the perfect couple living the perfect life. When I asked when she planned on coming back home she replied, "I don't know, it could be a while, it could be never." It was two weeks before Christmas and my wife of only four months had just left me.

I'd been in relationships that went sour, but usually you could see it coming. I couldn't understand how someone could call you the greatest husband one day and leave you the next. I thought to myself that I did everything in my power to be a good husband, but it still wasn't good enough. After the initial shock wore off I began to fall into a deep state of depression not wanting to go out or see anyone and didn't go to work for three days. The only time I left my apartment was to buy vodka and beer, which I was drinking every night. I sat in my apartment for a week drunk and depressed hoping that Toni would call. She never did. Toni's mother and stepfather were very sympathetic when I called them but couldn't tell me why Toni left so suddenly. Her mother told me that if I didn't go home for Christmas I was more than welcome to come to their house. Since I was too embarrassed to tell my family that my wife had left me, I decided to stay in Louisville for the holidays.

On Christmas Eve I went to the in-laws' house, although it felt very strange to be there without my wife. Toni was to arrive later, so I had some time to talk to her family about what had happened. Her two older sisters pulled me aside and told me something that Toni had conveniently kept from me. A little over a year earlier Toni had married a Marine who she only knew for months and divorced him soon after. Her sisters wanted to tell me before the wedding but didn't because they truly believed that I was right for Toni and didn't want to scare me away. I felt a little betrayed, but I still wanted Toni to come back to me. I wasn't concerned about her past since I still hadn't told my wife everything about my life in Canarsie. About an hour later Toni finally showed up.

When I saw her come down the steps into the basement I wanted nothing more than to hug and kiss her but didn't know how she would react. She did give me a slight hug and a peck on the cheek, which was disappointing considering how much I missed her. After some small talk with the rest of her family, I pulled Toni aside and asked her directly, "Do you plan on coming home anytime soon?" She told me she still wasn't sure and needed more time to think about it. When I asked her if she still loved me she said, "I do love you Rob, but I feel like we got married too fast. You're a great guy, but I really don't know much about you."

I immediately remembered the New York trip, and asked, "Does it have anything to do with some of the stories I told you when we were in Canarsie?" She replied, "Yeah they scared me a little." "I'm not that guy anymore," I assured her. "We all have a past," I mentioned while transitioning to hers. When I brought up her previous marriage she didn't seem surprised that I knew, and used the same excuse her sisters did, that she didn't want to scare me away. I told her I was ready to forgive her, and whenever she was ready I would sit down and tell her anything she wanted to know about me. I also told her that I wasn't going to wait forever. I gave her until New Year's Day to decide, and if she didn't return home by then I would consider the marriage over.

At about four in the afternoon on New Year's Day, Toni came home with all her belongings. I was ecstatic about her return and decided to back off and give her some space. A few days later she sat me down and told me what had happened when she was away.

She moved in with her friend and her friend's boyfriend who were sharing an apartment. She said that about a few weeks ago her girlfriend moved out leaving her alone with this guy. According to Toni, this guy tricked her into taking some acid and then had sex with her while she was tripping. I was furious at first, but when she started crying I felt bad for her and was ready to forgive and forget. I also didn't want to be a hypocrite since I had slept with one of the waitresses at my job in one of my drunken stupors. Within a few weeks, everything started to go back to the way it was.

After a few days, as promised I began telling Toni about my past. I told her about my drug use but couldn't get myself to tell her about my former crack habit as I was still too embarrassed. I told her about the wiseguys and wannabes, and some of the illegal things I did with them. I finally admitted to her that I watched Joe Milo die, and how his death may have led to my drug use. I also admitted to her that I was suffering from nightmares related to my experience in the Gulf. She mentioned how I would talk in my sleep about dead bodies but was too afraid to ask me about it knowing I'd been to war. I told her that they started about six months after the war ended and got progressively worse during her absence leading me to drink more than I ever did. She strongly encouraged me to speak to someone about the problem, but I dismissed the idea and said, "I volunteered to go, I knew what I was getting in to. I'm not gonna go crying to some doctor about bad dreams." I was more concerned about starting my new job and getting on with my life.

Following my graduation from the Corrections Academy in February I received amazing news. I was going to be a father! Toni told me that she was six weeks pregnant and that she was due in August. I immediately began thinking of names for the baby although we didn't know the sex yet because both of us wanted the surprise. Of course, I was hoping for a boy, as neither of my brothers had any children, and I wanted to pass on my family name. Toni told me to only tell immediate family until we were sure everything was okay. The nightmare of December was now a distant memory, and I could now resume the life I always imagined for myself. I graduated from the Corrections Academy at the top of my class and received an assignment at the Kentucky Correctional Institution for Women.

# Chapter 23
# The Stepmother Murder

KCIW was the only women's prison in the state. Located in Shelby County near the town of Pee Wee Valley, it housed over five hundred inmates who were doing time for charges ranging from writing bad checks to murder. Following my three weeks of training at the academy, I had to complete another three weeks of on-the-job training at the prison working alongside a veteran officer. The prison consisted of multiple housing units including a building located outside of the front gate that housed about fifteen non-violent short-timers. The main building was where most of the inmates lived military style including the most violent inmates. Some were on death row. The prison had another large housing unit which accommodated the inmates who were serving long sentences but considered low risk. The women in these units had their own private rooms and were allowed televisions, refrigerators, and microwave ovens.

As soon as I arrived at the prison I became quite popular with the inmates. They were intrigued with my long Italian last name and thick New York accent. The fact that I was in great shape didn't hurt either. I did, however, experience what many women go through every day with the inmates whistling at me or making crude, sexually suggestive comments. The officer who was training me told me that the only way to get them to stop is to write them up, as making inappropriate comments to an officer is punishable by time in segregation or the "hole." He also told me that I had to establish right away which type of officer I would be; the kind the inmates hated after writing them up for every little infraction or the laid-back friendly guard. Knowing that I would bolt from this job as soon as another department called me I decided to be the nice guard. It was more my personality and made the job a lot easier.

Following my three-week apprenticeship, they gave me a badge, and I was now eligible to work at any housing unit without direct supervision. The inmates immediately tested me to see what they could get away with. As a new officer, I was still on probation, so I made sure that the girls followed most of the rules. The difference was in the way I let them talk to me unless it got too aggressive or vulgar. I wasn't going to write up someone for profanity when I cursed on a regular basis. I also didn't mind when the girls flirted with me or made sexual comments. I enjoyed it. But when they would proposition me, which they often did, I would hold up my hand showing my wedding ring and tell them I was happily married.

Things at home couldn't have been better. Toni and I were getting along just as we did prior to her leaving as if nothing had happened. She was now about eleven weeks pregnant, and we started to think about where we might live permanently. I loved living in Kentucky especially since the cost of living was considerably less than what I was used to back East. I started the process of using my Veterans Administration loan to purchase a home, and Toni and I would drive around Louisville looking for the perfect neighborhood. We looked at some great properties that were affordable in Kentucky but would've been a pipe dream in New Jersey. Our troubles seemed far behind us, and our future looked extremely promising. Then I received the phone call that would change everything.

About an hour into my midnight shift at the prison my supervisor called me to the main office and told me I had an emergency phone call. I somehow knew that it involved my wife and sprinted as fast as I could from the unit I was working at. When I got to the phone Toni's mother told me that Toni had experienced some vaginal bleeding and was at the local hospital. I got to the hospital as fast as I could and found Toni lying in the hospital bed crying hysterically. She had suffered a miscarriage. As disappointed as I was about losing the child, I was relieved that Toni was okay. She was extremely distraught, and I tried to console her the best I could. I assured her that everything would be okay and that we could try to have a baby again soon. Following her discharge later that morning I took Toni home. She didn't say two words during the car ride home so I made her a cocktail to calm her down. She finally fell asleep but was never the same after that night.

Toni was obviously quite upset and didn't say much to me in the days following the miscarriage. I was equally upset, but tried to be strong for her. I thought it best to give her a few days to herself, but when a week had passed and she was still acting very distant I confronted her about it. "Toni, we can't live like this. We need to move on. You're only twenty-one. You can have all the kids you want," I calmly assured her. She became agitated and snapped back, "It's not just about the baby." I immediately sensed what was coming next. "Everything is different now," she replied. "I'm not sure if I still want to be married." As much as those words felt like a knife piercing my heart, I didn't show any emotion. "If you wanna leave me then just go now," I flatly stated. She went into the bedroom and grabbed a bunch of things before walking out. I knew right then and there that my marriage was over for good.

This time I wasn't only depressed, I was embarrassed and angry. I was angry with myself for getting married to someone I hardly knew. I felt that I was duped by a BAQ bandit who never liked the fact that I had left the service. I was embarrassed that my marriage had lasted less than five months, and I wasn't looking forward to the "I told you so" from my sister. My parents were supportive, although I knew my father was upset as he was a devout Catholic and divorce usually wasn't an option. My mother wanted me to move back to New Jersey, but I was too embarrassed to return home a failure. I decided to stay in Kentucky as I had a good job and was still hoping to be called by another department. I also wanted to stay in Louisville because as angry as I was at Toni for leaving, I realized that I was still madly in love with her and held onto the slightest hope that she would come back to me.

I tried calling her at her mom's a few times, but she wouldn't take my calls. I even went to her mom's house to try and talk to her, but she refused. I couldn't understand how I became the bad guy as if I'd done something horrible to her. I was miffed and began drinking heavily again. Not wanting to wallow in my sorrows at home like the last time, I began hanging out in the local bars. Other than going to the gym, it seemed that I spent all my free time drinking which usually led to a one-night stand. Within weeks I found myself going to the gym less and less and drinking four and five nights a week. I was spending all my money at the bars, and sometimes I used my badge to persuade the manager to run me a tab until payday. As my drinking got worse so did my nightmares about the mutilated burnt corpses. One night I scared the hell out of some girl I brought home from the bar when I woke up screaming and yelling about dead bodies.

It was obvious to everyone at work that something was wrong with me. I wasn't my usual talkative self and began distancing myself from the other guards. The inmates, who have nothing better to do than to observe the guards, immediately noticed that I was no longer wearing a wedding ring, and I was propositioned more than ever. I was tempted with some of the cuter ones there for minor offenses, but as lonely and depressed as I was I knew that the only thing I had in Kentucky was my job, and I couldn't risk it. I enjoyed talking with some of them since I had no one to talk to at home, and I began to get very friendly with one inmate who was a cute country girl who reminded me of Toni. I started to have feelings for this girl, as misguided as they were, and during one shift I did the worst thing a correction officer could do. When the girls were required to return to their beds for the count, I told her to stay behind and be the last to leave. I took her in the bathroom and made out with her for about thirty seconds before she had to get back.

This went on for about a week until they stopped assigning me to her dorm. There weren't any cameras in the trailer where the common area was, but there's always someone watching every move you make, and I'm sure that someone reported us. Since inmates regularly accuse guards of wrongdoing whether real or not, the warden can't punish the officer without concrete evidence which usually meant being on camera. They began assigning me to the yard where I had contact with inmates from all over the prison, some of whom I had never seen before. Although most of the women in this prison were undesirable, to say the least, there were a few who were cute, and I found myself flirting with them.

I knew if they caught me I would be fired immediately, and they could charge me criminally if there was any sexual contact with the inmates. After a while, I didn't care. My depression deepened, and I was self-medicating with alcohol almost every night as my nightmares continued to worsen. The thought of losing my job now meant nothing to me because I knew that without a reason to stay, I'd eventually leave Kentucky. During one shift on the yard when I was really feeling depressed, an inmate must have noticed something wrong and approached me.

Her name was Stephanie Spitser. She was tall, thin and stunningly beautiful with long brown hair, brown eyes, and a pleasant smile.

Although I had noticed her on the yard a few times, we had never had contact with each other as she lived in one of the lifer dorms. She said in a sweet subtle voice, and a slight Kentucky drawl, "You're too cute to look so sad." I told her flat out that she was gorgeous, and I thanked her for her concern. Then she said, "Word on the yard is that your wife left you. That's her loss. If you ever want to talk I have a good ear." I could tell right away by the way she spoke that she was educated and thought to myself, "What is this girl doing here?"

Since correction officers don't have access to inmate records, the only way to find out what an inmate was in for was to ask them since the rumor mill was unreliable. Discussing an inmate's record is against regulations, so you had to be careful of who you asked. The only other officers that I trusted were the ones I went to the academy with, and they knew about as much as I did. I couldn't stop thinking about Stephanie and became obsessed with trying to find out why she was there. From talking to other inmates all I could piece together was that Stephanie was doing life for murder but was appealing her conviction. It was hard to get information from the inmates because they didn't trust us and didn't want to be looked upon as snitches. There had been a recent news story out about a dozen women in Kentucky who were waiting on a court decision on whether they'd be released from prison, having murdered their abusers. Thinking that Stephanie was one of those inmates I felt sorry for her even though she did murder someone. A few days after meeting her in the yard they assigned me to her unit for the first time and was I looking forward to seeing her.

I had never worked the lifer unit before, and it was a little more relaxed than the other units. The building consisted of two floors with a command post and a common area on the first floor. There were dorm rooms on both floors, and each inmate had their own room with a door. When I arrived for my shift at the unit, Stephanie immediately came over to say hello. She was extremely flirty which made me a little uncomfortable around the other guards. I tried to play it off as if I was annoyed, but I loved every minute of it. After dinner, the inmates were allowed several hours to hang out in the common area before lights out, and Stephanie spent most of the time talking to me. I was hesitant to answer any of her questions, but soon fell victim to her beautiful face and sweet voice and began discussing my failed marriage. We talked for over three hours, and when the girls went to their bunks for lights out, one of the female officers said to me, "You better be careful with Spitser, there were two guards fired over her." I didn't give a shit.

Over the next few days, Stephanie would come speak to me whenever I was working on the yard. She became very flirtatious and told me that she thought about me all the time. She said that when she got out she'd love to be my girlfriend which I thought was strange since she was doing twenty-five years to life. Although she wasn't eligible for parole until 2017, she was convinced that she was getting out early on appeal. I knew deep down that it was crazy to think I could have a relationship with a convicted murderer, but I couldn't stop thinking about her. Seeing her was the only thing I looked forward to every day and I missed her on my days off. I had become so intrigued with her that I would go out of my way to see her whenever possible.

The next time I worked at her dorm we spoke for hours, and she told me that she had something for me during the count. I began counting the girls in their rooms through the glass window on their door, and when I got to Stephanie's room and looked through her window I just stood there with my mouth open. Stephanie was lying on her bed completely naked, rubbing her breasts with one hand, and her vagina with the other. As much as I wanted to stand there and stare at her I had to finish my count. The next time I worked in her dorm she decided to take it a step further, and I was more than game.

During the shift the officers on the dorm are required to do walkthroughs around the building, including the bathroom and shower stalls when they weren't in use. Since there were no cameras in the bathrooms, Stephanie told me that when I went to do my walkthrough she would be in the last shower stall waiting for me. When I walked in the bathroom she was standing up against the wall wearing an oversized t-shirt, looking like an innocent schoolgirl who was about to do something very naughty. I walked over to her, and without hesitation, began passionately making out with her with my hands underneath her shirt and all over her shapely body. Noticing her vagina was soaking wet I pulled out my penis through my uniform pants and was about to have sex with her.

Hearing a noise, we both panicked, and I immediately fixed my pants and left the stall, instructing her to wait for a few minutes. I checked myself in the mirror before walking out and continued my walkthrough. After a few minutes, Stephanie left the bathroom and went back to her room. We tried a few more times over the next few weeks, but we never had intercourse as I always got too paranoid. I was sure that nobody saw us in the bathroom together but would find out later that during one of our make-out sessions there was another inmate who was in the toilet and heard everything. It soon became obvious not only to the inmates but also to my supervisors that Stephanie and I were getting a little too cozy with each other. They soon stopped assigning me to work in her dorm.

I was still able to see her whenever I worked the yard but couldn't talk to her much since I knew they were watching me. Whenever she would pass by me she would smile, and either wink or blow a kiss at me. One afternoon on her way back to her dorm, she told me that she missed me and I should write to her using a phony name. I bought some corny Hallmark cards and wrote her a note in each one. Since the prison wouldn't accept mail without a return address, I used the name Chris Roberts and a random address in Louisville.

In the letter, I gave her my real address, and within a week we began corresponding by mail.

In one of my first letters to her, I asked her about her crime since she never discussed it with me. She did mention on a few occasions that her husband used to viciously beat her up. As I got to know Stephanie better I couldn't imagine that she would be able to murder another human being in cold blood. I had no reason not to believe her when she had told me she had been abused by her husband. A few days later I received a seven-page letter from Stephanie, in which she poured out her heart and explained everything to me, including the details of the murder she had committed. I had a hard time following the letter as it became extremely confusing.

She began the letter by telling me how she thought about me all the time, that she had strong feelings for me, and that she was hoping we could get together when she was released. She then began to describe the relationship with her second husband, Donnie. He was about fifteen years older than her and had a young son from a previous marriage. According to Stephanie, her husband was extremely jealous and wouldn't let her go out of the house without him. He made her quit college and her job and forbid her to associate with any of her old friends. She accused him of beating her as if he was fighting another man and claimed to be black and blue all the time. She told me that when she attempted to leave and return to her first husband, he tracked her down a few weeks later and dragged her back to the car threatening to kill her and her family if she didn't go back with him. When the divorce papers that she had filed a few weeks earlier came in the mail, she claims her husband beat her to a pulp and made her eat the papers.

She went on to tell me that her best friend Susie suggested that they kill Donnie. According to her, she was "afraid that he wouldn't die and then he'd kill us both," which sounded strange to me. She then wrote that two days before the crime she took a pregnancy test, which came back positive, but claims that the baby belonged to her first husband and not Donnie. She said that when she told Donnie about the baby, he freaked out and forced Stephanie to start calling abortion clinics or he would make sure that the baby didn't live. That's when the letter became very confusing as she went from plotting to kill her husband to picking up his ten-year-old son from school with her friend Susie. Then she described the murder in detail, and after reading it several times I finally pieced it together. I got sick from what I read. She wrote:

> On the way home, I mentioned to him that I was gonna have a baby. I had hoped he would be excited about it and maybe that would change Donnie's mind. Well, he wasn't happy, he was angry and wanted to go back to his house at his grandma's. He was upset and reached for the door handle. My co-defendant was driving, and he was upfront with her. She grabbed him by the collar and started screaming at me to grab him before he made her wreck. At that point, I don't know what happened. My mind just snapped, and I knew what I had to do to get away from him (Donnie) forever. Susie screamed, "Kill him Steph! I'll go with you!" It was all over before I even realized anything. It was like I was watching someone else do it.

She didn't murder her husband. She strangled her ten-year-old stepson to death in the car that day. What had confused me was that Stephanie placed Donnie's name in parenthesis when she wrote that she "knew that she had to get away from 'him.'" Although she tried to make it look like she was referring to Donnie after writing the sentence, since it was in small letters above the word "him," it was obvious to me that she was referring to his son and wanted the child out of the picture.

Mortified and disgusted by what I had read I wanted to make sure that I was reading the letter correctly. I had recently found out about this new thing called the internet where you could search for information on almost any topic. Since I didn't own a computer I went to the local library. I did a search on Stephanie Spitser, but nothing came up. I then started to search the local newspaper archives looking for any stories dealing with the murder of a child. To my horror, I found a newspaper article about two girls who murdered a ten-year-old boy and then tried to cover up the crime by burning the body in a deserted area. Right next to the article was a picture of the two girls charged with the crime. One of the girls was Stephanie Baker, who after the trial went back to using her maiden name of Spitser. In almost every story that I read, it stated that Stephanie killed her stepson because she was jealous of his relationship with his father and wanted her husband all for herself. Never once did they mention any abuse by her ex-husband.

What I couldn't understand was why nobody ever mentioned that she had killed a child, especially since it was such a high-profile case. When I called a friend who worked with me at the prison and asked him about Spitser, he was surprised that I didn't know anything about her case since it was all over the news. It turns out that the murder and trial had occurred while I was in Germany, and I never once heard about it even though it had become a national story. I guess everyone just assumed that it was common knowledge, and never really discussed it since it was against regulations to do so. Now that I knew that Stephanie was a child killer I refused to look at her the next day at work. Once she realized I didn't want anything to do with her anymore, she decided to bring me down.

Towards the end of my shift, I heard over the radio that they were bringing Stephanie Spitser to the warden's office. She must have spilled the beans about us because when I showed up for work the next day, they assigned me to guard the septic tank, which meant

I was in trouble and couldn't be around inmates. I really didn't care about the job, as I was more upset that I was stupid enough to let a conniving child killer seduce me, and that I had feelings for such a person. Not wanting to deal with all the nonsense at work I resigned the next day but was too embarrassed to see anyone so I didn't even bother to do it in person. I dropped off my uniforms and badge with the officer at the front gate and left the Kentucky Correctional Institution for Women for the last time.

My troubles were far from over as the guilt I felt from getting involved with Spitser just added to the misery of my divorce. On top of that, I was still having nightmares about the war, which were happening more frequently. I was running out of money, but was able to run a few tabs at the bars since they thought I was a still cop. After waking up from a disturbing nightmare I'd start drinking from the moment I woke up which I'd never done before. After polishing off half a bottle of vodka I decided to go to one of the bars in Louisville where I still had credit. I got so drunk that the bartender refused to serve me anymore and tried to keep me from leaving in my car. I don't remember how I did it, but I was able to sneak away and get to my car. I woke up the next morning with no knowledge of how I had gotten home.

The fact that I couldn't remember how I drove home really scared me, especially since I could have killed someone. Looking to hear a familiar voice I called my friend Robby in New York and told him what was going on. The first thing out of his mouth was, "What the fuck are you still doing there?" That must have hit a chord with me because as soon as I hung up with him I called my mother and asked her to lend me money to come home. She wired me two thousand dollars which I used to rent a U-Haul truck. I was all ready to leave, but still had one of the cats that Toni left with me. I asked everyone in the complex if anyone wanted her, but nobody obliged. Not wanting to abandon the cat I put her in the cab of the truck and left Kentucky for good. During the seventeen-hour trip to New Jersey the cat sat on my shoulder and didn't budge. I had her for seventeen years.

# Chapter 24
# A Deathbed Promise

I returned to New Jersey in July 1996, and along with my feline friend moved into the spare bedroom in my parents' condominium. The move must have had a cleansing effect on me as I stayed home the first week and didn't go out drinking. Just being away from Kentucky and back home with my family took me out of my deep depression. I spent that week working out and considering what I might do for the rest of my life. I knew that I had to stop or at least curtail my drinking, or eventually I'd end up right back where I started. What I really wanted to do was work for my brother Warren, either as his assistant or possibly in a security position. Working with my brother was something I thought a lot about, and I'd always dreamed about going on tour with him ever since his Missing Persons days.

Duran Duran's popularity had waned since their last hits, and the band was coming off a disastrous covers album. With no tour scheduled Warren was unable to give me a job, so I needed to look elsewhere. The only skills I had other than defusing landmines was making cocktails, and soon found a job as a bartender in a local restaurant. Working around alcohol wasn't a problem as the bartenders couldn't drink on the job, so I decided to work as much as possible, requesting a six-day work week. I wasn't drinking as heavily as I had been in Kentucky but would still have a few drinks on my day off. My goal was to work as much as possible so I'd be able to save enough money to secure my own apartment. Within six weeks I had the cash and told my parents I'd be moving out soon. It was then that my mother gave me the worst news of my life.

My father was dying from prostate cancer. They had known about it for a few weeks but were waiting on a second opinion. The doctors gave my father anywhere from two to five years to live. They said that with chemotherapy they might be able to prolong his life, but the cancer had spread too far and was inoperable. As I was crying uncontrollably and barely able to speak, my father asked me not to move out. I agreed. When I asked if the rest of the family knew, they told me I was the last one told as my mother didn't want to break the news over the phone. As the weight of my father's illness started to sink in, I began to see my divorce as a blessing. I was still distraught that my marriage had ended, but felt that fate had brought me back home to be with my father.

The news of my father's impending death was devastating and the thought of him not being around anymore was too much for me to handle. Combined with my divorce and my recurring nightmares I had become an emotional wreck. Whenever I was off I spent as much time with my father as I could, as he was getting weaker from the chemo and spent most of his time at home. But as soon as he'd fall asleep I'd leave and head straight to the bar to get shit-faced drunk. I was driving home extremely intoxicated, and sometimes had no memory of how I made it back. Watching my father deteriorate from cancer was chipping away at me, and I soon began to fall into a deep state of depression. I decided to deal with it the only way I knew how.

I called out of work on a Friday night infuriating my boss and used some of the money that I had saved up for an apartment to party my ass off. I started the night at a local pub and became friendly with a group of younger guys who were sitting next to me at the bar. After doing several shots with them, one of the guys asked me if I did cocaine. I hadn't done coke since my bachelor party over ten months ago, and before that, it had been over two years. I was extremely intoxicated and immediately said yes. One of them brought me into the bathroom, and both of us went inside a stall. He took out a small plastic bag filled with coke and poured some on my hand so I could snort it. I continued to drink with these guys for hours while they kept feeding me lines. When the club closed at 2 am I was still wired out of my mind and had no intention of going home. Not only did I want to do more cocaine, I wanted to have sex.

With no female prospects in the bar, I decided to drive to an area in Long Branch where I had seen prostitutes working. Whenever I would drive home from work late at night I would see girls on Joline Avenue waving to all the men who drove by. Within minutes of arriving in the area, I spotted a delicate, light-skinned black girl who must have been in her mid-twenties. She waved at me as soon as I came into view. I pulled over to let her in my car and immediately noticed an eerie resemblance to the Puerto Rican crack whore that I used to get high with in Canarsie. I asked her if she knew where to get some coke, and if she wanted to go to a motel. She told me she could get crack but didn't know anyone who sold powder. She also said we could smoke there and didn't need a room. As much as I was still afraid to smoke crack I was drunk and horny enough to agree.

She took me to an apartment complex in the worst part of Long Branch where we parked my car and had to walk to the other side of the building. As soon as we turned the corner towards the apartment we ran into a gang of about twenty black and Spanish men in their early twenties who looked shocked to see a white person walking through their complex at two o'clock in the morning. I thought for sure I was going to die, and decided that I had nothing to lose, so I tried to give them the impression that I was an off-duty cop since I still looked like one. One of the Spanish guys came walking directly at me and began yelling, "What the fuck are you doing here white boy?" I calmly placed my hand inside my jacket, which froze him for a second, and said in a loud confident voice, "I got no beef with you guys; I'm not working right now. I'm just trying to get laid," as I pointed to the black girl who was trying to usher me away. When the Spanish guy continued towards me, obviously not afraid of my imaginary gun, I thought the only way I could get out of this was to knock him over and run to my car. Before I could even react, something miraculous happened.

Out of nowhere one of the guys in the crowd sucker punched another guy who was standing right next to him, turning everyone's attention away from me and towards the fight. In the ensuing commotion, the prostitute grabbed my arm and pulled me away. As we were walking into the apartment the Spanish guy who had gotten in my face was still yelling that he was going to kill me for disrespecting him. Just as we safely got inside the apartment, he yelled out, "I'm going to be here when you get out mother fucker, you're dead." I could have easily fought this man since he wasn't very big, but he was still with four of his friends and knew I had no chance. I decided to wait it out hoping they'd eventually leave.

When the black girl asked me for the money to get the drugs, I reluctantly gave it to her, as the incident had sobered me up. All I could think about was getting out of that complex alive. As the girl and her friend were smoking crack, I sat on the couch convinced there was no way out, and that eventually I'd have to leave. After about an hour or so I couldn't take the waiting anymore and knew that the only way I was going to get to my car safely was to get the police to escort me. The only problem was that my companions were smoking crack in the house, and although I hadn't smoked any, I didn't want to risk arrest. When I went to use the second-floor bathroom, I looked out the window and saw the Spanish guy and his friends still sitting outside. I called the Long Branch police department from the bathroom using my new cell phone that I had just gotten two days earlier.

I told the officer on the phone where I was and that there were people waiting outside looking to harm to me. Without telling the girls that I had called the police, I went downstairs to wait for them. When a police officer knocked on the door about ten minutes later I immediately jumped up and answered the door to keep the officer from coming inside. The girl who lived there almost had a heart attack when she saw the cop through the window and scurried to hide any evidence of drugs. When I walked outside I showed the officer my retired military ID card and told him who I was. Instead of the friendly response that I thought being military would get me, the officer seemed to be angry with me, wanting to know why I was there. He began to chastise me saying that I didn't belong there and was risking my life just being in the complex that late at night. When I tried to lie and explain that I was just trying to get laid with a girl I met in a bar, the officer replied, "You're lucky they didn't break into the house and kill you." With that image running through my head, the officer walked me to my car and I was finally able to leave.

If there was anything positive that happened that night, it was that I never smoked any crack. The incident kept me from going back into that neighborhood, but it didn't keep me from drinking. I was coming to work on my morning shifts hungover and smelling like alcohol. Instead of firing me my boss changed my schedule giving me most of the slower shifts as a punishment. As soon as he posted the changes, I became extremely belligerent with him and told him to go fuck himself. I turned around and walked out right in the middle of my shift. Not wanting to worry my parents, when I returned home I made up some excuse about reading the schedule wrong. I had quit my job a month before Christmas, and with my money dwindling I couldn't go out much. That was also a blessing as I got to spend more time with my dying father.

By Thanksgiving, it was obvious that my father had only days to live. He was a shell of his former self, having dropped from over 200 pounds to about 125. He was too weak to leave his bed and had a full-time nurse taking care of him during his final weeks. Jerry, Stephanie and I would take turns sitting with our father and keeping him company in his final days. Warren was on tour and said he was unable to leave which angered me as I felt that our father was much more important than any concert. My father was drugged up from the morphine patch he was wearing, but he would occasionally wake up looking to talk. A few days before he died, as I was sitting alongside his bed, he gently grabbed my hand and in a barely audible voice asked me to make him a promise.

He wanted me to assure him that one day I would have a son to carry on the family name. He knew that Warren and Jerry didn't intend on having any children, and although my sister had two young girls they would never be able to pass on the Cuccurullo name. My father reminded me of the story of how *his* father had decided to come back into his life after originally abandoning him because he knew that his son was the only hope to continue the family name. I reminded my father that I didn't have a girlfriend and wasn't planning to have kids anytime soon. Before he nodded off he squeezed my hand as hard as he could and just said, "Please, have a son for me." "I will Dad, I promise," I assured him as he fell asleep.

Jerald "Gennaro" Cuccurullo passed away from prostate cancer on December 5, 1997 at the age of 63. The night before the funeral my friend Robby came down to New Jersey to spend a few days with me and kept me from going on another bender. I was besieged by grief, and also furious that Warren never made it to the funeral. As they brought my father's casket into the church the organist was playing the most beautiful version of Ordinary World, which was his favorite song. After my father's friend Dennis eulogized him, all my immediate family members placed a memento into his casket. I left him a stack of my military ribbons, which were not only my prized possessions, but represented the moment in my life when I gained my father's respect.

# Chapter 25
# Come Undone

I may have been miserable inside, but as a bartender I was quite adept at putting on a good front. I got a new job at a place called Redheads in Eatontown, New Jersey and was soon working all the busiest shifts and making a thousand dollars a week. Unfortunately, I was spending it as fast as I was making it. As I got to know more people in the bar business, I soon had several cocaine connections, and they'd deliver it to me at the bar. I didn't do coke while I worked, but the second the last customer left I went right to the bathroom to do a few lines. We were allowed a drink or two while we cleaned but had to leave when the manager did. The bars were closed by the time we got off, so we'd go across the street to the Holiday Inn and drink in the lobby for hours with the bar staff of the hotel, doing lines until we ran out. I spent my off days partying at the Headliner nightclub, being the big shot and buying everyone drinks. I no longer had to resort to picking up prostitutes, as there were always girls in the bar looking to hang and party.

Several weeks after my father's death I met a girl named Joanne at the bar who wanted me to come back to her house after my shift.

As usual, I did a few lines and had a few drinks before I left and arrived at her house high as a kite and horny as hell. After polishing off a half bottle of Jack Daniel's we went to her bedroom to have sex. As drunk as I was I realized I didn't have any condoms, and I told her just to give me a blowjob. She said she was on the pill, and even showed them to me, and we proceeded to have unprotected sex. I went over her house a few more times over the next few weeks, but suddenly stopped seeing her in the bar. I called her up to see if everything was okay, and she told me that she wasn't interested in seeing me anymore. Then she told me that she was pregnant and that I was the father.

She got angry when I asked, "Are you sure it's mine?" and assured me I was the only one she was sleeping with. "Wait…aren't you on the pill?" I asked. "They're not foolproof, you can still get pregnant," she shot back. When she informed me that she was four weeks pregnant I realized it was possible but couldn't know for sure if she'd slept with anyone else. I told her that I would obviously want to take a paternity test. She understood. She said I could either hang up the phone and never talk to her again, or I could be involved in the baby's life and help raise it. Without hesitation, I said that I would never abandon any child that was mine, and quickly agreed to her second option thinking of my father and the promise I'd made to him. She said she would keep me posted on her developments, and that we would eventually work out an agreement. When I asked her if she knew the baby's gender she told me that she didn't and that she had no intention of finding out before the baby was born. A few weeks later she called and told me that she was going to give the baby her last name.

I became livid and started freaking out. "You fuckin' bitch!" I screamed. "You can't fuckin' do that! No son of mine is gonna have an Irish last name!" She snapped back in a nasty tone, "You don't know it's going to be a boy." I continued to argue with her about it until she finally said, "I'll call you in a few weeks," and hung up. The thought of my son having a different last name began to consume me, and I even began hoping for a girl. I even contemplated asking her to marry me even though I had no feelings for her. When I casually brought up the idea when we spoke next, she immediately shot it down saying, "I don't need a husband." As the weeks went by I grew deeper into depression, and my drinking and cocaine habit worsened.

This wasn't how I wanted to have a child. I didn't just want my kid to have my name, I wanted to be part of a family, and raise the child full time. I was supposed to be excited about becoming a father, but instead, I was miserable. Four months after getting Joanne pregnant I began bartending at a new club called Jersey Girls that my boss had just opened. I was making double the money I was making at the other bar, but the routine stayed the same. With my boss out of the club most nights, I began doing coke during my shift and doing shots with the customers. By the end of the shift, I was so plastered that I did more coke and drank in the bar until the sun came up. The place was always packed with women, and I usually had no problem hooking up. During one shift an attractive girl came to the bar, introduced herself as Melanie, and asked me directly if I dated black girls. I told her that I dated all girls, and we soon began going out. After a few weeks, I really started to like her and decided to tell her about my impending fatherhood. She was very understanding, and to my surprise, still wanted to date.

Melanie was multi-ethnic, and ten years younger than me. She was well educated and had a three-year-old son with her ex-husband whom she had recently divorced. She smoked pot with me on occasion but had mentioned when I first met her that she despised hard drugs. That turned out to be a good thing because when I was with her, which was several times a week, I stayed away from cocaine. When we started sleeping together I always used a condom even though she didn't insist on it. After a night of drinking and doing cocaine, I knocked on her window at 3 am looking to get laid.

We tiptoed past her sleeping son and had sex in her bedroom. I was so high that the thought of using a condom never entered my mind. Three weeks later Melanie informed me that she was pregnant.

She seemed happy about it and told me she intended to keep the baby even though I encouraged her to have an abortion. I was in complete shock, and kept saying to myself, "This isn't happening." I denied the child was mine, but deep down I knew it was. I soon became withdrawn from everyone including Melanie and continued to drink heavily and snort cocaine. She called and left a message telling me she would give the child my last name, and that she wanted to stay in a relationship with me. She was offering me a chance at the life I was looking for, and the possibility of having a son to pass on my name, but the embarrassment of fathering two children with two different women within four months was too overwhelming. As word spread around the bar I denied to everyone that the child was mine, and I stopped talking to Melanie altogether.

In early October 1998 I got a call from Joanne telling me that she was due in a few weeks, but three days later she called me and said they were going to induce labor. She said I could be there, but not in the delivery room which infuriated me as her friend was allowed instead. As I waited outside the delivery room with my mother, Joanne gave birth to a beautiful healthy girl, which was a relief even though I still wanted her to have my last name. Following the birth Joanne allowed me to come over to her house and bond with the baby for a few hours each week. I was still spending my money like a drunken sailor but made enough to give Joanne money every week. I guess Melanie found out through the grapevine that my daughter had been born, and since I refused to return her calls, she came to my job.

It was Halloween night, and Melanie came to the bar dressed as a nun who was six months pregnant. She went around the bar telling everyone that I was the father and that I just had a baby with another woman. I had people I knew coming up to me and asking, "Did you get two girls pregnant at the same time?" I denied it. I told everyone she was delusional and that I wasn't the father. I was so humiliated and embarrassed that I felt like everyone in the bar was looking at me and talking behind my back. I started doing shot after shot and polished off the half of gram of cocaine I had for after work before the bar closed. After my shift I was so drunk, I wanted to do more cocaine, so I went to the only place I knew where I could get some. I drove to Long Branch and picked up a prostitute on Joline Ave, who took me back to the same apartment complex where I was almost killed months earlier. She took me into an apartment with complete strangers, and I smoked crack for the first time in seven years.

I woke up the next day severely depressed. I couldn't believe I had gone back to that apartment complex, and to add gasoline to the fire, smoked crack. It was too much for me to handle and I felt like my head was going to explode. I still wasn't over my father's death, and no matter how much pot I smoked I still couldn't shake the nightmares from the war. It seemed that every dream I had involved charred bodies and body parts. I had dreams that started off normal, and suddenly the person I was talking to was burnt to a crisp and still having a normal conversation. I had other nightmares where I would be helping the charred woman and her baby out of the wreckage, and they would fall apart as I picked them up. It got to a point where I didn't want to go to sleep, and I was becoming easily agitated and short-tempered with everyone at work. One day I came in late for my shift, and my boss started reaming me out in front of the other employees. I got so angry that I started yelling back at him. He yelled back, "One more word and you're fired!" Seething in anger I just looked at him and yelled," Go fuck yourself!" and walked out.

Now that I was unemployed I decided to use my rare Saturday night off and go to the other bar where I used to work. I got to the bar early, so I could eat dinner before the restaurant transformed into a club. As soon as I walked in many of my old customers greeted me warmly as they hadn't seen me in months, and everyone wanted to buy me a shot. I instantly got the cocaine itch and started looking around the bar for some. I saw the guy who used to sell me cocaine, but he was dealing ecstasy now, which I had never done before. I was hesitant at first, but when he told me the drug was much better than cocaine I decided to do it. He said the drug also made you drink more as it dehydrated you, so I thought I should eat before it kicked in.

I had planned on eating at the bar, but a girl who I knew invited me to sit with her and her friend in the restaurant. Halfway through my meal, I started to feel the effects of the Ecstasy, which gave me a warm fuzzy feeling, and I couldn't stop smiling. It felt like mescaline without the paranoia and was a hundred times better than cocaine ever made me feel. As the crowd got larger former customers kept coming over to my table to say hello, and I felt like a mafia don. I was having what felt like the greatest night ever, and I didn't have a care in the world. I didn't think about my father or getting two girls pregnant, or those fucking charred bodies that haunted my nights. No longer hungry I pushed my dinner to the side and started drinking again. Along with my two companions, I got up to use the bathroom. As I was walking back to my table I noticed that the girls hadn't come back yet, and to my amazement, there was a strange guy sitting in my chair.

He was a Hispanic male in his early twenties and even sitting down I could tell he was a big guy. As I stood over him, he seemed as if he was purposely ignoring me as I politely told him he was sitting in my seat. When he didn't respond at all I tapped him on the shoulder and said to him in a friendly tone, "Excuse me pal, you're sitting in my chair." He looked up at me laughing and said, "Go find another seat." My good mood soon turned to anger, and I said in a more forceful voice, "This is my table guy, that's my unfinished dinner you're sitting in front of, and those are my cigarettes and car keys next to you." He totally ignored me and made as if I wasn't even standing there, laughing and bouncing in the chair. When I looked up I noticed his two friends standing next to him laughing hysterically and looking right at me. My anger turned to rage, and I started breathing heavily anticipating a fight. Then I just snapped.

I slammed the beer bottle that I was holding across the side of his face as hard as I could while blood splattered all over me. He tried to get up but instantly fell backward into the chair. Within seconds I felt someone punch me right in the mouth, and as I covered up my face I felt another three or four punches hit me. With that, the head bouncer who knew me pulled me out of the ruckus and into a safe area. I remember yelling repeatedly, "I was hit, I was hit, somebody punched me," as if I was already trying to cover up what I had done. With the bar still in chaos, I decided to sneak out the side door and leave before the police arrived. I got in my car and drove home thinking I had gotten away with it. A few hours later a cop from the Eatontown Police Department came to my house to question me. He immediately noticed the blood all over my shirt that I foolishly forgot to take off, and he had no choice but to arrest me.

I was charged with Assault with a Deadly Weapon, a felony punishable by up to eight years in prison. My bail was set at $25,000, and I was denied the ten percent option as the guy I hit was hurt badly. Luckily, I had a friend who agreed to put up his house as my bail, as I didn't want to ask my mother. I found out later that the guy I hit received thirty-six stitches to close the gash on his face, but there was no permanent damage. That guy may have been an asshole, but he didn't deserve what I did to him. I don't recall if I made a conscious decision to hit him with the bottle, but I think if I wasn't holding it I might have just punched him. I was beside myself and re-played the incident in my head for days after it happened. It eerily reminded me of the time Robby and I beat up that guy in Canarsie. In both instances, my demeanor turned from friendly to extremely violent in a matter of seconds. Besides my excessive drinking and raging cocaine habit, I knew there was something going on in my head that I didn't understand.

Since I was a first-time offender I was eligible for Pre-Trial Intervention or PTI, which would keep me out of jail, and eventually be expunged from my record. The conditions of PTI were that I plead no contest and that I perform seventy-five hours of community service. I was also required to attend anger management counseling once a week for eight weeks which was run by a Catholic charity. I thought it was a waste of time, but it turned out to be quite the opposite, as talking about my problems with the group seemed to have a healing effect. I seemed to do most of the talking as the group seemed to enjoy my stories. During my last session, I began telling them about an adventure I had while serving in the war. Suddenly I flashed back to the carnage and began sobbing uncontrollably, unable to finish the story. Following the session, the counselor suggested I go to the VA, as he believed I suffered from Post-Traumatic Stress Disorder.

In the weeks following the incident, I stayed far away from the bars and the cocaine. I was afraid to drink thinking I could snap again and was unemployed and broke anyway. I did smoke pot to help me sleep and began working out again to keep me busy. After making an appointment with the VA psychiatrist I decided to call Melanie as she was due to give birth to my child in about a month. I hadn't spoken to her in months and wasn't sure she would take my call. I left her a long message telling her I was sorry, and that I wanted nothing more than to be a part of my child's life. I also admitted I had a drug problem, and mentioned I was getting help for my PTSD. She never responded.

During my first session with the doctor, we talked about my service during Desert Storm. I was under the impression that only soldiers who experienced heavy combat suffered from PTSD, but the doctor informed me that individuals who witness terrifying or horrific scenes are also prone to the mental illness. Without treatment, PTSD can lead to nightmares, anxiety, depression, and flashbacks which could trigger violent episodes. Many times, the disease leads to drug and alcohol abuse, and in some cases suicide. I broke down crying hysterically and threw up on the office floor recalling the horrors of moving mutilated bodies and the burnt corpses of the woman holding her baby.

In my second visit, we talked about my childhood, and I discussed the Joe Milo murder with him. The doctor told me what I had already figured out, that I suffered from PTSD as a teenager which probably exasperated my drug use. We went on to discuss how other traumatic experiences such as the death of my close friends, my divorce, and the death of my father all contributed to my self-destructive behavior. In my last visit before the Christmas break, we spent most of the session talking about my relationship with my father. I told him that I felt I'd spent my entire life competing with Warren for my father's admiration. I admitted for the first time that the reason I volunteered for Desert Storm wasn't out of any sense of patriotism, but to gain my father's respect, seeking the accolades and attention that came along with being a war hero.

At the end of the session, the doctor suggested I admit myself to a drug rehabilitation clinic but knowing the birth of my son was only weeks away I decided not to. I told him I had been sober since the incident, only smoking marijuana to help me sleep. I told the doctor that I felt marijuana kept my nightmares to a minimum, but he told me he had no choice but to recommend I quit immediately. He then said off the record if I wasn't abusing it and if it kept me away from alcohol and cocaine that it wouldn't be such a bad thing. That incident scared me to a point where I was afraid to go out drinking, and with my mind clearer than it had been in years all I could think about was my daughter and the upcoming birth of my son. I made another attempt at contacting Melanie, and this time she called me back.

I apologized repeatedly and I begged her forgiveness, admitting that ignoring her and denying the child was mine was a horrible thing to do. I explained in detail my sessions with the psychologist and my struggles with PTSD. I told her I wanted nothing more than to be part of my son's life, and that I was committed to being a father. She inquired about my drug use, and I assured her I hadn't done any in weeks, and that I had no desire. I invited her and her young son to meet my mother at her condo where she cooked us a big Italian dinner. After dinner, Melanie and I discussed what we would do after the baby was born. I suggested that I move in with her and that she could quit her job to take care of the kids. I had just gotten a new job bartending at the Holiday Inn and was making good money again. I told her that if it didn't work out between us I would always be there for our son, regardless. After a little hesitation, she realized it was beneficial for everyone involved, and agreed to let me move in.

I was working my shift at the bar when I received a phone call from Melanie's sister that Melanie's water had broken, and they were taking her to the hospital in Red Bank. I rushed out of work driving like a lunatic to the hospital which was about ten minutes away. When I arrived, the nurse told me that she was already in the delivery room and that the baby was due any minute. After washing my hands and being given a surgical mask, they took me to the delivery room where Melanie was spread eagle on the table screaming in pain. Moments later I watched my son enter this world. Then the doctor encouraged me to cut his umbilical cord. After they cleaned him up they gave him to his mother, who after a few minutes handed the baby to me. We named him Robert Gennaro Cuccurullo. As I held Robert in my hands for the very first time, I began to sob uncontrollably thinking of my father and the deathbed promise I was able to keep.

# Epilogue

Melanie and I would eventually break up, but I was awarded joint custody and she allowed me to pick up my son as I pleased. She also allowed me to take her son, Collin, as we had gotten attached to each other, and he soon started calling me dad. I also had joint custody of my daughter Ava, and I would pick up all three of them on my days off. I was doing well at the hotel, working my way up from bartender to General Manager in less than two years. When my children started school, I began missing important functions because of my hectic work schedule, which bothered me to no end. It was bad enough I was missing my daughter's dance recitals, but when Robert was old enough to play baseball I decided I was done with the restaurant business and wanted to follow my dreams. I quit my job at the hotel and found a job waiting tables at a busy Italian restaurant working nights and weekends. During the day I attended Brookdale Community College full time pursuing a double major in both Education and History.

During my first year back in school I was awarded full custody of my son. It happened following an incident where his mother left

Robert, who was eight at the time, home alone with his younger half-brother while she went out to a bar. I would've never known if Robert hadn't called me at work telling me he was afraid. I found myself as a full-time father while working two jobs and trying to finish my degree. Almost obsessed with finishing, I completed two years of college in eighteen months and graduated with honors. I transferred to Georgian Court University full time at night to complete my degree, and worked as a substitute teacher during the day, waiting tables on the weekends. I was a street kid from Canarsie who had never finished the tenth grade but after completing my student teaching I received a bachelor's degree in History and Education, graduating magna cum laude with a 3.82 GPA. The most rewarding part was that my seventy-nine-year-old mother, who used to dream of this day, was able to attend my graduation ceremony the following spring.

My first job was at a charter school in Asbury Park, New Jersey, an oceanfront town besieged by gangs and drugs. While I was teaching at the charter school I was hired as the girls' softball coach at Asbury Park Middle School and also coached the high school football team. I eventually transferred to the middle school where I worked as a special education teacher, mentoring students who suffered from behavioral disorders, many who struggled with drugs just as I had at their age. The job could be quite rewarding at times, but it was also very stressful as most of the students I taught came from despicable and heartbreaking home circumstances.

I served as the girls' basketball coach winning a championship my first year, but my greatest accomplishment in coaching came as the middle school baseball coach. I took over a program that at one point hadn't won a game in fifteen years and had never once made the playoffs in the school's 41-year history. As in many inner-city neighborhoods, football and basketball were popular, but baseball was always an afterthought. We finished with a record of 10-6 and went to the finals in my first year. The team was featured in an article that appeared on the front page of the Asbury Park Press Sunday sports section. The following year we only lost one game and won the school district's first ever baseball championship. In my final year as the coach, I helped a young lady play on the boy's baseball team when the athletic director insisted she had to play softball. After two years at the school, the district laid me off as part of a reduction in force.

A year later I decided to leave New Jersey and moved to Las Vegas with my son, Robert. I was hired as a middle school social studies teacher and coached three sports. With no middle school softball programs for the girls, I started my own team and spearheaded the creation of a brand-new league with some of the other schools. In my first year, I won a Teacher of the Year contest, having been nominated by over forty of my students. A week later I appeared as a guest on the live television news show Las Vegas Now. I currently teach honors U.S. History and coach both baseball and football at Coronado High School in Henderson, Nevada.

I never did go back to a drug rehab clinic as my doctor suggested. Fatherhood had sobered me up. I continued to smoke small amounts of marijuana at night as it helped control my nightmares but when I became a teacher, I decided to quit as I was concerned about drug testing. About a month after I stopped smoking pot I noticed my anxiety had gotten worse, and I was getting easily agitated. My son noticed a change in my demeanor and complained that I was getting mad over trivial things. I also noticed that my war nightmares were more frequent, and I wasn't sleeping well. When I resorted to alcohol to help me sleep I knew I needed help, and went back to the VA.

According to my doctor, there was evidence that marijuana helped suppress PTSD, and the VA was still doing studies. He couldn't prescribe it as a federal employee as marijuana was still illegal but offered me prescription pills instead. I knew too many people who became addicted and I turned them down. I went to see a civilian doctor to get a prescription for medical marijuana which was now legal in New Jersey. Within a week both my son and I noticed a major difference in my behavior, and I was able to sleep again with minimal dreams. Ironically, the drug I always blamed for the beginning of my downfall was now helping to make me feel normal.

Robert completed his senior year of high school in Las Vegas, and after graduation enlisted in the U.S. Army Reserve as a Military Police Officer. He had played high school football, and he seemed to inherit some of my speed, although he's a lot bigger than me. It was my son's constant hounding that led me to quit smoking cigarettes on his tenth birthday after twenty-eight years. I always attributed Robert's birth as my motivation for finally changing my life around. I consider him my best friend, and my only regret is that my father never got to meet him. Maybe when my father asked me to have a son on his deathbed, it wasn't just to pass on the name, but because he knew that fatherhood would change me in a way that nothing else could.

Following the death of my father, I was still livid with my brother Warren for not attending the funeral but didn't confront him about it. When I finally did a few years later I told him I thought that he should've been at the funeral regardless of any concert. He told me that dad wanted him to stay on tour, something I never knew. At the concert following my father's death, Warren paid tribute to him by dedicating and playing Ordinary World, a song that made my father cry. I was able to get closure on something that had bothered me for years.

Warren continued to play with Duran Duran until 1999. Later that year he was informed that the five original members of the band would be reuniting and he was being let go. Through the help of his good friend Nick Rhodes, MTV awarded Warren a Lifetime

Achievement Award for his work with Duran Duran. In 2002 Warren became the co-owner of an Italian restaurant called Via Veneto in Santa Monica and continues to write music and lives on the beach in Malibu, California with his girlfriend, Donna. Unfortunately, Warren became preoccupied with 9/11 conspiracy theories, and we soon drifted apart. I've made a few attempts at reconciliation, but as of this writing, he still refuses to speak to me.

My brother Jerry was never able to achieve the musical success that Warren did, and later became a stockbroker. He currently lives on Long Island with his wife of over thirty years. He continues to play for various local bands and gives drum lessons on the side. Jerry always expected Warren to help him with his career, and I truly believe he tried. Warren felt that he got burned too many times, but in Jerry's defense, Warren always treated him like shit from the time they were teenagers playing in our basement. They don't speak to each other. My sister Stephanie got married and had three beautiful extremely smart daughters and lives on the Jersey Shore. My eighty-six-year-old mother is alive and well living with her boyfriend of eighteen years in Baltimore, Maryland.

As for the old Canarsie crew, I lost touch with many from the old neighborhood until social media connected us again. Through Facebook, I was able to track down my old friend Randy, who I had lost touch with for over twenty years. He was able to kick his crack addiction and currently lives in Arizona. My pal Mario married his high school girlfriend and used his cocaine earnings to buy a house in Brooklyn, and later moved to Long Island. My friend Henry moved to Staten Island with his family and started his own business. He also became a bookie and was involved with an illegal online gambling operation. Jose got a job with the sanitation department but was retired after suffering a heart attack and receiving four stents in his heart. He's still loud as ever and plays softball almost every day. Robby has remained one of my closest friends over the years, and currently works security in New Jersey. He was the very last of my friends to move out of Canarsie.

By the end of the 20th century, Canarsie had changed dramatically as many of the longtime residents left in droves. Just as with many of the surrounding neighborhoods in Brooklyn, "White Flight" had caused many of the Canarsie residents to flee to neighborhoods on Long Island, Staten Island, and in New Jersey. Many of the new Canarsie residents were recent immigrants from the Caribbean and parts of Western Africa. Most of my family members had already moved out of Brooklyn except for my aunt and cousins who still lived in nearby Starrett City. On one of my recent trips back East I visited Canarsie for the first time in years and spent the day entire day with my buddy Jose as we reminisced about the good, the bad, and the ugly.

"By Way of Canarsie" is a mid-twentieth century American English figure of speech meaning, "to come to one's destination by a roundabout way or from a distant point." I spent the first twenty-eight years of life in my Brooklyn neighborhood with a few side trips and adventures along the way. It wasn't until I finally found my place and purpose in life that I knew I'd arrived By Way of Canarsie.

Made in the USA
Lexington, KY
10 July 2019